"This is not the republic I came to see; this is not the republic of my imagination. . . . The more I think of its youth and strength, the poorer and more trifling in a thousand aspects it appears in my eyes."
—CHARLES DICKENS, *1842*

Dickens was disappointed in America. But we are now able to understand why Dickens, like so many other visitors—then and now—felt as he did. If the literature left by travelers in America is literature predominantly of disappointment, it is because the expectation of America invariably exceeds the reality, and the promise invariably exceeds the fact.

Any country regarded by so much of the world as a land of special promise and opportunity should expect to find itself judged by standards more exacting than those applied to countries which do not have to live up to such an exalted reputation. If people criticize us with particular violence, we should be reassured even though we may suffer pangs of shame; the violence of the criticism implies that the old promise still raises hopes throughout the world.

We should be grateful for our critics. We need them to hold us to the mark. Americans needed Dickens in 1842, and they need him again today.
—*Christopher Lasch*

AMERICAN NOTES

BY CHARLES DICKENS

INTRODUCTION BY CHRISTOPHER LASCH
DEPARTMENT OF HISTORY, ROOSEVELT UNIVERSITY

GLOUCESTER, MASS.

PETER SMITH

1968

CONTENTS

ILLUSTRATIONS

INTRODUCTION

CHARLES Dickens came to America in January, 1842, in
the footsteps of Tocqueville, Fanny Trollope, and Harriet
Martineau. If he was not the first European to find himself drawn by an irresistible curiosity to examine at first
hand the evidences of God's wonder-working providence in
the New World (as Americans liked to think of their
country), neither was he the first to set out in the high
hope that, of all such visitors, he alone would succeed in
sufficiently detaching himself from his European prejudices to send home a true and unbiased report of his
travels.

Having read Mrs. Trollope's *Domestic Manners of the
Americans* and Harriet Martineau's *Society in America*,
Dickens was aware of the pitfalls of comparison. "In going
to the New World," he wrote in anticipation of his visit,
"one must for the time being utterly forget and push out
of sight the Old one and bring none of its customs or observances into the comparison."

This advice proved as hard to follow as it was easy to
give. Comparisons, Dickens discovered as soon as he set
foot in America, inevitably suggested themselves. The difficulty lay in the fact that America, while a new and
strange society in many respects, was yet too much like
Europe to be judged except as an outpost of the Old
World. New England in particular, to which Dickens first
came, reminded an Englishman in a hundred ways of
home. It therefore invited comparisons with home—comparisons which, in the nature of the case, were invariably
damaging to New England.

Seeking culture and refinement, New Englanders—indeed all Americans—invariably fell short of them, if
judged by English standards. Desperately and almost

pitiably eager for the approval of the visitor from abroad, they invited his scorn; and sensing that, they proceeded loudly to proclaim anew their independence from Europe: what they lacked in experience and elegance, they let the visitor know, they made up in virtue and simplicity. But Americans, when they assumed the role of noble savages, merely called down upon themselves a redoubled contempt, and found themselves in travellers' accounts caricatured as bear-baiting, slave-driving, tobacco-spitting boors—savage indeed, but lacking any semblance of nobility.

Driven by such ridicule to prove the contrary, to establish beyond question their refinement and sensibility, they came full circle, whereupon the whole process by which they alternately courted Europe and rejected it started up again.

The ambivalent emotions with which Americans greeted visitors to their country was enough to undermine anyone's objectivity. But Dickens was subjected to other difficulties as well, peculiar to his own case. For one thing, he was received as an international celebrity—not so much on account of his novels (although he had already published *Pickwick Papers, Nicholas Nickleby* and *The Old Curiosity Shop*) as for his reputation as a social reformer.

In Boston, the assembled dignitaries of New England greeted him as a renowned humanitarian. He had "done more to ameliorate the condition of the English poor," said Daniel Webster at a banquet in his honor, "than all the statesmen that Great Britain had sent into Parliament."

Josiah Quincy declared that Dickens infused "a moral tone into everything. . . . He is a reformer," Quincy concluded in triumph, as if nothing further could possibly be said in tribute. Dickens was flattered; but after a few weeks of this he became more and more oppressed by uplift.

Wherever they went, Dickens and his wife were greeted by throngs of admirers. "I can give you no conception of my reception here," he wrote home from Boston. "There never was a king or emperor upon the earth so cheered and followed by crowds. If I go out in a carriage, the crowds surround me and escort me home; if I go

to the theatre, the whole house (crowded to the roof)
rises as one man."

It was immensely exciting, until Dickens discovered that
his admirers all insisted on shaking his hand. His first
obligation, upon entering a city, was to hold an enormous
"*levée*," at which he was introduced to hundreds of people—in some places, it seemed, the entire population. By
the end of March he was shaking hands, he complained,
"on an average with five or six hundred people" every
day. Thus his tour rapidly became a grinding physical
ordeal. In New Haven he was almost mobbed by throngs
so ardent in their admiration that they appropriated
handfuls of his fur coat as souvenirs of the occasion. In
New York he was introduced to society at a ball in the
Carlton Hotel, after which he took to his bed for four
days. "Poor man, he is literally used up," wrote Mrs.
John Motley to her husband, ". . . giving himself up as a
spectacle."

The enthusiasm of the crowds, overwhelming as it was,
might have been borne in good spirits. But the enthusiasm
itself was in fact, as Dickens discovered, a light and airy
thing, which could be dissipated by the merest breeze of
criticism on his part. The moment he ventured upon a
topic in which American pride was involved, a perceptible
chill set in. Such a topic, unfortunately, was always at
hand, for Dickens had come to America in part to convince Americans that the law of international copyright
should be changed so as to prevent the pirating of European authors by American publishers. Several of his own
works had suffered in this fashion. He was not bitter; he
merely wished, as he told his listeners wherever he went,
to lay the matter before their consideration.

Whenever Dickens made this speech—and he made it
wherever he found an audience assembled—he was treated
as if he had committed an outrageous breach of taste.
The Bostonians were embarrassed, and squirmed in their
seats. In Hartford the inhabitants were more outspoken
in their disapproval. "It happens that we want no advice
on this subject," said the Hartford *Times*, "and it will be
better for Mr. D. if he refrains from introducing the
subject hereafter." It was the effort to shut him up, much
more than the disapproval itself, which gradually convinced Dickens, as it had convinced Tocqueville, that

there was far less freedom of opinion in America than Americans imagined.

An Englishman likes his privacy, and he likes to speak his mind. Dickens decided that America offered neither privacy nor opportunities for the free exchange of ideas. By the time he reached Baltimore, he confessed that he was disappointed in the New World. "This is not the republic I came to see; this is not the republic of my imagination." A liberal monarchy, he decided, was "infinitely" preferable to "such a government as this." The people themselves he found "affectionate, generous, open-hearted, hospitable, enthusiastic, good-humoured, anxious to oblige, far less prejudiced than they have been described to be, frequently polished and refined, very seldom rude or disagreeable."

It was not the "ingredients" but the "dish" that he objected to—the meanness of the press, the low tone of public discussion, the tyranny of public opinion. The last of these in particular continued to disturb him; he had himself been the victim of it. "I speak of Bancroft, and am advised to be silent on that subject, for he is 'a black sheep—a Democrat.' I speak of Bryant, and am entreated to be more careful, for the same reason. I speak of international copyright, and am implored not to ruin myself outright."

After these experiences, Dickens was heartily sick of America. To a friend in England he declared: "I would not condemn you to a year's residence on this side of the Atlantic for any money." It was with a tremendous sense of relief that he and his wife finally arrived in Canada, where they delighted in an excursion to Niagara Falls—their first privacy in four months—before sailing for England in June.

Before leaving England Dickens had arranged with his publisher to write his American experiences for publication. Upon his return he began work on the book, although somewhat half-heartedly; he would have preferred to forget the whole business. He did not, however, allow his disappointment to creep into the work. On one subject only—Negro slavery, to which, like most Europeans, he reacted with loathing—did he allow himself to speak out. For the rest, he confined himself to what he could praise —to prisons and reformatories and schools for the handicapped; to just those evidences of the spirit of uplift which he had privately deplored, but with which he was, nevertheless, in fundamental sympathy.

He said nothing of the copyright issue, or of the absence of freedom of opinion, and though he noted with disgust the prevalence of tobacco-spitting, he was careful to balance censure of American manners with approval. The book, after all, had to pay for his trip.

Commercially *American Notes* was a success. Four editions sold out by the end of the year, at a profit to the author of £4,000, a tidy sum even for Dickens. But critics on both sides of the Atlantic received it without excitement. Thackeray refused even to review it. He thought it "at once frivolous and dull. . . . What is meant to be easy and sprightly," he observed with considerable justice, "is vulgar and flippant."

The vulgarity, it should be noted, was the result of Dickens' efforts to avoid giving offense, which led him to depict himself as a comic victim of circumstances that were merely unfamiliar and awkward, when in fact they had been deeply distasteful.

It was in *Martin Chuzzlewit,* begun at the same time as *American Notes,* that Dickens took his literary revenge on the United States. There he forced his hero to share his American ordeal, step by step. He holds a *levée* for a crowd of uncouth provincials who rove about him "with watchful eyes and itching fingers," and "audibly exchange opinions on his looks." He buys a tract of land in Illinois, "Eden," only to find on his arrival that the place is a "hideous swamp . . . choked with slime and matted growth."

In these pages Dickens depicts Americans as utterly lacking either in taste or in imagination. The men bolt their food and spit tobacco; the women attend elevating lectures. Dreariness and mediocrity hang over everything. America is disgusting, but what is worse, it is dull.

Chuzzlewit, said Carlyle, caused "all Yankee-doodledum to fizz like one universal sodawater bottle." Preachers preached against it; angry citizens consigned it to flames. *American Notes* encountered no such violence, but neither did it excite approbation; and the two books gave Dickens the reputation, in the United States, of a cantankerous critic whose strictures merely confirmed the impression that Europeans were too far gone in wickedness to appreciate the advantages of the American way.

Yet in 1867, when Dickens made a second visit to the United States, another generation of Americans gave him a rousing welcome. This time Dickens avoided *levées,* and confined himself to giving a series of public readings from his works. Nothing could better have served to convince him that Americans were at last ready for the refinements of culture than the applause which his readings everywhere evoked. But if Dickens was moved to relent somewhat in his earlier denunciations of the New World, he nowhere published his revised opinions.

CHRISTOPHER LASCH
Roosevelt University

I DEDICATE THIS BOOK

TO

THOSE FRIENDS OF MINE
IN AMERICA,

*Who, giving me a welcome I must ever
gratefully and proudly remember,
left my judgment
FREE;
and who, loving their country, can bear
the truth, when it is told good
humouredly, and in a
kind spirit.*

PREFACE

My readers have opportunities of judging for themselves whether the influences and tendencies which I distrusted in America had any existence but in my imagination. They can examine for themselves whether there has been anything in the public career of that country since, at home or abroad, which suggests that those influences and tendencies really did exist. As they find the fact, they will judge me. If they discern any evidences of wrong-going, in any direction that I have indicated, they will acknowledge that I had reason in what I wrote. If they discern no such thing, they will consider me altogether mistaken—but not wilfully.

Prejudiced I am not, and never have been, otherwise than in favor of the United States. I have many friends in America, I feel a grateful interest in the country, I hope and believe it will successfully work out a problem of the highest importance to the whole human race. To represent me as viewing AMERICA with ill-nature, coldness, or animosity, is merely to do a very foolish thing, which is always a very easy one.

CHAPTER 1

Going Away.

I SHALL never forget the one-fourth serious and three-fourths comical astonishment with which, on the morning of the third of January, eighteen hundred and forty-two, I opened the door of, and put my head into, a "state-room" on board the Britannia steam-packet, twelve hundred tons burden per register, bound for Halifax and Boston, and carrying her Majesty's mails.

That this state-room had been specially engaged for "Charles Dickens, Esquire, and Lady," was rendered sufficiently clear even to my scared intellect by a very small manuscript, announcing the fact, which was pinned on a very flat quilt, covering a very thin mattress, spread like a surgical plaster on a most inaccessible shelf. But that this was the state-room concerning which Charles Dickens, Esquire, and Lady, had held daily and nightly conferences for at least four months preceding: that this could by any possibility be that small snug chamber of the imagination, which Charles Dickens, Esquire, with the spirit of prophecy strong upon him, had always foretold would contain at least one little sofa, and which his lady, with a modest yet most magnificent sense of its limited dimensions, had from the first opined would not hold more than two enormous portmanteaus in some odd corner out of sight (portmanteaus which could now no more be got in at the door, not to say stowed away, than a giraffe could be persuaded or forced into a flower-pot) : that this utterly impracticable, thoroughly hopeless, and profoundly preposterous box had the remotest reference to, or connec-

15

tion with, those chaste and pretty, not to say gorgeous little bowers, sketched by a masterly hand, in the highly varnished lithographic plan hanging up in the agent's counting-house in the city of London: that this room of state, in short, could be anything but a pleasant fiction and cheerful jest of the captain's, invented and put in practice for the better relish and enjoyment of the real state-room presently to be disclosed:—these were truths which I really could not, for the moment, bring my mind at all to bear upon or comprehend. And I sat down upon a kind of horsehair slab, or perch, of which there were two within; and looked, without any expression of countenance whatever, at some friends who had come on board with us, and who were crushing their faces into all manner of shapes by endeavoring to squeeze them through the small doorway.

We had experienced a pretty smart shock before coming below, which, but that we were the most sanguine people living, might . have prepared us for the worst. The imaginative artist to whom I have already made allusion has depicted, in the same great work, a chamber of almost interminable perspective, furnished, as Mr. Robins would say, in a style of more than Eastern splendor, and filled (but not inconveniently so) with groups of ladies and gentlemen, in the very highest state of enjoyment and vivacity. Before descending into the bowels of the ship, we had passed from the deck into a long narrow apartment, not unlike a gigantic hearse with windows in the sides; having at the upper end a melancholy stove, at which three or four chilly stewards were warming their hands; while on either side, extending down its whole dreary length, was a long, long table, over each of which a rack, fixed to the low roof, and stuck full of drinking-glasses and cruet-stands, hinted dismally at rolling seas and heavy weather. I had not at that time seen the ideal presentment of this chamber which has since gratified me so much, but I observed that one of our friends, who had made the arrangements for our voyage, turned pale on entering, retreated on the friend behind him, smote his forehead involuntarily, and said below his breath, "Impossible! it cannot be!" or words to that effect. He recovered himself, however, by a great effort, and, after a preparatory cough or two, cried, with a ghastly smile which is still before me, looking at the same time round the walls, "Ha! the breakfast-room, steward, eh?" We all foresaw what the answer must be: we knew the agony he suffered. He had often spoken of *the saloon;* had taken in and lived upon the pictorial idea; had usually given us to understand, at home, that to form a just conception of it, it would be necessary to multiply the size and furniture of an ordinary drawing-room by seven, and then fall short of the reality. When the man in reply avowed the truth: the blunt, remorseless, naked truth: "This is the saloon, sir"—he actually reeled beneath the blow.

In persons who were so soon to part, and interpose between their else daily communication the formidable barrier of many thousand miles of stormy space, and who were for that reason anxious to cast no other cloud, not even the passing shadow of a moment's disappointment or discomfiture, upon the short interval of happy companionship that yet remained to them—in persons so situated, the natural transition from these first surprises was obviously into peals of hearty laughter; and I can report that I, for one, being still seated upon the slab or perch before mentioned, roared outright until the vessel rang again. Thus, in less than two minutes after coming upon it for the first time, we all by common consent agreed that this state-room was the pleasantest and most facetious and capital contrivance possible, and that to have had it one inch larger would have been quite a disagreeable and deplorable state of things. And with this; and with showing how—by very nearly closing the door, and twining in and out like serpents, and by counting the little washing slab as standing-room—we could manage to insinuate four people into it, all at one time; and entreating each other to observe how very airy it was (in dock), and how there was a beautiful port-hole which could be kept open all day (weather permitting), and how there was quite a large bull's-eye just over the looking-glass, which would render shaving a perfectly easy and delightful process (when the ship didn't roll too much); we arrived, at last, at the unanimous conclusion that it was rather spacious than otherwise: though I do verily believe that, deducting the two berths, one above the other, than which nothing smaller for sleeping in was ever made except coffins, it was no bigger than one of those hackney cabriolets which have the door behind, and shoot their fares out like sacks of coals upon the pavement.

Having settled this point to the perfect satisfaction of all parties, concerned or unconcerned, we sat down round the fire in the ladies' cabin—just to try the effect. It was rather dark, certainly; but somebody said, "Of course it would be light at sea," a proposition to which we all assented; echoing "Of course, of course;" though it would be exceedingly difficult to say why we thought so. I remember, too, when we had discovered and exhausted another topic of consolation in the circumstance of this ladies' cabin adjoining our state-room, and the consequently immense feasibility of sitting there at all times and seasons, and had fallen into a momentary silence, leaning our faces on our hands and looking at the fire, one of our party said, with the solemn air of a man who had made a discovery, "What a relish mulled claret will have down here!" which appeared to strike us all most forcibly; as though there were something spicy and high-flavored in cabins, which essentially improved that composition, and rendered it quite incapable of perfection anywhere else.

There was a stewardess, too, actively engaged in producing clean sheets and table-cloths from the very entrails of the sofas, and from unexpected lockers, of such artful mechanism that it made one's head ache to see them opened one after another, and rendered it quite a distracting circumstance to follow her proceedings, and to find that every nook and corner and individual piece of furniture was something else besides what it pretended to be, and was a mere trap and deception and place of secret stowage, whose ostensible purpose was its least useful one.

God bless that stewardess for her piously fraudulent account of January voyages! God bless her for her clear recollection of the companion passage of last year, when nobody was ill, and everybody danced from morning till night, and it was "a run" of twelve days, and a piece of the purest frolic, and delight, and jollity! All happiness be with her for her bright face and her pleasant Scotch tongue, which had sounds of old Home in it for my fellow-traveller; and for her predictions of fair winds and fine weather (all wrong, or I shouldn't be half so fond of her); and for the ten thousand small fragments of genuine womanly tact by which, without piecing them elaborately together, and patching them up into shape and form and case and pointed application, she nevertheless did plainly show that all young mothers on one side of the Atlantic were near and close at hand to their little children left upon the other; and that what seemed to the uninitiated a serious journey, was, to those who were in the secret, a mere frolic, to be sung about and whistled at! Light be her heart, and gay her merry eyes, for years!

The state-room had grown pretty fast; but by this time it had expanded into something quite bulky, and almost boasted a bay-window to view the sea from. So we went upon deck again in high spirits; and there everything was in such a state of bustle and active preparation, that the blood quickened its pace, and whirled through one's veins on that clear frosty morning with involuntary mirthfulness. For every gallant ship was riding slowly up and down, and every little boat was plashing noisily in the water; and knots of people stood upon the wharf, gazing with a kind of "dread delight" on the far-famed fast American steamer; and one party of men were "taking in the milk," or, in other words, getting the cow on board; and another were filling the ice-houses to the very throat with fresh provisions; with butcher's meat and garden stuff, pale sucking-pigs, calves' heads in scores, beef, veal, and pork, and poultry out of all proportion; and others were coiling ropes, and busy with oakum yarns; and others were lowering heavy packages into the hold; and the purser's head was barely visible as it loomed in a state of exquisite perplexity from the midst of a vast pile of passengers' luggage; and there seemed to be nothing going on anywhere, or uppermost in the mind of anybody, but preparations for this mighty voyage. This, with the bright cold sun, the bracing air, the crisply curling water, the thin white crust of morning ice upon the decks which crackled with a sharp and cheerful sound beneath the lightest tread, was irresistible. And when, again upon the shore, we turned and saw from the vessel's mast her name signalled in flags of joyous colors, and fluttering by their side the beautiful American banner with its stars and stripes,—the long three thousand miles and more, and, longer still, the six whole months of absence, so dwindled and faded that the ship had gone out and come home again, and it was broad spring already in the Coburg Dock at Liverpool.

I have not inquired among my medical acquaintance whether Turtle, and cold Punch, with Hock, Champagne, and Claret, and all the slight et cetera usually included in an unlimited order for a good dinner—especially when it is left to the liberal construction of my faultless friend, Mr. Radley of the Adelphi Hotel—are peculiarly calculated to suffer a sea-change; or whether a plain mutton chop, and a glass or two of sherry, would be less likely of conversion into foreign and disconcerting material. My own opinion is, that whether one is discreet or indiscreet in these particulars, on the eve of a sea voyage, is a matter of little consequence; and that, to use a common phrase, "it comes to very much the same thing in the end." Be this as it may, I know that the dinner of that day was undeniably perfect; that it comprehended all these items, and a great many more; and that we all did ample justice to it. And I know, too, that, bating a certain tacit avoidance of any allusion to to-morrow; such as may be supposed to prevail between delicate-minded turnkeys and a sensitive prisoner who is to be hanged next morning; we got on very well, and, all things considered, were merry enough.

When the morning—*the* morning—came, and we met at breakfast, it was curious to see how eager we all were to prevent a moment's pause in the conversation, and how astoundingly gay everybody was: the forced spirits of each member of the little party having as much likeness to his natural mirth, as hothouse peas at five guineas the quart resemble in flavor the growth of the dews, and air, and rain of Heaven. But as one o'clock, the hour for going aboard, drew near, this volubility dwindled away by little and little, despite the most persevering efforts to the contrary, until at last, the matter being now quite desperate, we threw off all disguise; openly speculated upon where we should be this time to-morrow, this time next day, and so forth; and intrusted a vast number of messages to those who intended returning to town that night, which were to be delivered at home and elsewhere, without fail, within the very shortest possible space of time after the arrival of the railway train at Euston Square. And commissions and remembrances do so crowd upon one at such a time, that we were still busied with this employment when we found ourselves fused, as it were, into a dense conglomeration of passengers and passengers' friends and passengers' luggage, all jumbled together on the deck of a small steamboat, and panting and snorting off to the packet, which had worked out of dock yesterday afternoon, and was now lying at her moorings in the river.

And there she is! All eyes are turned to where she lies, dimly discernible through the gathering fog of the early winter afternoon; every finger is pointed in the same direction; and murmurs of interest and admiration—as "How beautiful she looks!" "How trim she is!"—are heard on every side. Even the lazy gentleman with his hat on one side and his hands in his pockets, who has dispensed so much consolation by inquiring with a yawn of another gentleman whether he is "going across"—as if it were a ferry—even he condescends to look that way, and nod his head, as who should say, "No mistake about *that:*" and not even the sage Lord Burleigh in his nod included half so much as this lazy gentleman of might who has made the passage (as everybody on board has found out already; it's impossible to say how) thirteen times without a single accident! There is another passenger very much wrapped up, who has been frowned down by the rest, and morally trampled upon and crushed, for presuming to inquire with a timid interest how long it is since the poor President went down. He is standing close to the lazy gentleman, and says with a faint smile that he believes She is a very strong Ship; to which the lazy gentleman, looking first in his questioner's eye and then very hard in the wind's, answers unexpectedly and ominously, that She need be. Upon this the lazy gentleman instantly falls very low in the popular estimation, and the passengers, with looks of defiance, whisper to each other that he is an ass and an impostor, and clearly don't know anything at all about it.

But we are made fast alongside the packet, whose huge red funnel is smoking bravely, giving rich promise of serious intentions. Packing-cases, portmanteaus, carpet bags, and boxes are already passed from hand to hand, and hauled on board with breathless rapidity. The officers, smartly dressed, are at the gangway, handing the passengers up the side, and hurrying the men. In five minutes' time the little steamer is utterly deserted, and the packet is beset and overrun by its late freight, who instantly pervade the whole ship, and are to be met with by the dozen in every nook and corner: swarming down below with their own baggage, and stumbling over other people's; disposing themselves comfortably in wrong cabins, and creating a most horrible confusion by having to turn out again; madly bent upon opening locked doors, and on forcing a passage into all kinds of out-of-the-way places where there is no thoroughfare; sending wild stewards, with elfin hair, to and fro upon the breezy decks on unintelligible errands, impossible of execution; and, in short, creating the most extraordinary and bewildering tumult. In the midst of all this, the lazy gentleman, who seems to have no luggage of any kind—not so much as a friend even—lounges up and down the hurricane deck, coolly puffing a cigar; and, as this unconcerned demeanor again exalts him in the opinion of those who have leisure to observe his proceedings, every time he looks up at the masts, or down at the decks, or over the side, they look there too, as wondering whether he sees anything wrong anywhere, and hoping that, in case he should, he will have the goodness to mention it.

What have we here? The captain's boat! and yonder the captain himself. Now, by all our hopes and wishes, the very man he ought to be! A well-made, tight-built, dapper little fellow; with a ruddy face, which is a letter of invitation to shake him by both hands at once; and with a clear blue, honest eye, that it does one good to see one's sparkling image in. "Ring the bell!" "Ding, ding, ding!" the very bell is in a hurry. "Now for the shore—who's for the shore?"—"These gentlemen, I am sorry to say." They are away, and never said Good-by. Ah! now they wave it from the little boat. "Good-by! Good-by!" Three cheers from them; three more from us; three more from them; and they are gone.

To and fro, to and fro, to and fro again a hundred times! This waiting for the latest mail-bags is worse than all. If we could have gone off in the midst of that last burst, we should have started triumphantly: but to lie here, two hours and more, in the damp fog, neither staying at home nor going abroad, is letting one gradually down into the very depths of dulness and low spirits. A speck in the mist, at last! That's something. It is the boat we wait for! That's more to the purpose. The captain appears on the paddle-box, with his speaking trumpet; the officers take their stations; all hands are on the alert; the flagging hopes of the passengers revive; the cooks pause in their savory work, and look out with faces full of interest. The boat comes alongside; the bags are dragged in anyhow, and flung down for the moment anywhere. Three cheers more: and, as the first one rings upon our ears, the vessel throbs like a strong giant that has just received the breath of life; the two great wheels turn fiercely round for the first time; and the noble ship, with wind and tide astern, breaks proudly through the lashed and foaming water.

CHAPTER 2

The Passage Out.

WE all dined together that day; and a rather formidable party we were: no fewer than eighty-six strong. The vessel being pretty deep in the water, with all her coals on board and so many passengers, and the weather being calm and quiet, there was but little motion; so that before the dinner was half over, even those passengers who were most distrustful of themselves plucked up amazingly; and those who in the morning had returned to the universal question, "Are you a good sailor?" a very decided negative, now either parried the inquiry with the evasive reply, "Oh! I suppose I'm no worse than anybody else;" or, reckless of all moral obligations, answered boldly, "Yes:" and with some irritation too, as though they would add, "I should like to know what you see in *me*, sir, particularly, to justify suspicion!"

Notwithstanding this high tone of courage and confidence, I could not but observe that very few remained long over their wine; and that everybody had an unusual love of the open air; and that the favorite and most coveted seats were invariably those nearest to the door. The tea-table, too, was by no means as well attended as the dinner-table; and there was less whist-playing than might have been expected. Still, with the exception of one lady, who had retired with some precipitation at dinner-time, immediately after being assisted to the finest cut of a very yellow boiled leg of mutton with very green capers, there were no invalids as yet; and walking, and smoking, and drinking of brandy and water (but always in the

open air), went on with unabated spirit until eleven
o'clock, or thereabouts, when "turning in"—no sailor of
seven hours' experience talks of going to bed—became
the order of the night. The perpetual tramp of boot-
heels on the decks gave place to a heavy silence, and the
whole human freight was stowed away below, excepting
a very few stragglers like myself, who were probably,
like me, afraid to go there.

To one unaccustomed to such scenes, this is a very striking time on shipboard. Afterwards, and when its novelty
had long worn off, it never ceased to have a peculiar interest and charm for me. The gloom through which the
great black mass holds its direct and certain course; the
rushing water, plainly heard, but dimly seen; the broad,
white, glistening track that follows in the vessel's wake;
the men on the look-out forward, who would be scarcely
visible against the dark sky, but for their blotting out
some score of glistening stars; the helmsman at the wheel,
with the illuminated card before him, shining, a speck of
light amidst the darkness, like something sentient and of
Divine intelligence; the melancholy sighing of the wind
through block, and rope, and chain; the gleaming forth
of light from every crevice, nook, and tiny piece of glass
about the decks, as though the ship were filled with fire
in hiding, ready to burst through any outlet, wild with
its resistless power of death and ruin. At first, too, and
even when the hour, and all the objects it exalts, have
come to be familiar, it is difficult, alone and thoughtful,
to hold them to their proper shapes and forms. They
change with the wandering fancy; assume the semblance
of things left far away; put on the well-remembered
aspect of favorite places dearly loved; and even people
them with shadows. Streets, houses, rooms; figures so
like their usual occupants, that they have startled me by
their reality, which far exceeded, as it seemed to me, all
power of mine to conjure up the absent; have, many and
many a time, at such an hour, grown suddenly out of objects with whose real look, use, and purpose I was as well
acquainted as with my own two hands.

My own two hands, and feet likewise, being very cold,
however, on this particular occasion, I crept below at
midnight. It was not exactly comfortable below. It was
decidedly close; and it was impossible to be unconscious

of the presence of that extraordinary compound of strange smells, which is to be found nowhere but on board ship, and which is such a subtle perfume that it seems to enter at every pore of the skin, and whisper of the hold. Two passengers' wives (one of them my own) lay already in silent agonies on the sofa; and one lady's maid (*my* lady's) was a mere bundle on the floor, execrating her destiny, and pounding her curl-papers among the stray boxes. Everything sloped the wrong way; which in itself was an aggravation scarcely to be borne. I had left the door open, a moment before, in the bosom of a gentle declivity, and, when I turned to shut it, it was on the summit of a lofty eminence. Now every plank and timber creaked, as if the ship were made of wicker-work; and now crackled like an enormous fire of the dryest possible twigs. There was nothing for it but bed; so I went to bed.

It was pretty much the same for the next two days, with a tolerably fair wind and dry weather. I read in bed (but to this hour I don't know what) a good deal; and reeled on deck a little; drank cold brandy and water with an unspeakable disgust, and ate hard biscuit perseveringly: not ill, but going to be.

It is the third morning. I am awakened out of my sleep by a dismal shriek from my wife, who demands to know whether there's any danger. I rouse myself, and look out of bed. The water-jug is plunging and leaping like a lively dolphin; all the smaller articles are afloat, except my shoes, which are stranded on a carpet bag, high and dry, like a couple of coal-barges. Suddenly I see them spring into the air, and behold the looking-glass, which is nailed to the wall, sticking fast upon the ceiling. At the same time the door entirely disappears, and a new one is opened in the floor. Then I begin to comprehend that the state-room is standing on its head.

Before it is possible to make any arrangement at all compatible with this novel state of things, the ship rights. Before one can say "Thank Heaven!" she wrongs again. Before one can cry she *is* wrong, she seems to have started forward, and to be a creature actively running of its own accord, with broken knees and failing legs, through every variety of hole and pitfall, and stumbling constantly. Before one can so much as wonder, she takes a high leap into the air. Before she has well done that, she takes a

deep dive into the water. Before she has gained the surface, she throws a summerset. The instant she is on her
legs, she rushes backward. And so she goes on staggering,
heaving, wrestling, leaping, diving, jumping, pitching,
throbbing, rolling, and rocking: and going through all
these movements, sometimes by turns, and sometimes all
together: until one feels disposed to roar for mercy.

A steward passes. "Steward!" "Sir?" "What *is* the matter? what *do* you call this?" "Rather a heavy sea on,
sir, and a head wind."

A head wind! Imagine a human face upon the vessel's
prow, with fifteen thousand Samsons in one bent upon
driving her back, and hitting her exactly between the
eyes whenever she attempts to advance an inch. Imagine
the ship herself, with every pulse and artery of her huge
body swollen and bursting under this maltreatment, sworn
to go on or die. Imagine the wind howling, the sea roaring, the rain beating: all in furious array against her.
Picture the sky both dark and wild, and the clouds, in
fearful sympathy with the waves, making another ocean
in the air. Add to all this the clattering on deck and
down below; the tread of hurried feet; the loud hoarse
shouts of seamen; the gurgling in and out of water
through the scuppers; with every now and then the striking of a heavy sea upon the planks above, with the deep,
dead, heavy sound of thunder heard within a vault; and
there is the head wind of that January morning.

I say nothing of what may be called the domestic noises
of the ship: such as the breaking of glass and crockery,
the tumbling down of stewards, the gambols, overhead, of
loose casks and truant dozens of bottled porter, and the
very remarkable and far from exhilarating sounds raised
in their various state-rooms by the seventy passengers who
were too ill to get up to breakfast. I say nothing of them:
for although I lay listening to this concert for three or
four days, I don't think I heard it for more than a quarter of a minute, at the expiration of which term, I lay
down again, excessively sea-sick.

Not sea-sick, be it understood, in the ordinary accepta-
tion of the term: I wish I had been: but in a form which
I have never seen or heard described, though I have no
doubt it is very common. I lay there, all the day long,
quite coolly and contentedly; with no sense of weariness,

with no desire to get up, or get better, or take the air; with no curiosity, or care, or regret, of any sort or degree, saving that I think I can remember, in this universal indifference, having a kind of lazy joy—of fiendish delight, if anything so lethargic can be dignified with the title—in the fact of my wife being too ill to talk to me. If I may be allowed to illustrate my state of mind by such an example, I should say that I was exactly in the condition of the elder Mr. Willet, after the incursion of the rioters into his bar at Chigwell. Nothing would have surprised me. If, in the momentary illumination of any ray of intelligence that may have come upon me in the way of thoughts of Home, a goblin postman, with a scarlet coat and bell, had come into that little kennel before me, broad awake, in broad day, and, apologizing for being damp through walking in the sea, had handed me a letter, directed to myself, in familiar characters, I am certain I should not have felt one atom of astonishment: I should have been perfectly satisfied. If Neptune himself had walked in, with a toasted shark on his trident, I should have looked upon the event as one of the very commonest every-day occurrences.

Once—once—I found myself on deck. I don't know how I got there, or what possessed me to go there, but there I was; and completely dressed too, with a huge pea-coat on, and a pair of boots such as no weak man in his senses could ever have got into. I found myself standing, when a gleam of consciousness came upon me, holding on to something. I don't know what. I think it was the boatswain: or it may have been the pump: or possibly the cow. I can't say how long I had been there; whether a day or a minute. I recollect trying to think about something (about anything in the whole wide world, I was not particular) without the smallest effect. I could not even make out which was the sea, and which the sky; for the horizon seemed drunk, and was flying wildly about in all directions. Even in that incapable state, however, I recognized the lazy gentleman standing before me: nautically clad in a suit of shaggy blue, with an oil-skin hat. But I was too imbecile, although I knew it to be he, to separate him from his dress; and tried to call him, I remember, *Pilot*. After another interval of total unconsciousness, I found he had gone, and recognized another figure in its place. It seemed to wave and fluctuate before me as though I saw it reflected in an unsteady looking-glass; but I knew it for the captain; and such was the cheerful influence of his face, that I tried to smile: yes, even then I tried to smile. I saw by his gestures that he addressed me; but it was a long time before I could make out that he remonstrated against my standing up to my knees in water —as I was; of course I don't know why. I tried to thank him, but couldn't. I could only point to my boots—or wherever I supposed my boots to be—and say in a plaintive voice, "Cork soles:" at the same time endeavoring, I am told, to sit down in the pool. Finding that I was quite insensible, and for the time a maniac, he humanely conducted me below.

There I remained until I got better: suffering, whenever I was recommended to eat anything, an amount of anguish only second to that which is said to be endured by the apparently drowned, in the process of restoration to life. One gentleman on board had a letter of introduction to me from a mutual friend in London. He sent it below with his card, on the morning of the head wind; and I was long troubled with the idea that he might be up, and well, and a hundred times a day expecting me to call upon him in the saloon. I imagined him one of those cast-iron images—I will not call them men—who ask, with red faces and lusty voices, what sea-sickness means, and whether it really is as bad as it is represented to be. This was very torturing indeed; and I don't think I ever felt such perfect gratification and gratitude of heart as I did when I heard from the ship's doctor that he had been obliged to put a large mustard poultice on this very gentleman's stomach. I date my recovery from the receipt of that intelligence.

It was materially assisted though, I have no doubt, by a heavy gale of wind, which came slowly up at sunset, when we were about ten days out, and raged with gradually increasing fury until morning, saving that it lulled for an hour a little before midnight. There was something in the unnatural repose of that hour, and in the after gathering of the storm, so inconceivably awful and tremendous, that its bursting into full violence was almost a relief.

The laboring of the ship in the troubled sea on this

night I shall never forget. "Will it ever be worse than this?" was a question I had often heard asked, when everything was sliding and bumping about, and when it certainly did seem difficult to comprehend the possibility of anything afloat being more disturbed, without toppling over and going down. But what the agitation of a steam-vessel is, on a bad winter's night in the wild Atlantic, it is impossible for the most vivid imagination to conceive. To say that she is flung down on her side in the waves, with her masts dipping into them, and that, springing up again, she rolls over on the other side, until a heavy sea strikes her with the noise of a hundred great guns, and hurls her back—that she stops, and staggers, and shivers, as though stunned, and then, with a violent throbbing at her heart, darts onward like a monster goaded into madness, to be beaten down, and battered, and crushed, and leaped on by the angry sea—that thunder, lightning, hail, and rain, and wind are all in fierce contention for the mastery—that every plank has its groan, every nail its shriek, and every drop of water in the great ocean its howling voice—is nothing. To say that all is grand, and all appalling and horrible in the last degree, is nothing. Words cannot express it. Thoughts cannot convey it. Only a dream can call it up again in all its fury, rage, and passion.

And yet, in the very midst of these terrors, I was placed in a situation so exquisitely ridiculous, that even then I had as strong a sense of its absurdity as I have now: and could no more help laughing than I can at any other comical incident, happening under circumstances the most favorable to its enjoyment. About midnight we shipped a sea, which forced its way through the skylights, burst open the doors above, and came raging and roaring down into the ladies' cabin, to the unspeakable consternation of my wife and a little Scotch lady—who, by the way, had previously sent a message to the captain by the stewardess, requesting him, with her compliments, to have a steel conductor immediately attached to the top of every mast, and to the chimney, in order that the ship might not be struck by lightning. They, and the handmaid before mentioned, being in such ecstasies of fear that I scarcely knew what to do with them, I naturally bethought myself of some restorative or comfortable cordial; and nothing better occurring to me, at the moment, than hot brandy and water, I procured a tumblerful without delay. It being impossible to stand or sit without holding on, they were all heaped together in one corner of a long sofa—a fixture, extending entirely across the cabin—where they clung to each other in momentary expectation of being drowned. When I approached this place with my specific, and was about to administer it, with many consolatory expressions, to the nearest sufferer, what was my dismay to see them all roll slowly down to the other end! And when I staggered to that end, and held out the glass once more, how immensely baffled were my good intentions by the ship giving another lurch, and their all rolling back again! I suppose I dodged them up and down this sofa for at least a quarter of an hour, without reaching them once; and, by the time I did catch them, the brandy and water was diminished, by constant spilling, to a teaspoonful. To complete the group, it is necessary to recognize, in this disconcerted dodger, an individual very pale from sea-sickness, who had shaved his beard and brushed his hair last at Liverpool: and whose only articles of dress (linen not included) were a pair of dreadnaught trousers; a blue jacket, formerly admired upon the Thames at Richmond; no stockings; and one slipper.

Of the outrageous antics performed by that ship next morning; which made bed a practical joke, and getting up, by any process short of falling out, an impossibility; I say nothing. But anything like the utter dreariness and desolation that met my eyes when I literally "tumbled up" on deck at noon, I never saw. Ocean and sky were all of one dull, heavy, uniform lead color. There was no extent of prospect even over the dreary waste that lay around us, for the sea ran high, and the horizon encompassed us like a large black hoop. Viewed from the air, or some tall bluff on shore, it would have been imposing and stupendous, no doubt; but seen from the wet and rolling decks, it only impressed one giddily and painfully. In the gale of last night the life-boat had been crushed by one blow of the sea like a walnut shell; and there it hung dangling in the air: a mere fagot of crazy boards. The planking of the paddle-boxes had been torn sheer away. The wheels were exposed and bare; and they whirled and dashed their spray about the decks at random. Chimney white with crusted salt; top-masts struck; storm-sails set; rigging all knotted, tangled, wet, and drooping: a gloomier picture it would be hard to look upon.

I was now comfortably established by courtesy in the ladies' cabin, where, besides ourselves, there were only four other passengers. First, the little Scotch lady before mentioned, on her way to join her husband at New York, who had settled there three years before. Secondly and thirdly, an honest young Yorkshireman, connected with some American house; domiciled in that same city, and carrying thither his beautiful young wife, to whom he had been married but a fortnight, and who was the fairest specimen of a comely English country girl I have ever seen. Fourthly, fifthly, and lastly, another couple: newly married too, if one might judge from the endearments they frequently interchanged: of whom I know no more than that they were rather a mysterious, runaway kind of couple; that the lady had great personal attractions also; and that the gentleman carried more guns with him than Robinson Crusoe, wore a shooting coat, and had two great dogs on board. On further consideration, I remember that he tried hot roast pig and bottled ale as a cure for sea-sickness; and that he took these remedies (usually in bed) day after day, with astonishing perseverance. I may add, for the information of the curious, that they decidedly failed.

The weather continuing obstinately and almost unprecedentedly bad, we usually straggled into this cabin, more or less faint and miserable, about an hour before noon, and lay down on the sofas to recover; during which interval the captain would look in to communicate the state of the wind, the moral certainty of its changing to-morrow (the weather is always going to improve to-morrow, at sea), the vessel's rate of sailing, and so forth. Observations there were none to tell us of, for there was no sun to take them by. But a description of one day will serve for all the rest. Here it is.

The captain being gone, we compose ourselves to read, if the place be light enough; and if not, we doze and talk alternately. At one a bell rings, and the stewardess comes down with a steaming dish of baked potatoes, and another of roasted apples; and plates of pig's face, cold ham, salt beef; or perhaps a smoking mess of rare hot collops. We fall to upon these dainties; eat as much as we can (we have great appetites now); and are as long as possible about it. If the fire will burn (it *will* sometimes), we are pretty cheerful. If it won't, we all remark to each other that it's very cold, rub our hands, cover ourselves with coats and cloaks, and lie down again to doze, talk, and read (provided as aforesaid), until dinner-time. At five another bell rings, and the stewardess reappears with another dish of potatoes—boiled this time—and store of hot meat of various kinds: not forgetting the roast pig, to be taken medicinally. We sit down at table again (rather more cheerfully than before); prolong the meal with a rather mouldy dessert of apples, grapes, and oranges; and drink our wine and brandy and water. The bottles and glasses are still upon the table, and the oranges and so forth are rolling about according to their fancy and the ship's way, when the doctor comes down, by special nightly invitation, to join our evening rubber: immediately on whose arrival we make a party at whist, and, as it is a rough night and the cards will not lie on the cloth, we put the tricks in our pockets as we take them. At whist we remain with exemplary gravity (deducting a short time for tea and toast) until eleven o'clock, or thereabouts; when the captain comes down again, in a sou'-wester hat tied under his chin, and a pilot coat: making the ground wet where he stands. By this time the card-playing is over, and the bottles and glasses are again upon the table; and after an hour's pleasant conversation about the ship, the passengers, and things in general, the captain (who never goes to bed, and is never out of humor) turns up his coat collar for the deck again; shakes hands all round; and goes laughing out into the weather as merrily as to a birthday party.

As to daily news, there is no dearth of that commodity. This passenger is reported to have lost fourteen pounds at Vingt-et-un in the saloon yesterday; and that passenger drinks his bottle of champagne every day, and how he does it (being only a clerk) nobody knows. The head engineer has distinctly said that there never was such times—meaning weather—and four good hands are ill, and have given in, dead beat. Several berths are full of water, and all the cabins are leaky. The ship's cook, se-

cretly swigging damaged whiskey, has been found drunk;
and has been played upon by the fire-engine until quite
sober. All the stewards have fallen downstairs at various
dinner-times, and go about with plasters in various places.
The baker is ill, and so is the pastrycook. A new man,
horribly indisposed, has been required to fill the place of
the latter officer; and has been propped and jammed up
with empty casks in a little house upon deck, and commanded to roll out pie-crusts, which he protests (being
highly bilious) it is death to him to look at. News! A
dozen murders on shore would lack the interest of these
slight incidents at sea.

Divided between our rubber and such topics as these,
we were running (as we thought) into Halifax Harbor,
on the fifteenth night, with little wind and a bright moon
—indeed, we had made the Light at its outer entrance,
and put the pilot in charge—when suddenly the ship
struck upon a bank of mud. An immediate rush on deck
took place, of course; the sides were crowded in an instant; and for a few minutes we were in as lively a state
of confusion as the greatest lover of disorder would desire to see. The passengers, and guns, and water casks,
and other heavy matters, being all huddled together aft,
however, to lighten her in the head, she was soon got off;
and after some driving on towards an uncomfortable
line of objects (whose vicinity had been announced very
early in the disaster by a loud cry of "Breakers ahead!")
and much backing of paddles, and heaving of the lead
into a constantly decreasing depth of water, we dropped
anchor in a strange outlandish-looking nook which nobody on board could recognize, although there was land
all about us, and so close that we could plainly see the
waving branches of the trees.

It was strange onough, in the silence of midnight, and
the dead stillness that seemed to be created by the sudden
and unexpected stoppage of the engine, which had been
clanking and blasting in our ears incessantly for so many
days, to watch the look of blank astonishment expressed
in every face; beginning with the officers, tracing it
through all the passengers, and descending to the very
stokers and furnace-men, who emerged from below, one
by one, and clustered together in a smoky group about
the hatchway of the engine-room, comparing notes in

whispers. After throwing up a few rockets and firing signal guns in the hope of being hailed from the land, or at least of seeing a light—but without any other sight or sound presenting itself—it was determined to send a boat on shore. It was amusing to observe how very kind some of the passengers were, in volunteering to go ashore in this same boat: for the general good, of course; not by any means because they thought the ship in an unsafe position, or contemplated the possibility of her heeling over in case the tide were running out. Nor was it less amusing to remark how desperately unpopular the poor pilot became in one short minute. He had had his passage out from Liverpool, and during the whole voyage had been quite a notorious character, as a teller of anecdotes and cracker of jokes. Yet here were the very men who had laughed the loudest at his jests, now flourishing their fists in his face, loading him with imprecations, and defying him to his teeth as a villain!

The boat soon shoved off, with a lantern and sundry blue lights on board; and in less than an hour returned; the officer in command bringing with him a tolerably tall young tree, which he had plucked up by the roots, to satisfy certain distrustful passengers whose minds misgave them that they were to be imposed upon and shipwrecked, and who would on no other terms believe that he had been ashore, or had done anything but fraudulently row a little way into the mist, specially to deceive them and compass their deaths. Our captain had foreseen from the first that we must be in a place called the Eastern passage; and so we were. It was about the last place in the world in which we had any business or reason to be, but a sudden fog, and some error on the pilot's part, were the cause. We were surrounded by banks, and rocks, and shoals of all kinds, but had happily drifted, it seemed, upon the only safe speck that was to be found thereabouts. Eased by this report, and by the assurance that the tide was past the ebb, we turned in at three o'clock in the morning.

I was dressing about half-past nine next day, when the noise above hurried me on deck. When I had left it overnight, it was dark, foggy, and damp, and there were bleak hills all round us. Now, we were gliding down a smooth, broad stream, at the rate of eleven miles an hour: our colors flying gayly; our crew rigged out in their smartest clothes; our officers in uniform again; the sun shining as on a brilliant April day in England; the land stretched out on either side, streaked with light patches of snow; white wooden houses; people at their doors; telegraphs working; flags hoisted; wharves appearing; ships; quays crowded with people; distant noises; shouts; men and boys running down steep places towards the pier; all more bright and gay and fresh to our unused eyes than words can paint them. We came to a wharf, paved with uplifted faces; got alongside, and were made fast, after some shouting and straining of cables; darted, a score of us, along the gangway, almost as soon as it was thrust out to meet us, and before it had reached the ship—and leaped upon the firm glad earth again!

I suppose this Halifax would have appeared an Elysium, though it had been a curiosity of ugly dulness. But I carried away with me a most pleasant impression of the town and its inhabitants, and have preserved it to this hour. Nor was it without regret that I came home, without having found an opportunity of returning thither, and once more shaking hands with the friends I made that day.

It happened to be the opening of the Legislative Council and General Assembly, at which ceremonial the forms observed on the commencement of a new Session of Parliament in England were so closely copied, and so gravely presented on a small scale, that it was like looking at Westminster through the wrong end of a telescope. The governor, as her Majesty's representative, delivered what may be called the Speech from the Throne. He said what he had to say manfully and well. The military band outside the building struck up "God save the Queen" with great vigor before his Excellency had quite finished; the people shouted; the ins rubbed their hands; the outs shook their heads; the Government party said there never was such a good speech; the opposition declared there never was such a bad one; the Speaker and members of the House of Assembly withdrew from the bar to say a great deal among themselves, and do a little; and, in short, everything went on, and promised to go on, just as it does at home upon the like occasions.

The town is built on the side of a hill, the highest point

being commanded by a strong fortress, not yet quite finished. Several streets of good breadth and appearance
extend from its summit to the water-side, and are inter-
sected by cross-streets running parallel with the river.
The houses are chiefly of wood. The market is abundantly
supplied: and provisions are exceedingly cheap. The
weather being unusually mild at that time for the season
of the year, there was no sleighing: but there were plenty
of those vehicles in yards and by-places, and some of
them, from the gorgeous quality of their decorations,
might have "gone on" without alteration as triumphal
cars in a melodrama at Astley's. The day was uncommonly
fine; the air bracing and healthful; the whole aspect of
the town cheerful, thriving, and industrious.

We lay there seven hours, to deliver and exchange the
mails. At length, having collected all our bags and all our
passengers (including two or three choice spirits, who,
having indulged too freely in oysters and champagne,
were found lying insensible on their backs in unfrequented
streets), the engines were again put in motion, and we
stood off for Boston.

Encountering squally weather again in the Bay of
Fundy, we tumbled and rolled about as usual all that
night and all next day. On the next afternoon—that is to
say, on Saturday, the twenty-second of January—an American pilot-boat came alongside, and soon afterwards the
Britannia steam-packet from Liverpool, eighteen days out,
was telegraphed at Boston.

The indescribable interest with which I strained my
eyes, as the first patches of American soil peeped like
molehills from the green sea, and followed them, as they
swelled, by slow and almost imperceptible degrees, into a
continuous line of coast, can hardly be exaggerated. A
sharp keen wind blew dead against us; a hard frost prevailed on shore; and the cold was most severe. Yet the
air was so intensely clear, and dry, and bright, that the
temperature was not only endurable, but delicious.

How I remained on deck, staring about me, until we
came alongside the dock, and how, though I had had as
many eyes as Argus, I should have had them all wide
open, and all employed on new objects—are topics which
I will not prolong this chapter to discuss. Neither will I
more than hint at my foreigner-like mistake, in supposing

that a party of most active persons, who scrambled on board at the peril of their lives as we approached the wharf, were newsmen, answering to that industrious class at home; whereas, despite the leathern wallets of news slung about the necks of some, and the broad-sheets in the hands of all, they were Editors, who boarded ships in person (as one gentleman in a worsted comforter informed me), "because they like the excitement of it." Suffice it in this place to say, that one of these invaders, with a ready courtesy for which I thank him here most gratefully, went on before to order rooms at the hotel; and that when I followed, as I soon did, I found myself rolling through the long passages with an involuntary imitation of the gait of Mr. T. P. Cooke, in a new nautical melodrama.

"Dinner, if you please," said I to the waiter.

"When?" said the waiter.

"As quick as possible," said I.

"Right away?" said the waiter.

After a moment's hesitation, I answered, "No," at hazard.

"*Not* right away?" cried the waiter, with an amount of surprise that made me start.

I looked at him doubtfully, and returned, "No; I would rather have it in this private room. I like it very much."

At this I really thought the waiter must have gone out of his mind: as I believe he would have done, but for the interposition of another man, who whispered in his ear, "Directly."

"Well! and that's a fact!" said the waiter, looking helplessly at me. "Right away."

I saw now that "Right away" and "Directly" were one and the same thing. So I reversed my previous answer, and sat down to dinner in ten minutes afterwards; and a capital dinner it was.

The hotel (a very excellent one) is called the Tremont House. It has more galleries, colonnades, piazzas, and passages than I can remember, or the reader would believe.

CHAPTER 3

Boston.

In all the public establishments of America the utmost courtesy prevails. Most of our Departments are susceptible of considerable improvement in this respect, but the Custom House, above all others, would do well to take example from the United States, and render itself somewhat less odious and offensive to foreigners. The servile rapacity of the French officials is sufficiently contemptible; but there is a surly, boorish incivility about our men, alike disgusting to all persons who fall into their hands, and discreditable to the nation that keeps such ill-conditioned curs snarling about its gates.

When I landed in America, I could not help being strongly impressed with the contrast their Custom House presented, and the attention, politeness, and good-humor with which its officers discharged their duty.

As we did not land at Boston, in consequence of some detention at the wharf, until after dark, I received my first impressions of the city in walking down to the Custom House on the morning after our arrival, which was Sunday. I am afraid to say, by the way, how many offers of pews and seats in church for that morning were made to us, by formal note of invitation, before we had half finished our first dinner in America; but if I may be allowed to make a moderate guess, without going into nicer calculation, I should say that at least as many sittings were proffered us as would have accommodated a score or two of grown-up families. The number of creeds and forms of religion to which the pleasure of our company was requested was in very fair proportion.

Not being able, in the absence of any change of clothes, to go to church that day, we were compelled to decline these kindnesses, one and all; and I was reluctantly obliged to forego the delight of hearing Dr. Channing, who happened to preach that morning for the first time in a very long interval. I mention the name of this distinguished and accomplished man (with whom I soon afterwards had the pleasure of becoming personally acquainted), that I may have the gratification of recording my humble tribute of admiration and respect for his high abilities and character; and for the bold philanthropy with which he has ever opposed himself to that most hideous blot and foul disgrace—Slavery.

To return to Boston. When I got into the streets upon this Sunday morning, the air was so clear, the houses were so bright and gay; the sign-boards were painted in such gaudy colors; the gilded letters were so very golden; the bricks were so very red, the stone was so very white, the blinds and area railings were so very green, the knobs and plates upon the street-doors so marvellously bright and twinkling; and all so slight and unsubstantial in appearance—that every thoroughfare in the city looked exactly like a scene in a pantomime. It rarely happens in the business streets that a tradesman—if I may venture to call anybody a tradesman, where everybody is a merchant —resides above his store; so that many occupations are often carried on in one house, and the whole front is covered with boards and inscriptions. As I walked along, I kept glancing up at these boards, confidently expecting to see a few of them change into something; and I never turned a corner suddenly without looking out for the Clown and Pantaloon, who, I had no doubt, were hiding in a doorway or behind some pillar close at hand. As to Harlequin and Columbine, I discovered immediately that they lodged (they are always looking after lodgings in a pantomime) at a very small clock-maker's, one story high, near the hotel; which, in addition to various symbols and devices, almost covering the whole front, had a great dial hanging out—to be jumped through, of course.

The suburbs are, if possible, even more unsubstantial-looking than the city. The white wooden houses (so white that it makes one wink to look at them), with their green jalousie blinds, are so sprinkled and dropped about in all directions, without seeming to have any root at all in the ground; and the small churches and chapels are so prim, and bright, and highly varnished; that I almost believed the whole affair could be taken up piecemeal like a child's toy, and crammed into a little box.

The city is a beautiful one, and cannot fail, I should imagine, to impress all strangers very favorably. The private dwelling-houses are, for the most part, large and elegant; the shops extremely good; and the public buildings handsome. The State House is built upon the summit of a hill, which rises gradually at first, and afterwards by a steep ascent, almost from the water's edge. In front is a green enclosure, called the Common. The site is beautiful: and from the top there is a charming panoramic view of the whole town and neighborhood. In addition to a variety of commodious offices, it contains two handsome chambers: in one the House of Representatives of the State hold their meetings: in the other, the Senate. Such proceedings as I saw here were conducted with perfect gravity and decorum; and were certainly calculated to inspire attention and respect.

There is no doubt that much of the intellectual refinement and superiority of Boston is referable to the quiet influence of the University of Cambridge, which is within three or four miles of the city. The resident professors at that university are gentlemen of learning and varied attainments; and are, without one exception that I can call to mind, men who would shed a grace upon, and do honor to, any society in the civilized world. Many of the resident gentry in Boston and its neighborhood, and I think I am not mistaken in adding, a large majority of those who are attached to the liberal professions there, have been educated at this same school. Whatever the defects of American universities may be, they disseminate no prejudices; rear no bigots; dig up the buried ashes of no old superstitions; never interpose between the people and their improvement; exclude no man because of his religious opinions; above all, in their whole course of study and instruction, recognize a world, and a broad one too, lying beyond the college walls.

It was a source of inexpressible pleasure to me to observe the almost imperceptible, but not less certain effect, wrought by this institution among the small community of Boston; and to note at every turn the humanizing tastes and desires it has engendered; the affectionate friendships to which it has given rise; the amount of vanity and prejudice it has dispelled. The golden calf they worship at Boston is a pygmy compared with the giant effigies set up in other parts of that vast counting-house which lies beyond the Atlantic; and the almighty dollar sinks into something comparatively insignificant, amidst a whole Pantheon of better gods.

Above all, I sincerely believe that the public institutions and charities of this capital of Massachusetts are as nearly perfect as the most considerate wisdom, benevolence, and humanity can make them. I never in my life was more affected by the contemplation of happiness, under circumstances of privation and bereavement, than in my visits to these establishments.

It is a great and pleasant feature of all such institutions in America, that they are either supported by the State or assisted by the State; or (in the event of their not needing its helping hand) that they act in concert with it, and are emphatically the people's. I cannot but think, with a view to the principle and its tendency to elevate or depress the character of the industrious classes, that a Public Charity is immeasurably better than a Private Foundation, no matter how munificently the latter may be endowed. In our own country, where it has not, until within these later days, been a very popular fashion with governments to display any extraordinary regard for the great mass of the people, or to recognize their existence as improvable creatures, private charities, unexampled in the history of the earth, have arisen, to do an incalculable amount of good among the destitute and afflicted. But the government of the country, having neither act nor part in them, is not in the receipt of any portion of the gratitude they inspire; and, offering very little shelter or relief beyond that which is to be found in the workhouse and the jail, has come, not unnaturally, to be looked upon by the poor rather as a stern master, quick to correct and punish, than a kind protector, merciful and vigilant in their hour of need.

The maxim, that out of evil cometh good, is strongly

illustrated by these establishments at home; as the records of the Prerogative Office in Doctors' Commons can abundantly prove. Some immensely rich old gentleman or lady, surrounded by needy relatives, makes, upon a low average, a will a week. The old gentleman or lady, never very remarkable in the best of times for good temper, is full of aches and pains from head to foot; full of fancies and caprices; full of spleen, distrust, suspicion, and dislike. To cancel old wills, and invent new ones, is at last the sole business of such a testator's existence; and relations and friends (some of whom have been bred up distinctly to inherit a large share of the property, and have been, from their cradles, specially disqualified from devoting themselves to any useful pursuit, on that account) are so often and so unexpectedly and summarily cut off, and reinstated, and cut off again, that the whole family, down to the remotest cousin, is kept in a perpetual fever. At length it becomes plain that the old lady or gentleman has not long to live; and the plainer this becomes, the more clearly the old lady or gentleman perceives that everybody is in a conspiracy against their poor old dying relative; wherefore the old lady or gentleman makes another last will—positively the last this time—conceals the same in a china teapot, and expires next day. Then it turns out, that the whole of the real and personal estate is divided between half a dozen charities; and that the dead and gone testator has in pure spite helped to do a great deal of good, at the cost of an immense amount of evil passion and misery.

The Perkins Institution and Massachusetts Asylum for the Blind, at Boston, is superintended by a body of trustees who make an annual report to the corporation. The indigent blind of that State are admitted gratuitously. Those from the adjoining State of Connecticut, or from the States of Maine, Vermont, or New Hampshire, are admitted by a warrant from the State to which they respectively belong; or, failing that, must find security among their friends, for the payment of about twenty pounds English for their first year's board and instruction, and ten for the second. "After the first year," say the trustees, "an account current will be opened with each pupil; he will be charged with the actual cost of his board, which will not exceed two dollars per week;" a trifle more than eight shillings English; "and he will be credited with the amount paid for him by the State, or by his friends; also with his earnings over and above the cost of the stock which he uses; so that. all his earnings over one dollar per week will be his own. By the third year it will be known whether his earnings will more than pay the actual cost of his board; if they should, he will have it at his option to remain and receive his earnings, or not. Those who prove unable to earn their own livelihood will not be retained; as it is not desirable to convert the establishment into an almshouse, or to retain any but working bees in the hive. Those who, by physical or mental imbecility, are disqualified for work, are thereby disqualified from being members of an industrious community; and they can be better provided for in establishments fitted for the infirm."

I went to see this place one very fine winter morning: an Italian sky above, and the air so clear and bright on every side, that even my eyes, which are none of the best, could follow the minute lines and scraps of tracery in distant buildings. Like most other public institutions in America of the same class, it stands a mile or two without the town, in a cheerful, healthy spot; and is an airy, spacious, handsome edifice. It is built upon a height, commanding the harbor. When I paused for a moment at the door, and marked how fresh and free the whole scene was—what sparkling bubbles glanced upon the waves, and welled up every moment to the surface, as though the world below, like that above, were radiant with the bright day, and gushing over in its fulness of light: when I gazed from sail to sail away upon a ship at sea, a tiny speck of shining white, the only cloud upon the still, deep, distant blue—and, turning, saw a blind boy with his sightless face addressed that way, as though he too had some sense within him of the glorious distance: I felt a kind of sorrow that the place should be so very light, and a strange wish that for his sake it were darker. It was but momentary, of course, and a mere fancy, but I felt it keenly for all that.

The children were at their daily tasks in different rooms, except a few who were already dismissed, and were at play. Here, as in many institutions, no uniform is worn; and I was very glad of it, for two reasons. Firstly, because

I am sure that nothing but senseless custom and want of thought would reconcile us to the liveries and badges we are so fond of at home. Secondly, because the absence of these things presents each child to the visitor in his or her own proper character, with its individuality unimpaired; not lost in a dull, ugly, monotonous repetition of the same unmeaning garb: which is really an important consideration. The wisdom of encouraging a little harmless pride in personal appearance even among the blind, or the whimsical absurdity of considering charity and leather breeches inseparable companions, as we do, requires no comment.

Good order, cleanliness, and comfort pervaded every corner of the building. The various classes, who were gathered round their teachers, answered the questions put to them with readiness and intelligence, and in a spirit of cheerful contest for precedence which pleased me very much. Those who were at play were gleesome and noisy as other children. More spiritual and affectionate friendships appeared to exist among them than would be found among other young persons suffering under no deprivation; but this I expected and was prepared to find. It is a part of the great scheme of Heaven's merciful consideration for the afflicted.

In a portion of the building, set apart for that purpose, are workshops for blind persons whose education is finished, and who have acquired a trade, but who cannot pursue it in an ordinary manufactory because of their deprivation. Several people were at work here; making brushes, mattresses, and so forth; and the cheerfulness, industry, and good order discernible in every other part of the building, extended to this department also.

On the ringing of a bell, the pupils all repaired, without any guide or leader, to a spacious music-hall, where they took their seats in an orchestra erected for that purpose, and listened with manifest delight to a voluntary on the organ, played by one of themselves. At its conclusion, the performer, a boy of nineteen or twenty, gave place to a girl; and to her accompaniment they all sang a hymn, and afterwards a sort of chorus. It was very sad to look upon and hear them, happy though their condition unquestionably was; and I saw that one blind girl, who (being for the time deprived of the use of her limbs by illness) sat close beside me with her face towards them, wept silently the while she listened.

It is strange to watch the faces of the blind, and see how free they are from all concealment of what is passing in their thoughts; observing which, a man with eyes may blush to contemplate the mask he wears. Allowing her one shade of anxious expression which is never absent from their countenances, and the like of which we may readily detect in our own faces if we try to feel our way in the dark, every idea, as it rises within them, is expressed with the lightning's speed, and nature's truth. If the company at a rout, or drawing-room at court, could only for one time be as unconscious of the eyes upon them as blind men and women are, what secrets would come out, and what a worker of hypocrisy this sight, the loss of which we so much pity, would appear to be!

The thought occurred to me as I sat down in another room, before a girl blind, deaf, and dumb; destitute of smell; and nearly so of taste: before a fair young creature with every human faculty, and hope, and power of goodness and affection, enclosed within her delicate frame, and but one outward sense—the sense of touch. There she was, before me: built up, as it were, in a marble cell, impervious to any ray of light, or particle of sound; with her poor white hand peeping through a chink in the wall, beckoning to some good man for help, that an Immortal soul might be awakened.

Long before I looked upon her, the help had come. Her face was radiant with intelligence and pleasure. Her hair, braided by her own hands, was bound about a head whose intellectual capacity and development were beautifully expressed in its graceful outline, and its broad open brow; her dress, arranged by herself, was a pattern of neatness and simplicity; the work she had knitted lay beside her; her writing-book was on the desk she leaned upon. From the mournful ruin of such bereavement, there had slowly risen up this gentle, tender, guileless, grateful-hearted being.

Like other inmates of that house, she had a green ribbon bound round her eyelids. A doll she had dressed lay near upon the ground. I took it up, and saw that she had made a green fillet such as she wore herself, and fastened it about its mimic eyes.

She was seated in a little enclosure, made by school desks and forms, writing her daily journal. But, soon finishing this pursuit, she engaged in an animated communication with a teacher who sat beside her. This was a favorite mistress with the poor pupil. If she could see the face of her fair instructress, she would not love her less, I am sure.

I have extracted a few disjointed fragments of her history, from an account written by that one man who has made her what she is. It is a very beautiful and touching narrative; and I wish I could present it entire.

Her name is Laura Bridgman. "She was born in Hanover, New Hampshire, on the twenty-first of December, 1829. She is described as having been a very sprightly and pretty infant, with bright blue eyes. She was, however, so puny and feeble until she was a year and a half old, that her parents hardly hoped to rear her. She was subject to severe fits, which seemed to rack her frame almost beyond her power of endurance: and life was held by the feeblest tenure: but, when a year and a half old, she seemed to rally; the dangerous symptoms subsided; and, at twenty months old, she was perfectly well.

"Then her mental powers, hitherto stinted in their growth, rapidly developed themselves; and during the four months of health which she enjoyed, she appears (making due allowance for a fond mother's account) to have displayed a considerable degree of intelligence.

"But suddenly she sickened again; her disease raged with great violence during five weeks, when her eyes and ears were inflamed, suppurated, and their contents were discharged. But though sight and hearing were gone forever, the poor child's sufferings were not ended. The fever raged during seven weeks; for five months she was kept in bed in a darkened room; it was a year before she could walk unsupported, and two years before she could sit up all day. It was now observed that her sense of smell was almost entirely destroyed; and, consequently, that her taste was much blunted.

"It was not until four years of age that the poor child's bodily health seemed restored, and she was able to enter upon her apprenticeship of life and the world.

"But what a situation was hers! The darkness and the silence of the tomb were around her: no mother's smile called forth her answering smile, no father's voice taught her to imitate his sounds:—they, brothers and sisters, were but forms of matter which resisted her touch, but which differed not from the furniture of the house, save in warmth, and in the power of locomotion; and not even in these respects from the dog and the cat.

"But the immortal spirit which had been implanted within her could not die, nor be maimed nor mutilated; and though most of its avenues of communication with the world were cut off, it began to manifest itself through the others. As soon as she could walk, she began to explore the room, and then the house; she became familiar with the form, density, weight, and heat of every article she could lay her hands upon. She followed her mother, and felt her hands and arms, as she was occupied about the house; and her disposition to imitate, led her to repeat everything herself. She even learned to sew a little, and to knit."

The reader will scarcely need to be told, however, that the opportunities of communicating with her were very, very limited; and that the moral effects of her wretched state soon began to appear. Those who cannot be enlightened by reason can only be controlled by force; and this, coupled with her great privations, must soon have reduced her to a worse condition than that of the beasts that perish, but for timely and unhoped-for aid.

"At this time I was so fortunate as to hear of the child, and immediately hastened to Hanover to see her. I found her with a well-formed figure; a strongly marked, nervous-sanguine temperament; a large and beautifully shaped head; and the whole system in healthy action. The parents were easily induced to consent to her coming to Boston, and on the 4th of October, 1837, they brought her to the Institution.

"For a while she was much bewildered; and after waiting about two weeks, until she became acquainted with her new locality, and somewhat familiar with the inmates, the attempt was made to give her knowledge of arbitrary signs, by which she could interchange thoughts with others.

"There was one of two ways to be adopted: either to go on to build up a language of signs on the basis of the natural language which she had already commenced herself, or to teach her the purely arbitrary language in common use: that is, to give her a sign for every individual thing, or to give her a knowledge of letters by combination of which she might express her idea of the existence, and the mode and condition of existence, of any thing. The former would have been easy, but very ineffectual; the latter seemed very difficult, but, if accomplished, very effectual. I determined, therefore, to try the latter.

"The first experiments were made by taking articles in common use, such as knives, forks, spoons, keys, etc., and pasting upon them labels with their names printed in raised letters. These she felt very carefully, and soon, of course, distinguished that the crooked lines *s p o o n* differed as much from the crooked lines *k e y,* as the spoon differed from the key in form.

"Then small detached labels, with the same words printed upon them, were put into her hands; and she soon observed that they were similar to the ones pasted on the articles. She showed her perception of this similarity by laying the label *k e y* upon the key, and the label *s p o o n* upon the spoon. She was encouraged here by the natural sign of approbation, patting on the head.

"The same process was then repeated with all the articles which she could handle; and she very easily learned to place the proper labels upon them. It was evident, however, that the only intellectual exercise was that of imitation and memory. She recollected that the label *b o o k* was placed upon a book, and she repeated the process first from imitation, next from memory, with only the motive of love of approbation, but apparently without the intellectual perception of any relation between the things.

"After a while, instead of labels, the individual letters were given to her on detached bits of paper: they were arranged side by side so as to spell *b o o k, k e y,* etc.; then they were mixed up in a heap, and a sign was made for her to arrange them herself, so as to express the words *b o o k, k e y,* etc.; and she did so.

"Hitherto the process had been mechanical, and the success about as great as teaching a very knowing dog a variety of tricks. The poor child had sat in mute amazement, and patiently imitated everything her teacher did; but now the truth began to flash upon her: her intellect began to work: she perceived that here was a way by which she could herself make up a sign of anything that was in her own mind, and show it to another mind; and at once her countenance lighted up with a human expression: it was no longer a dog, or parrot: it was an immortal spirit, eagerly seizing upon a new link of union with other spirits! I could almost fix upon the moment when this truth dawned upon her mind, and spread its light to her countenance; I saw that the great obstacle was overcome; and that henceforward nothing but patient and persevering, but plain and straightforward, efforts were to be used.

"The result, thus far, is quickly related, and easily conceived; but not so was the process; for many weeks of apparently unprofitable labor were passed before it was effected.

"When it was said above, that a sign was made, it was intended to say that the action was performed by her teacher, she feeling his hands, and then imitating the motion.

"The next step was to procure a set of metal types, with the different letters of the alphabet cast upon their ends; also a board, in which were square holes, into which holes she could set the types; so that the letters on their ends could alone be felt above the surface.

"Then, on any article being handed to her,—for instance, a pencil, or a watch,—she would select the component letters, and arrange them on her board, and read them with apparent pleasure.

"She was exercised for several weeks in this way, until her vocabulary became extensive; and then the important step was taken of teaching her how to represent the different letters by the position of her fingers, instead of the cumbrous apparatus of the board and types. She accomplished this speedily and easily, for her intellect had begun to work in aid of her teacher, and her progress was rapid.

"This was the period, about three months after she had commenced, that the first report of her case was made, in which it is stated that 'she has just learned the manual alphabet, as used by the deaf mutes, and it is a subject of delight and wonder to see how rapidly, correctly, and eagerly she goes on with her labors. Her teacher gives her a new object,—for instance, a pencil,—

first lets her examine it, and get an idea of its use, then teaches her how to spell it by making the signs for the letters with her own fingers: the child grasps her hand, and feels her fingers, as the different letters are formed; she turns her head a little on one side, like a person listening closely; her lips are apart; she seems scarcely to breathe; and her countenance, at first anxious, gradually changes to a smile, as she comprehends the lesson. She then holds up her tiny fingers, and spells the word in the manual alphabet; next, she takes her types and arranges her letters; and last, to make sure that she is right, she takes the whole of the types composing the word, and places them upon or in contact with the pencil, or whatever the object may be.'

"The whole of the succeeding year was passed in gratifying her eager inquiries for the names of every object which she could possibly handle; in exercising her in the use of the manual alphabet; in extending in every possible way her knowledge of the physical relations of things; and in proper care of her health.

"At the end of the year a report of her case was made, from which the following is an extract.

" 'It has been ascertained, beyond the possibility of doubt, that she cannot see a ray of light, cannot hear the least sound, and never exercises her sense of smell, if she have any. Thus her mind dwells in darkness and stillness, as profound as that of a closed tomb at midnight. Of beautiful sights, and sweet sounds, and pleasant odors she has no conception; nevertheless, she seems as happy and playful as a bird or a lamb; and the employment of her intellectual faculties, or the acquirement of a new idea, gives her a vivid pleasure, which is plainly marked in her expressive features. She never seems to repine, but has all the buoyancy and gayety of childhood. She is fond of fun and frolic, and, when playing with the rest of the children, her shrill laugh sounds loudest of the group.

" 'When left alone, she seems very happy if she have her knitting or sewing, and will busy herself for hours: if she have no occupation, she evidently amuses herself by imaginary dialogues, or by recalling past impressions; she counts with her fingers, or spells out names of things which she has recently learned, in the manual alphabet of the deaf mutes. In this lonely self-communion she seems to reason, reflect, and argue: if she spell a word wrong with the fingers of her right hand, she instantly strikes it with her left, as her teacher does, in sign of disapprobation; if right, then she pats herself upon the head and looks pleased. She sometimes purposely spells a word wrong with the left hand, looks roguish for a moment and laughs, and then with the right hand strikes the left, as if to correct it.

" 'During the year she has attained great dexterity in the use of the manual alphabet of the deaf mutes; and she spells out the words and sentences which she knows, so fast and so deftly, that only those accustomed to this language can follow with the eye the rapid motions of her fingers.

" 'But wonderful as is the rapidity with which she writes her thoughts upon the air, still more so is the ease and accuracy with which she reads the words thus written by another; grasping their hands in hers, and following every movement of their fingers, as letter after letter conveys their meaning to her mind. It is in this way that she converses with her blind playmates, and nothing can more forcibly show the power of mind in forcing matter to its purpose than a meeting between them. For if great talent and skill are necessary for two pantomimes to paint their thoughts and feelings by the movements of the body, and the expression of the countenance, how much greater the difficulty when darkness shrouds them both, and the one can hear no sound!

" 'When Laura is walking through a passage-way, with her hands spread before her, she knows instantly every one she meets, and passes them with a sign of recognition: but if it be a girl of her own age, and especially if it be one of her favorites, there is instantly a bright smile of recognition, and a twining of arms, a grasping of hands, and a swift telegraphing upon the tiny fingers; whose rapid evolutions convey the thoughts and feelings from the outposts of one mind to those of the other. There are questions and answers, exchanges of joy or sorrow, there are kissings and partings, just as between little children with all their senses.'

"During this year, and six months after she had left home, her mother came to visit her, and the scene of their meeting was an interesting one.

"The mother stood some time, gazing with overflowing eyes upon her unfortunate child, who, all unconscious of her presence, was playing about the room. Presently Laura ran against her, and at once began feeling her hands, examining her dress, and trying to find out if she knew her; but not succeeding in this, she turned away as from a stranger, and the poor woman could not conceal the pang she felt at finding that her beloved child did not know her.

"She then gave Laura a string of beads which she used to wear at home, which were recognized by the child at once, who, with much joy, put them around her neck, and sought me eagerly to say she understood the string was from her home.

"The mother now tried to caress her, but poor Laura repelled her, preferring to be with her acquaintances.

"Another article from home was now given her, and she began to look much interested; she examined the stranger much closer, and gave me to understand that she knew she came from Hanover; she even endured her caresses, but would leave her with indifference at the slightest signal. The distress of the mother was now painful to behold; for, although she had feared that she should not be recognized, the painful reality of being treated with cold indifference by a darling child was too much for woman's nature to bear.

"After a while, on the mother taking hold of her again, a vague idea seemed to flit across Laura's mind that this could not be a stranger; she therefore felt her hands very eagerly, while her countenance assumed an expression of intense interest; she became very pale, and then suddenly red; hope seemed struggling with doubt and anxiety, and never were contending emotions more strongly painted upon the human face: at this moment of painful uncertainty, the mother drew her close to her side, and kissed her fondly, when at once the truth flashed upon the child, and all mistrust and anxiety disappeared from her face, as with an expression of exceeding joy she eagerly nestled to the bosom of her parent, and yielded herself to her fond embraces.

"After this the beads were all unheeded; the playthings which were offered to her were utterly disregarded; her playmates, for whom but a moment before she gladly left the stranger, now vainly strove to pull her from her mother; and though she yielded her usual instantaneous obedience to my signal to follow me, it was evidently with painful reluctance. She clung close to me, as if bewildered and fearful; and when, after a moment, I took her to her mother, she sprang to her arms, and clung to her with eager joy.

"The subsequent parting between them showed alike the affection, the intelligence, and the resolution of the child.

"Laura accompanied her mother to the door, clinging close to her all the way, until they arrived at the threshold, where she paused, and felt around to ascertain who was near her. Perceiving the matron, of whom she is very fond, she grasped her with one hand, holding on convulsively to her mother with the other; and thus she stood for a moment: then she dropped her mother's hand; put her handkerchief to her eyes; and, turning round, clung sobbing to the matron; while her mother departed, with emotions as deep as those of her child.

"It has been remarked, in former reports, that she can distinguish different degrees of intellect in others, and that she soon regarded almost with contempt a newcomer, when, after a few days, she discovered her weakness of mind. This unamiable part of her character has been more strongly developed during the past year.

"She chooses for her friends and companions those children who are intelligent, and can talk best with her; and she evidently dislikes to be with those who are deficient in intellect, unless, indeed, she can make them serve her purposes, which she is evidently inclined to do. She takes advantage of them, and makes them wait upon her, in a manner that she knows she could not exact of others; and in various ways she shows her Saxon blood.

"She is fond of having other children noticed and caressed by the teachers, and those whom she respects; but this must not be carried too far, or she becomes jealous. She wants to have her share, which, if not the lion's, is the greater part; and if she does not get it, she says, *'My mother will love me.'*

"Her tendency to imitation is so strong that it leads her to actions which must be entirely incomprehensible to her, and which can give her no other pleasure than the gratification of an internal faculty. She has been known to sit for half an hour, holding a book before her sightless eyes, and moving her lips, as she has observed seeing people do when reading.

"She one day pretended that her doll was sick; and went through all the motions of tending it, and giving it medicine; she then put it carefully to bed, and placed a bottle of hot water to its feet, laughing all the time most heartily. When I came home, she insisted upon my going to see it, and feel its pulse; and when I told her to put a blister on its back, she seemed to enjoy it amazingly, and almost screamed with delight.

"Her social feelings, and her affections, are very strong; and when she is sitting at work, or at her studies, by the side of one of her little friends, she will break off from her task every few moments, to hug and kiss them with an earnestness and warmth that is touching to behold.

"When left alone, she occupies, and apparently amuses herself, and seems quite contented; and so strong seems to be the natural tendency of thought to put on the garb of language, that she often soliloquizes in the *finger language,* slow and tedious as it is. But it is only when alone that she is quiet: for if she becomes sensible of the presence of any one near her, she is restless until she can sit close beside them, hold their hand, and converse with them by signs.

"In her intellectual character it is pleasing to observe an insatiable thirst for knowledge, and a quick perception of the relations of things. In her moral character, it is beautiful to behold her continual gladness, her keen enjoyment of existence, her expansive love, her unhesitating confidence, her sympathy with suffering, her conscientiousness, truthfulness, and hopefulness."

Such are a few fragments from the simple but most interesting and instructive history of Laura Bridgman. The name of her great benefactor and friend, who writes it, is Doctor Howe. There are not many persons, I hope and believe, who, after reading these passages, can ever hear that name with indifference.

A further account has been published by Doctor Howe, since the report from which I have just quoted. It describes her rapid mental growth and improvement during twelve months more, and brings her little history down to the end of last year. It is very remarkable that as we dream in words, and carry on imaginary conversations, in which we speak both for ourselves and for the shadows who appear to us in those visions of the night, so she, having no words, uses her finger alphabet in her sleep. And it has been ascertained that when her slumber is broken, and is much disturbed by dreams, she expresses her thoughts in an irregular and confused manner on her fingers: just as we should murmur and mutter them indistinctly in the like circumstances.

I turned over the leaves of her Diary, and found it written in a fair, legible, square hand, and expressed in terms which were quite intelligible without any explanation. On my saying that I should like to see her write again, the teacher who sat beside her bade her, in their language, sign her name upon a slip of paper twice or thrice. In doing so, I observed that she kept her left hand always touching and following up her right, in which, of course, she held the pen. No line was indicated by any contrivance, but she wrote straight and freely.

She had, until now, been quite unconscious of the presence of visitors; but, having her hand placed in that of the gentleman who accompanied me, she immediately expressed his name upon her teacher's palm. Indeed, her sense of touch is now so exquisite, that having been acquainted with a person once, she can recognize him or her after almost any interval. This gentleman had been in her company, I believe, but very seldom, and certainly had not seen her for many months. My hand she rejected at once, as she does that of any man who is a stranger to her. But she retained my wife's with evident pleasure, kissed her, and examined her dress with a girl's curiosity and interest.

She was merry and cheerful, and showed much innocent playfulness in her intercourse with her teacher. Her delight on recognizing a favorite playfellow and companion—herself a blind girl—who silently, and with an equal enjoyment of the coming surprise, took a seat beside her, was beautiful to witness. It elicited from her at first, as other slight circumstances did twice or thrice during my visit, an uncouth noise which was rather painful to hear. But, on her teacher touching her lips, she immediately desisted, and embraced her laughingly and affectionately.

I had previously been into another chamber, where a number of blind boys were swinging, and climbing, and engaged in various sports. They all clamored, as we entered, to the assistant master, who accompanied us, "Look at me, Mr. Hart! Please, Mr. Hart, look at me!" evincing, I thought, even in this, an anxiety peculiar to their condition, that their little feats of agility should be *seen*. Among them was a small laughing fellow, who stood aloof, entertaining himself with a gymnastic exercise for bringing the arms and chest into play; which he enjoyed mightily; especially when, in thrusting out his right arm, he brought it into contact with another boy. Like Laura Bridgman, this young child was deaf, and dumb, and blind.

Doctor Howe's account of this pupil's first instruction is so very striking, and so intimately connected with Laura herself, that I cannot refrain from a short extract. I may premise that the poor boy's name is Oliver Caswell; that he is thirteen years of age; and that he was in full possession of all his faculties until three years and four months old. He was then attacked by scarlet fever: in four weeks became deaf; in a few weeks more, blind; in six months, dumb. He showed his anxious sense of this last deprivation by often feeling the lips of other persons when they were talking, and then putting his hand upon his own, as if to assure himself that he had them in the right position.

"His thirst for knowledge," says Doctor Howe, "proclaimed itself as soon as he entered the house, by his eager examination of everything he could feel or smell in his new location. For instance, treading upon the register of a furnace, he instantly stooped down and began to feel it, and soon discovered the way in which the upper plate moved upon the lower one; but this was not enough for him, so, lying down upon his face, he applied his tongue first to one, then to the other, and seemed to discover that they were of different kinds of metal.

"His signs were expressive: and the strictly natural language, laughing, crying, sighing, kissing, embracing, etc., was perfect.

"Some of the analogical signs which (guided by his

faculty of imitation) he had contrived, were comprehensible; such as the waving motion of his hand for the motion of a boat, the circular one for a wheel, etc.

"The first object was to break up the use of these signs, and to substitute for them the use of purely arbitrary ones.

"Profiting by the experience I had gained in the other cases, I omitted several steps of the process before employed, and commenced at once with the finger language. Taking, therefore, several articles having short names, such as key, cup, mug, etc., and with Laura for an auxiliary, I sat down, and, taking his hand, placed it upon one of them, and then with my own made the letters k e y. He felt my hands eagerly with both of his, and, on my repeating the process, he evidently tried to imitate the motions of my fingers. In a few minutes he contrived to feel the motions of my fingers with one hand, and, holding out the other, he tried to imitate them, laughing most heartily when he succeeded. Laura was by, interested even to agitation; and the two presented a singular sight: her face was flushed and anxious, and her fingers twined in among ours so closely as to follow every motion, but so lightly as not to embarrass them; while Oliver stood attentive, his head a little aside, his face turned up, his left hand grasping mine, and his right held out; at every motion of my fingers his countenance betokened keen attention; there was an expression of anxiety as he tried to imitate the motions; then a smile came stealing out as he thought he could do so, and spread into a joyous laugh the moment he succeeded, and felt me pat his head, and Laura clap him heartily upon the back, and jump up and down in her joy.

"He learned more than a half-dozen letters in half an hour, and seemed delighted with his success, at least in gaining approbation. His attention then began to flag, and I commenced playing with him. It was evident that in all this he had merely been imitating the motions of my fingers, and placing his hand upon the key, cup, etc., as part of the process, without any perception of the relation between the sign and the object.

"When he was tired with play I took him back to the table, and he was quite ready to begin again his process of imitation. He soon learned to make the letters for

key, pen, pin; and, by having the object repeatedly placed
in his hand, he at last perceived the relation I wished to
establish between them. This was evident, because when
I made the letters *p i n,* or *p e n,* or *c u p,* he would
select the article.

"The perception of this relation was not accompanied
by that radiant flash of intelligence, and that glow of joy,
which marked the delightful moment when Laura first
perceived it. I then placed all the articles on the table,
and going away a little distance with the children, placed
Oliver's fingers in the positions to spell *key,* on which
Laura went and brought the article: the little fellow
seemed to be much amused by this, and looked very attentive and smiling. I then caused him to make the letters
b r e a d, and in an instant Laura went and brought
him a piece; he smelled at it; put it to his lips; cocked
up his head with a most knowing look; seemed to reflect
a moment; and then laughed outright, as much as to say,
'Aha! I understand now how something may be made
out of this.'

"It was now clear that he had the capacity and inclination to learn, that he was a proper subject for instruction, and needed only persevering attention. I therefore
put him in the hands of an intelligent teacher, nothing
doubting of his rapid progress."

Well may this gentleman call that a delightful moment,
in which some distant promise of her present state first
gleamed upon the darkened mind of Laura Bridgman.
Throughout his life, the recollection of that moment will
be to him a source of pure, unfading happiness; nor will
it shine least brightly on the evening of his days of Noble
Usefulness.

The affection that exists between these two—the master
and the pupil—is as far removed from all ordinary care
and regard, as the circumstances in which it has had its
growth are apart from the common occurrences of life.
He is occupied now in devising means of imparting to her
higher knowledge, and of conveying to her some adequate idea of the Great Creator of that universe in which,
dark and silent and scentless though it be to her, she has
such deep delight and glad enjoyment.

Ye who have eyes and see not, and have ears and hear
not; ye who are as the hypocrites of sad countenances,

and disfigure your faces that ye may seem unto men to fast;
learn healthy cheerfulness, and mild contentment, from
the deaf, and dumb, and blind! Self-elected saints with
gloomy brows, this sightless, earless, voiceless child may
teach you lessons you will do well to follow. Let that poor
hand of hers lie gently on your hearts; for there may
be something in its healing touch akin to that of the
Great Master whose precepts you misconstrue, whose lessons you pervert, of whose charity and sympathy with
all the world not one among you, in his daily practice,
knows as much as many of the worst among those fallen
sinners, to whom you are liberal in nothing but the preach-
ment of perdition!

As I rose to quit the room, a pretty little child of one
of the attendants came running in to greet its father.
For the moment, a child with eyes among the sightless
crowd impressed me almost as painfully as the blind boy
in the porch had done, two hours ago. Ah! how much
brighter and more deeply blue, glowing and rich though
it had been before, was the scene without, contrasting with
the darkness of so many youthful lives within!

At SOUTH BOSTON, as it is called, in a situation excellently adapted for the purpose, several charitable institutions are clustered together. One of these is the State
Hospital for the insane; admirably conducted on those enlightened principles of conciliation and kindness, which
twenty years ago would have been worse than heretical,
and which have been acted upon with so much success in
our own pauper asylum at Hanwell. "Evince a desire to
show some confidence, and repose some trust, even in
mad people," said the resident physician, as we walked
along the galleries, his patients flocking round us unre-
strained. Of those who deny or doubt the wisdom of this
maxim after witnessing its effects, if there be such people
still alive, I can only say that I hope I may never be summoned as a Juryman on a Commission of Lunacy whereof
they are the subjects; for I should certainly find them out
of their senses, on such evidence alone.

Each ward in this institution is shaped like a long
gallery or hall, with the dormitories of the patients opening from it on either hand. Here they work, read, play at
skittles and other games; and, when the weather does not

admit of their taking exercise out of doors, pass the day together. In one of these rooms, seated calmly, and quite as a matter of course, among a throng of madwomen, black and white, were the physician's wife and another lady with a couple of children. These ladies were graceful and handsome; and it was not difficult to perceive, at a glance, that even their presence there had a highly beneficial influence on the patients who were grouped about them.

Leaning her head against the chimney-piece, with a great assumption of dignity and refinement of manner, sat an elderly female, in as many scraps of finery as Madge Wildfire herself. Her head in particular was so strewn with scraps of gauze and cotton and bits of paper, and had so many queer odds and ends stuck all about it, that it looked like a bird's nest. She was radiant with imaginary jewels; wore a rich pair of undoubted gold spectacles; and gracefully dropped upon her lap, as we approached, a very old, greasy newspaper, in which I dare say she had been reading an account of her own presentation at some Foreign Court.

I have been thus particular in describing her, because she will serve to exemplify the physician's manner of acquiring and retaining the confidence of his patients.

"This," he said aloud, taking me by the hand, and advancing to the fantastic figure with great politeness—not raising her suspicions by the slightest look or whisper, or any kind of aside, to me: "this lady is the hostess of this mansion, sir. It belongs to her. Nobody else has anything whatever to do with it. It is a large establishment, as you see, and requires a great number of attendants. She lives, you observe, in the very first style. She is kind enough to receive my visits, and to permit my wife and family to reside here; for which, it is hardly necessary to say, we are much indebted to her. She is exceedingly courteous, you perceive,"—on this hint she bowed condescendingly,—"and will permit me to have the pleasure of introducing you: a gentleman from England, ma'am: newly arrived from England, after a very tempestuous passage: Mr. Dickens—the lady of the house!"

We exchanged the most dignified salutations with profound gravity and respect, and so went on. The rest of the madwomen seemed to understand the joke perfectly (not

only in this case, but in all the others, except their own),
and to be highly amused by it. The nature of their several
kinds of insanity was made known to me in the same way,
and we left each of them in high good-humor. Not only is
a thorough confidence established, by these means, between physician and patient, in respect of the nature and
extent of their hallucinations, but it is easy to understand
that opportunities are afforded for seizing any moment of
reason, to startle them by placing their own delusion before them in its most incongruous and ridiculous light.

Every patient in this asylum sits down to dinner every
day with a knife and fork; and in the midst of them
sits the gentleman, whose manner of dealing with his
charges I have just described. At every meal, moral
influence alone restrains the more violent among them
from cutting the throats of the rest; but the effect of that
influence is reduced to an absolute certainty, and is found,
even as a means of restraint, to say nothing of it as a means
of cure, a hundred times more efficacious than all the
strait-waistcoats, fetters and handcuffs that ignorance,
prejudice, and cruelty have manufactured since the
creation of the world.

In the labor department, every patient is as freely
trusted with the tools of his trade as if he were a sane
man. In the garden, and on the farm, they work with
spades, rakes, and hoes. For amusement, they walk, run,
fish, paint, read, and ride out to take the air in carriages
provided for the purpose. They have among themselves
a sewing society to make clothes for the poor, which holds
meetings, passes resolutions, never comes to fisticuffs or
bowie-knives, as sane assemblies have been known to do
elsewhere; and conducts all its proceedings with the
greatest decorum. The irritability, which would otherwise
be expended on their own flesh, clothes, and furniture, is
dissipated in these pursuits. They are cheerful, tranquil,
and healthy.

Once a week they have a ball, in which the Doctor and
his family, with all the nurses and attendants, take an
active part. Dances and marches are performed alternately, to the enlivening strains of a piano; and now and
then some gentleman or lady (whose proficiency has been
previously ascertained) obliges the company with a song;
nor does it ever degenerate, at a tender crisis, into a

screech or a howl; wherein, I must confess, I should have thought the danger lay. At an early hour they all meet together for these festive purposes; at eight o'clock refreshments are served; and at nine they separate.

Immense politeness and good-breeding are observed throughout. They all take their tone from the Doctor; and he moves a very Chesterfield among the company. Like other assemblies, these entertainments afford a fruitful topic of conversation among the ladies for some days; and the gentlemen are so anxious to shine on these occasions, that they have been sometimes found "practising their steps" in private, to cut a more distinguished figure in the dance.

It is obvious that one great feature of this system is the inculcation and encouragement, even among such unhappy persons, of a decent self-respect. Something of the same spirit pervades all the Institutions at South Boston.

There is the House of Industry. In that branch of it which is devoted to the reception of old or otherwise helpless paupers, these words are painted on the walls: "WORTHY OF NOTICE. SELF-GOVERNMENT, QUIETUDE, AND PEACE ARE BLESSINGS." It is not assumed and taken for granted that, being there, they must be evil-disposed and wicked people, before whose vicious eyes it is necessary to flourish threats and harsh restraints. They are met at the very threshold with this mild appeal. All within doors is very plain and simple, as it ought to be, but arranged with a view to peace and comfort. It costs no more than any other plan of arrangement, but it bespeaks an amount of consideration for those who are reduced to seek a shelter there, which puts them at once upon their gratitude and good behavior. Instead of being parcelled out in great, long, rambling wards, where a certain amount of weazen life may mope, and pine, and shiver all day long, the building is divided into separate rooms, each with its share of light and air. In these the better kind of paupers live. They have a motive for exertion and becoming pride, in the desire to make these little chambers comfortable and decent. I do not remember one but it was clean and neat, and had its plant or two upon the window-sill, or row of crockery upon the shelf, or small display of colored prints upon the white-washed wall, or, perhaps, its wooden clock behind the door.

The orphans and young children are in an adjoining building; separate from this, but a part of the same Institution. Some are such little creatures that the stairs are of Lilliputian measurement, fitted to their tiny strides. The same consideration for their years and weakness is expressed in their very seats, which are perfect curiosities, and look like articles of furniture for a pauper doll's house. I can imagine the glee of our Poor-Law Commissioners at the notion of these seats having arms and backs; but small spines being of older date than their occupation of the Board-room at Somerset House, I thought even this provision very merciful and kind.

Here, again, I was greatly pleased with the inscriptions on the wall, which were scraps of plain morality, easily remembered and understood: such as "Love one another" —"God remembers the smallest creature in his creation:" and straightforward advice of that nature. The books and tasks of these smallest of scholars were adapted, in the same judicious manner, to their childish powers. When we had examined these lessons, four morsels of girls (of whom one was blind) sang a little song about the merry month of May, which I thought (being extremely dismal) would have suited an English November better. That done, we went to see their sleeping-rooms on the floor above, in which the arrangements were no less excellent and gentle than those we had seen below. And after observing that the teachers were of a class and character well suited to the spirit of the place, I took leave of the infants with a lighter heart than ever I have taken leave of pauper infants yet.

Connected with the House of Industry, there is also a Hospital, which was in the best order, and had, I am glad to say, many beds unoccupied. It had one fault, however, which is common to all American interiors: the presence of the eternal, accursed, suffocating, red-hot demon of a stove, whose breath would blight the purest air under Heaven.

There are two establishments for boys in this same neighborhood. One is called the Boylston School, and is an asylum for neglected and indigent boys who have committed no crime, but who, in the ordinary course of things, would very soon be purged of that distinction if they were not taken from the hungry streets and sent here. The other is a House of Reformation for Juvenile Offenders. They are both under the same roof, but the two classes of boys never come in contact.

The Boylston boys, as may be readily supposed, have very much the advantage of the others in point of personal appearance. They were in their schoolroom when I came upon them, and answered correctly, without book, such questions as where was England; how far was it; what was its population; its capital city; its form of government; and so forth. They sang a song, too, about a farmer sowing his seed: with corresponding action at such parts as "'tis thus he sows," "he turns him round," "he claps his hands;" which gave it greater interest for them, and accustomed them to act together in an orderly manner. They appeared exceedingly well taught, and not better taught than fed; for a more chubby-looking, full-waist-coated set of boys I never saw.

The juvenile offenders had not such pleasant faces by a great deal, and in this establishment there were many boys of color. I saw them first at their work (basket-making, and the manufacture of palm-leaf hats), afterwards in their school, where they sang a chorus in praise of Liberty: an odd, and, one would think, rather aggravating, theme for prisoners. These boys were divided into four classes, each denoted by a numeral, worn on a badge upon the arm. On the arrival of a new-comer, he is put into the fourth or lowest class, and left, by good behavior, to work his way up into the first. The design and object of this Institution is to reclaim the youthful criminal by firm, but kind and judicious, treatment; to make his prison a place of purification and improvement, not of demoralization and corruption; to impress upon him that there is but one path, and that one sober industry, which can ever lead him to happiness; to teach him how it may be trodden, if his footsteps have never yet been led that way; and to lure him back to it, if they have strayed: in a word, to snatch him from destruction, and restore him to society a penitent and useful member. The importance of such an establishment, in every point of view, and with reference to every consideration of humanity and social policy, requires no comment.

One other establishment closes the catalogue. It is the House of Correction for the State, in which silence is strictly maintained, but where the prisoners have the comfort and mental relief of seeing each other, and of working together. This is the improved system of Prison Discipline which we have imported into England, and which has been in successful operation among us for some years past.

America, as a new and not over-populated country, has in all her prisons the one great advantage of being enabled to find useful and profitable work for the inmates: whereas, with us, the prejudice against prison labor is naturally very strong, and almost insurmountable, when honest men, who have not offended against the laws, are frequently doomed to seek employment in vain. Even in the United States, the principle of bringing convict labor and free labor into a competition which must obviously be to the disadvantage of the latter, has already found many opponents, whose number is not likely to diminish with access of years.

For this very reason, though, our best prisons would seem at the first glance to be better conducted than those of America. The treadmill is accompanied with little or no noise; five hundred men may pick oakum in the same room without a sound; and both kinds of labor admit of such keen and vigilant superintendence, as will render even a word of personal communication among the prisoners almost impossible. On the other hand, the noise of the loom, the forge, the carpenter's hammer, or the stone-mason's saw greatly favors those opportunities of intercourse—hurried and brief, no doubt, but opportunities still—which these several kinds of work, by rendering it necessary for men to be employed very near to each other, and often side by side, without any barrier or partition between them, in their very nature present. A visitor, too, requires to reason and reflect a little, before the sight of a number of men engaged in ordinary labor, such as he is accustomed to out of doors, will impress him half as strongly as the contemplation of the same persons in the same place and garb would, if they were occupied in some task, marked and degraded everywhere as belonging only to felons in jails. In an American State prison, or house of correction, I found it difficult at first to persuade myself that I was really in a jail: a place of ignominious punishment and endurance. And to this hour I very much question whether the humane boast, that it is not like one, has its root in the true wisdom or philosophy of the matter.

I hope I may not be misunderstood on this subject, for it is one in which I take a strong and deep interest. I incline as little to the sickly feeling which makes every canting lie or maudlin speech of a notorious criminal a subject of newspaper report and general sympathy, as I do to those good old customs of the good old times which made England, even so recently as in the reign of the Third King George, in respect of her criminal code and her prison regulations, one of the most bloody-minded and barbarous countries on the earth. If I thought it would do any good to the rising generation, I would cheerfully give my consent to the disinterment of the bones of any genteel highwayman (the more genteel, the more cheerfully), and to their exposure, piecemeal, on any sign-post, gate, or gibbet that might be deemed a good elevation for the purpose. My reason is as well convinced that these gentry were utterly worthless and debauched villains, as it is that the laws and jails hardened them in their evil courses, or that their wonderful escapes were effected by the prison turnkeys who, in those admirable days, had always been felons themselves, and were, to the last, their bosom friends and pot companions. At the same time, I know, as all men do or should, that the subject of Prison Discipline is one of the highest importance to any community; and that, in her sweeping reform and bright example to other countries on this head, America has shown great wisdom, great benevolence, and exalted policy. In contrasting her system with that which we have modelled upon it, I merely seek to show that, with all its drawbacks, ours has some advantages of its own.[1]

[1] Apart from profit made by the useful labor of prisoners, which we can never hope to realize to any great extent, and which it is perhaps not expedient for us to try to gain, there are two prisons in London, in all respects equal, and in some decidedly superior, to any I saw, or have ever heard or read of, in America. One is the Tothill Fields Bridewell, conducted by Lieutenant A. F. Tracey, R.N.; the other the Middlesex House of Correction, superintended by Mr. Chesterton. This gentleman also holds an appointment in the Public Service. Both are enlightened and superior men; and it would be as difficult to find persons better qualified for the functions they discharge with firmness, zeal, intelligence, and humanity, as it would be to exceed the perfect order and arrangement of the institutions they govern.

The House of Correction which has led to these remarks is not walled, like other prisons, but is palisaded
round about with tall rough stakes, something after the
manner of an enclosure for keeping elephants in, as we
see it represented in Eastern prints and pictures. The
prisoners wear a party-colored dress; and those who are
sentenced to hard labor work at nail-making or stone-
cutting. When I was there, the latter class of laborers
were employed upon the stone for a new Custom House in
course of erection at Boston. They appeared to shape it
skilfully and with expedition, though there were very few
among them (if any) who had not acquired the art
within the prison gates.

The women, all in one large room, were employed
in making light clothing for New Orleans and the Southern
States. They did their work in silence, like the men; and,
like them, were overlooked by the person contracting for
their labor, or by some agent of his appointment. In
addition to this, they are every moment liable to be
visited by the prison officers appointed for that purpose.

The arrangements for cooking, washing of clothes, and
so forth, are much upon the plan of those I have seen at
home. Their mode of bestowing the prisoners at night
(which is of general adoption) differs from ours, and
is both simple and effective. In the centre of a lofty area,
lighted by windows in the four walls, are five tiers of
cells, one above the other; each tier having before it a
light iron gallery, attainable by stairs of the same construction and material; excepting the lower one, which
is on the ground. Behind these, back to back with them,
and facing the opposite wall, are five corresponding rows
of cells, accessible by similar means: so that, supposing
the prisoners locked up in their cells, an officer stationed
on the ground, with his back to the wall, has half their
number under his eye at once; the remaining half being
equally under the observation of another officer on the
opposite side; and all in one great apartment. Unless this
watch be corrupted or sleeping on his post, it is impossible
for a man to escape; for even in the event of his forcing
the iron door of his cell without noise (which is exceedingly improbable), the moment he appears outside, and
steps into that one of the five galleries on which it is

situated, he must be plainly and fully visible to the officer below. Each of these cells holds a small truckle-bed, in which one prisoner sleeps; never more. It is small, of course; and the door being not solid, but grated, and without blind or curtain, the prisoner within is at all times exposed to the observation and inspection of any guard who may pass along that tier at any hour or minute of the night. Every day, the prisoners receive their dinner, singly, through a trap in the kitchen wall; and each man carries his to his sleeping cell to eat it, where he is locked up alone, for that purpose, one hour. The whole of this arrangement struck me as being admirable; and I hope that the next new prison we erect in England may be built on this plan.

I was given to understand that in this prison no swords or fire-arms, or even cudgels, are kept; nor is it probable that, so long as its present excellent management continues, any weapon, offensive or defensive, will ever be required within its bounds.

Such are the Institutions at South Boston! In all of them, the unfortunate or degenerate citizens of the State are carefully instructed in their duties both to God and man; are surrounded by all reasonable means of comfort and happiness that their condition will admit of; are appealed to as members of the great human family, however afflicted, indigent, or fallen; are ruled by the strong Heart, and not by the strong (though immeasurably weaker) Hand. I have described them at some length: firstly, because their worth demanded it; and secondly, because I mean to take them for a model, and to content myself with saying of others we may come to, whose design and purpose are the same, that in this or that respect they practically fail, or differ.

I wish by this account of them, imperfect in its execution, but, in its just intention, honest, I could hope to convey to my readers one hundredth part of the gratification the sights I have described afforded me.

To an Englishman, accustomed to the paraphernalia of Westminster Hall, an American Court of Law is as odd a sight as, I suppose, an English Court of Law would be to an American. Except in the Supreme Court at Washington (where the judges wear a plain black robe), there is no such thing as a wig or gown connected with the administration of justice. The gentlemen of the bar, being barristers and attorneys too (for there is no division of those functions as in England), are no more removed from their clients than attorneys in our Court for the Relief of Insolvent Debtors are from theirs. The jury are quite at home, and make themselves as comfortable as circumstances will permit. The witness is so little elevated above, or put aloof from, the crowd in the court, that a stranger entering during a pause in the proceedings would find it difficult to pick him out from the rest. And if it chanced to be a criminal trial, his eyes, in nine cases out of ten, would wander to the dock in search of the prisoner in vain; for that gentleman would most likely be lounging among the most distinguished ornaments of the legal profession, whispering suggestions in his counsel's ear, or making a toothpick out of an old quill with his penknife.

I could not but notice these differences when I visited the courts at Boston. I was much surprised at first, too, to observe that the counsel who interrogated the witness under examination at the time did so *sitting*. But seeing that he was also occupied in writing down the answers, and remembering that he was alone, and had no "junior," I quickly consoled myself with the reflection that law was not quite so expensive an article here as at home; and that the absence of sundry formalities, which we regard as indispensable, had doubtless a very favorable influence upon the bill of costs.

In every court ample and commodious provision is made for the accommodation of the citizens. This is the case all through America. In every Public Institution, the right of the people to attend, and to have an interest in the proceedings, is most fully and distinctly recognized. There are no grim door-keepers to dole out their tardy civility by the sixpennyworth; nor is there, I sincerely believe, any insolence of office of any kind. Nothing national is exhibited for money; and no public officer is a showman. We have begun, of late years, to imitate this good example. I hope we shall continue to do so; and that, in the fulness of time, even deans and chapters may be converted.

In the civil court an action was trying for damages

sustained in some accident upon a railway. The witnesses
had been examined, and counsel was addressing the jury.
The learned gentleman (like a few of his English brethren) was desperately long-winded, and had a remarkable
capacity of saying the same thing over and over again.
His great theme was "Warren the ĕn*gine* driver," whom
he pressed into the service of every sentence he uttered.

I listened to him for about a quarter of an hour; and,
coming out of court at the expiration of that time, without the faintest ray of enlightenment as to the merits of
the case, felt as if I were at home again.

In the prisoners' cell, waiting to be examined by the
magistrate on a charge of theft, was a boy. This lad,
instead of being committed to a common jail, would be
sent to the asylum at South Boston, and there taught a
trade; and, in the course of time, he would be bound
apprentice to some respectable master. Thus his detec-
tion in this offence, instead of being the prelude to a life
of infamy and a miserable death, would lead, there was a
reasonable hope, to his being reclaimed from vice, and
becoming a worthy member of society.

I am by no means a wholesale admirer of our legal
solemnities, many of which impress me as being exceedingly ludicrous. Strange as it may seem, too, there is undoubtedly a degree of protection in the wig and gown—a
dismissal of individual responsibility in dressing for the
part—which encourages that insolent bearing and language, and that gross perversion of the office of a pleader
for The Truth, so frequent in our courts of law. Still, I
cannot help doubting whether America, in her desire to
shake off the absurdities and abuses of the old system,
may not have gone too far into the opposite extreme; and
whether it is not desirable, especially in the small community of a city like this, where each man knows the
other, to surround the administration of justice with
some artificial barriers against the "Hail fellow, well met"
deportment of every-day life. All the aid it can have in
the very high character and ability of the Bench, not
only here, but elsewhere, it has, and well deserves to
have; but it may need something more: not to impress
the thoughtful and the well informed, but the ignorant
and heedless; a class which includes some prisoners and
many witnesses. These institutions were established, no

doubt, upon the principle that those who had so large a share in making the laws would certainly respect them. But experience has proved this hope to be fallacious; for no men know better than the judges of America, that on the occasion of any great popular excitement the law is powerless, and cannot, for the time, assert its own supremacy.

The tone of society in Boston is one of perfect politeness, courtesy, and good-breeding. The ladies are unquestionably very beautiful—in face: but there I am compelled to stop. Their education is much as with us; neither better nor worse. I had heard some very marvellous stories in this respect; but, not believing them, was not disappointed. Blue ladies there are in Boston; but, like philosophers of that color and sex in most other latitudes, they rather desire to be thought superior than to be so. Evangelical ladies there are, likewise, whose attachment to the forms of religion, and horror of theatrical entertainments, are most exemplary. Ladies who have a passion for attending lectures are to be found among all classes and all conditions. In the kind of provincial life which prevails in cities such as this, the Pulpit has great influence. The peculiar province of the Pulpit in New England (always excepting the Unitarian ministry) would appear to be the denouncement of all innocent and rational amusements. The church, the chapel, and the lecture-room are the only means of excitement excepted; and to the church, the chapel, and the lecture-room the ladies resort in crowds.

Wherever religion is resorted to as a strong drink, and as an escape from the dull, monotonous round of home, those of its ministers who pepper the highest will be the surest to please. They who strew the Eternal Path with the greatest amount of brimstone, and who most ruthlessly tread down the flowers and leaves that grow by the wayside, will be voted the most righteous; and they who enlarge with the greatest pertinacity on the difficulty of getting into heaven will be considered, by all true believers, certain of going there: though it would be hard to say by what process of reasoning this conclusion is arrived at. It is so at home, and it is so abroad. With regard to the other means of excitement, the Lecture, it has at least the merit of being always new. One lecture treads so quickly on the heels of another, that none are remembered; and the course of this month may be safely repeated next, with its charm of novelty unbroken, and its interest unabated.

The fruits of the earth have their growth in corruption. Out of the rottenness of these things there has sprung up in Boston a sect of philosophers known as Transcendentalists. On inquiring what this appellation might be supposed to signify, I was given to understand that whatever was unintelligible would be certainly transcendental. Not deriving much comfort from this elucidation, I pursued the inquiry still further, and found that the Transcendentalists are followers of my friend Mr. Carlyle, or I should rather say, of a follower of his, Mr. Ralph Waldo Emerson. This gentleman has written a volume of Essays, in which, among much that is dreamy and fanciful (if he will pardon me for saying so), there is much more that is true and manly, honest and bold. Transcendentalism has its occasional vagaries (what school has not?), but it has good healthful qualities in spite of them; not least among the number a hearty disgust of Cant, and an aptitude to detect her in all the million varieties of her everlasting wardrobe. And therefore, if I were a Bostonian, I think I would be a Transcendentalist.

The only preacher I heard in Boston was Mr. Taylor, who addresses himself peculiarly to seamen, and who was once a mariner himself. I found his chapel down among the shipping, in one of the narrow, old, water-side streets, with a gay blue flag waving freely from its roof. In the gallery opposite to the pulpit were a little choir of male and female singers, a violoncello, and a violin. The preacher already sat in the pulpit, which was raised on pillars, and ornamented behind him with painted drapery of a lively and somewhat theatrical appearance. He looked a weather-beaten, hard-featured man, of about six or eight and fifty; with deep lines graven as it were into his face, dark hair, and a stern, keen eye. Yet the general character of his countenance was pleasant and agreeable.

The service commenced with a hymn, to which succeeded an extemporary prayer. It had the fault of frequent repetition, incidental to all such prayers; but it was plain and comprehensive in its doctrines, and breathed a tone of general sympathy and charity, which is not so commonly a characteristic of this form of address to the Deity as it might be. That done, he opened his discourse, taking for his text a passage from the Song of Solomon, laid upon the desk before the commencement of the service by some unknown member of the congregation: "Who is this coming up from the wilderness, leaning on the arm of her beloved?"

He handled his text in all kinds of ways, and twisted it into all manner of shapes; but always ingeniously, and with a rude eloquence well adapted to the comprehension of his hearers. Indeed, if I be not mistaken, he studied their sympathies and understandings much more than the display of his own powers. His imagery was all drawn from the sea, and from the incidents of a seaman's life; and was often remarkably good. He spoke to them of "that glorious man, Lord Nelson," and of Collingwood; and drew nothing in, as the saying is, by the head and shoulders, but brought it to bear upon his purpose naturally, and with a sharp mind to its effect. Sometimes, when much excited with his subject, he had an odd way— compounded of John Bunyan and Balfour of Burley—of taking his great quarto Bible under his arm, and pacing up and down the pulpit with it; looking steadily down meantime, into the midst of the congregation. Thus, when he applied his text to the first assemblage of his hearers, and pictured the wonder of the church at their presumption in forming a congregation among themselves, he stopped short with his Bible under his arm in the manner I have described, and pursued his discourse after this manner:

"Who are these—who are they—who are these fellows? Where do they come from? Where are they going to?— Come from! What's the answer?" leaning out of the pulpit, and pointing downward with his right hand: "From below!"—starting back again, and looking at the sailors before him: "from below, my brethren. From under the hatches of sin, battened down above you by the evil one. That's where you came from!"—a walk up and down the pulpit: "and where are you going?"—stopping abruptly: "where are you going? Aloft!"—very softly, and pointing upward: "aloft!"—louder: "aloft!"— louder still: "that's where you are going—with a fair wind,—all taut and trim, steering direct for Heaven in its glory, where there are no storms or foul weather, and where the wicked cease from troubling, and the weary are at rest."—Another walk: "That's where you're going to, my friends. That's it. That's the place. That's the port. That's the haven. It's a blessed harbor—still water there, in all changes of the winds and tides; no driving ashore upon the rocks, or slipping your cables and running out to sea there: Peace—Peace—Peace—all peace!"—Another walk, and patting the Bible under his left arm: "What! These fellows are coming from the wilderness, are they? Yes. From the dreary, blighted wilderness of Iniquity, whose only crop is Death. But do they lean upon anything—do they lean upon nothing, these poor seamen?"—Three raps upon the Bible: "Oh, yes!—Yes.—They lean upon the arm of their Beloved"—three more raps: "upon the arm of their Beloved"—three more, and a walk: "Pilot, guiding-star, and compass, all in one, to all hands—here it is"—three more: "here it is. They can do their seaman's duty manfully, and be easy in their minds in the utmost peril and danger, with this"—two more: "they can come, even these poor fellows can come, from the wilderness, leaning on the arm of their Beloved, and go up—up—up!"—raising his hand higher and higher at every repetition of the word, so that he stood with it at last stretched above his head, regarding them in a strange, rapt manner, and pressing the book triumphantly to his breast until he gradually subsided into some other portion of his discourse.

I have cited this, rather as an instance of the preacher's eccentricities than his merits, though, taken in connection with his look and manner, and the character of his audience, even this was striking. It is possible, however, that my favorable impression of him may have been greatly influenced and strengthened, firstly, by his impressing upon his hearers that the true observance of religion was not inconsistent with a cheerful deportment and an exact discharge of the duties of their station, which, indeed, it scrupulously required of them; and secondly, by his cautioning them not to set up any monopoly in Paradise and its mercies. I never heard these two points so wisely touched (if, indeed, I have ever heard them touched at all) by any preacher of that kind before.

Having passed the time I spent in Boston in making

myself acquainted with these things, in settling the course I should take in my future travels, and in mixing constantly with its society, I am not aware that I have any occasion to prolong this chapter. Such of its social customs as I have not mentioned, however, may be told in a very few words.

The usual dinner hour is two o'clock. A dinner-party takes place at five; and at an evening party they seldom sup later than eleven; so that it goes hard but one gets home, even from a rout, by midnight. I never could find out any difference between a party at Boston and a party in London, saving that at the former place all assemblies are held at more rational hours; that the conversation may possibly be a little louder and more cheerful; that a guest is usually expected to ascend to the very top of the house to take his cloak off; that he is certain to see, at every dinner, an unusual amount of poultry on the table; and at every supper, at least two mighty bowls of hot stewed oysters, in any one of which a half-grown Duke of Clarence might be smothered easily.

There are two theatres in Boston, of good size and construction, but sadly in want of patronage. The few ladies who resort to them sit, as of right, in the front rows of the boxes.

The bar is a large room with a stone floor, and there people stand and smoke, and lounge about, all the evening: dropping in and out as the humor takes them. There, too, the stranger is initiated into the mysteries of Ginsling, Cocktail, Sangaree, Mint Julep, Sherry Cobbler, Timber Doodle, and other rare drinks. The house is full of boarders, both married and single, many of whom sleep upon the premises, and contract by the week for their board and lodging: the charge for which diminishes as they go nearer the sky to roost. A public table is laid in a very handsome hall for breakfast, and for dinner, and for supper. The party sitting down together to these meals will vary in number from one to two hundred: sometimes more. The advent of each of these epochs in the day is proclaimed by an awful gong, which shakes the very window frames as it reverberates through the house, and horribly disturbs nervous foreigners. There is an ordinary for ladies, and an ordinary for gentlemen.

In our private room the cloth could not, for any earthly

consideration, have been laid for dinner without a huge glass dish of cranberries in the middle of the table; and breakfast would have been no breakfast unless the principal dish were a deformed beef-steak with a great flat bone in the centre, swimming in hot butter, and sprinkled with the very blackest of all possible pepper. Our bedroom was spacious and airy, but (like every bedroom on this side of the Atlantic) very bare of furniture, having no curtains to the French bedstead or to the window. It had one unusual luxury, however, in the shape of a wardrobe of painted wood, something smaller than an English watch-box: or, if this comparison should be insufficient to convey a just idea of its dimensions, they may be estimated from the fact of my having lived for fourteen days and nights in the firm belief that it was a shower-bath.

CHAPTER 4

An American Railroad. Lowell and Its Factory System.

BEFORE leaving Boston, I devoted one day to an excursion to Lowell. I assign a separate chapter to this visit; not because I am about to describe it at any great length, but because I remember it as a thing by itself, and am desirous that my readers should do the same.

I made acquaintance with an American railroad on this occasion, for the first time. As these works are pretty much alike all through the States, their general characteristics are easily described.

There are no first and second class carriages as with us; but there is a gentlemen's car and a ladies' car: the main distinction between which is, that in the first everybody smokes; and in the second, nobody does. As a black man never travels with a white one, there is also a Negro car; which is a great, blundering, clumsy chest, such as Gulliver put to sea in from the kingdom of Brobdingnag. There is a great deal of jolting, a great deal of noise, a great deal of wall, not much window, a locomotive engine, a shriek, and a bell.

The cars are like shabby omnibuses, but larger: holding thirty, forty, fifty people. The seats, instead of stretching from end to end, are placed crosswise. Each seat holds two persons. There is a long row of them on each side of the caravan, a narrow passage up the middle, and a door at both ends. In the centre of the carriage there is usually a stove, fed with charcoal or anthracite coal; which is for the most part red-hot. It is insufferably close; and you see the hot air fluttering between yourself and any other object you may happen to look at, like the ghost of smoke.

In the ladies' car there are a great many gentlemen who have ladies with them. There are also a great many ladies who have nobody with them: for any lady may travel alone, from one end of the United States to the other, and be certain of the most courteous and considerate treatment everywhere. The conductor, or check-taker, or guard, or whatever he may be, wears no uniform. He walks up and down the car, and in and out of it, as his fancy dictates; leans against the door with his hands in his pockets, and stares at you, if you chance to be a stranger; or enters into conversation with the passengers about him. A great many newspapers are pulled out, and a few of them are read. Everybody talks to you, or to anybody else who hits his fancy. If you are an Englishman, he expects that that railroad is pretty much like an English railroad. If you say "No," he says "Yes?" (interrogatively), and asks in what respect they differ. You enumerate the heads of difference, one by one, and he says "Yes?" (still interrogatively) to each. Then he guesses that you don't travel faster in England; and on your replying that you do, says "Yes?" again (still interrogatively), and, it is quite evident, doesn't believe it. After a long pause he remarks, partly to you, and partly to the knob on the top of his stick, that "Yankees are reckoned to be considerable of a go-ahead people too;" upon which *you* say "Yes," and then *he* says "Yes" again (affirmatively this time); and upon your looking out of window, tells you that behind that hill, and some three miles from the next station, there is a clever town in a smart lo-ca-tion, where he expects you have con-cluded to stop. Your answer in the negative naturally leads to more questions in reference to your intended route (always pronounced rout); and wherever you are going, you invariably learn that you can't get there without immense difficulty and danger, and that all the great sights are somewhere else.

If a lady take a fancy to any male passenger's seat, the gentleman who accompanies her gives him notice of the fact, and he immediately vacates it with great politeness. Politics are much discussed; so are banks, so is cotton.

RAILWAY DIALOGUE.

Quiet people avoid the question of the Presidency, for there will be a new election in three years and a half, and party feeling runs very high: the great constitutional feature of this institution being, that directly the acrimony of the last election is over, the acrimony of the next one begins; which is an unspeakable comfort to all strong politicians and true lovers of their country: that is to say, to ninety-nine men and boys out of every ninety-nine and a quarter.

Except when a branch road joins the main one, there is seldom more than one track of rails; so that the road is very narrow, and the view, where there is a deep cutting, by no means extensive. When there is not, the character of the scenery is always the same. Mile after mile of stunted trees: some hewn down by the axe, some blown down by the wind, some half fallen and resting on their neighbors, many mere logs half hidden in the swamp, others mouldered away to spongy chips. The very soil of the earth is made up of minute fragments such as these; each pool of stagnant water has its crust of vegetable rottenness; on every side there are the boughs, and trunks, and stumps of trees, in every possible stage of decay, decomposition, and neglect. Now you emerge for a few brief minutes on an open country, glittering with some bright lake or pool, broad as many an English river, but so small here that it scarcely has a name; now catch hasty glimpses of a distant town, with its clean white houses and their cool piazzas, its prim New England church and schoolhouse; when whir-r-r-r! almost before you have seen them, comes the same dark screen: the stunted trees, the stumps, the logs, the stagnant water—all so like the last that you seem to have been transported back again by magic.

The train calls at stations in the woods, where the wild impossibility of anybody having the smallest reason to get out is only to be equalled by the apparently desperate hopelessness of there being anybody to get in. It rushes across the turnpike road, where there is no gate, no policeman, no signal: nothing but a rough wooden arch, on which is painted "WHEN THE BELL RINGS, LOOK OUT FOR THE LOCOMOTIVE." On it whirls headlong, dives through the woods again, emerges in the light, clatters over frail arches, rumbles upon the heavy ground, shoots beneath a wooden bridge which intercepts the light for a second like a wink, suddenly awakens all the slumbering echoes in the main street of a large town, and dashes on hap-hazard, pell-mell, neck or nothing, down the middle of the road. There—with mechanics working at their trades, and people leaning from their doors and windows, and boys flying kites and playing marbles, and men smoking, and women talking, and children crawling, and pigs burrowing, and unaccustomed horses plunging and rearing, close to the very rails—there—on, on, on—tears the mad dragon of an engine with its train of cars; scattering in all directions a shower of burning sparks from its wood fire; screeching, hissing, yelling, panting, until at last the thirsty monster stops beneath a covered way to drink, the people cluster round, and you have time to breathe again.

I was met at the station at Lowell by a gentleman intimately connected with the management of the factories there; and, gladly putting myself under his guidance, drove off at once to that quarter of the town in which the works, the object of my visit, were situated. Although only just of age—for, if my recollection serve me, it has been a manufacturing town barely one and twenty years—Lowell is a large, populous, thriving place. Those indications of its youth which first attract the eye, give it a quaintness and oddity of character which, to a visitor from the old country, is amusing enough. It was a very dirty winter's day, and nothing in the whole town looked old to me, except the mud, which in some parts was almost knee-deep, and might have been deposited there on the subsiding of the waters after the Deluge. In one place there was a new wooden church, which, having no steeple, and being yet unpainted, looked like an enormous packing-case without any direction upon it. In another there was a large hotel, whose walls and colonnades were so crisp, and thin, and slight, that it had exactly the appearance of being built with cards. I was careful not to draw my breath as we passed, and trembled when I saw a workman come out upon the roof, lest with one thoughtless stamp of his foot he should crush the structure beneath him, and bring it rattling down. The very river that moves the machinery in the mills (for they are all worked by water power) seems to acquire a new character from the fresh buildings of bright red brick and painted wood among which it takes its course; and to be as light-headed, thoughtless, and brisk a young river, in its murmurings and tumblings, as one would desire to see. One would swear that every "Bakery," "Grocery," and "Bookbindery," and other kind of store took its shutters down for the first time, and started in business yesterday. The golden pestles and mortars fixed as signs upon the sun-blind frames outside the Druggists' appear to have been just turned out of the United States Mint; and when I saw a baby of some week or ten days old in a woman's arms at a street corner, I found myself unconsciously wondering where it came from: never supposing for an instant that it could have been born in such a young town as that.

There are several factories in Lowell, each of which belongs to what we should term a Company of Proprietors, but what they call in America a Corporation. I went over several of these; such as a woollen factory, a carpet factory, and a cotton factory: examined them in every part; and saw them in their ordinary working aspect, with no preparation of any kind, or departure from their ordinary every-day proceedings. I may add that I am well acquainted with our manufacturing towns in England, and have visited many mills in Manchester and elsewhere in the same manner.

I happened to arrive at the first factory just as the dinner hour was over, and the girls were returning to their work; indeed, the stairs of the mill were thronged with them as I ascended. They were all well dressed, but not, to my thinking, above their condition: for I like to see the humbler classes of society careful of their dress and appearance, and even, if they please, decorated with such little trinkets as come within the compass of their means. Supposing it confined within reasonable limits, I would always encourage this kind of pride, as a worthy element of self-respect, in any person I employed; and should no more be deterred from doing so, because some wretched female referred her fall to a love of dress, than I would allow my construction of the real intent and meaning of the Sabbath to be influenced by any warning to the well disposed, founded on his backslidings on that

particular day, which might emanate from the rather
doubtful authority of a murderer in Newgate.

These girls, as I have said, were all well dressed: and
that phrase necessarily includes extreme cleanliness. They
had serviceable bonnets, good warm cloaks and shawls;
and were not above clogs and pattens. Moreover, there
were places in the mill in which they could deposit these
things without injury; and there were conveniences for
washing. They were healthy in appearance, many of them
remarkably so, and had the manners and deportment of
young women: not of degraded brutes of burden. If I
had seen in one of those mills (but I did not, though I
looked for something of this kind with a sharp eye) the
most lisping, mincing, affected, and ridiculous young creature that my imagination could suggest, I should have
thought of the careless, moping, slatternly, degraded, dull
reverse (I *have* seen that), and should have been still
well pleased to look upon her.

The rooms in which they worked were as well ordered
as themselves. In the windows of some there were green
plants, which were trained to shade the glass; in all, there
was as much fresh air, cleanliness, and comfort as the
nature of the occupation would possibly admit of. Out of
so large a number of females, many of whom were only
then just verging upon womanhood, it may be reasonably
supposed that some were delicate and fragile in appearance: no doubt there were. But I solemnly declare, that
from all the crowd I saw in the different factories that
day, I cannot recall or separate one young face that gave
me a painful impression; not one young girl whom, as-
suming it to be matter of necessity that she should gain
her daily bread by the labor of her hands, I would have
removed from those works if I had had the power.

They reside in various boarding-houses near at hand.
The owners of the mills are particularly careful to allow
no persons to enter upon the possession of these houses,
whose characters have not undergone the most searching
and thorough inquiry. Any complaint that is made against
them by the boarders, or by any one else, is fully investi-
gated; and if good ground of complaint be shown to exist
against them, they are removed, and their occupation is
handed over to some more deserving person. There are a
few children employed in these factories, but not many.

The laws of the State forbid their working more than nine months in the year, and require that they be educated during the other three. For this purpose there are schools in Lowell; and there are churches and chapels of various persuasions, in which the young women may observe that form of worship in which they have been educated.

At some distance from the factories, and on the highest and pleasantest ground in the neighborhood, stands their hospital, or boarding-house for the sick: it is the best house in those parts, and was built by an eminent merchant for his own residence. Like that institution at Boston, which I have before described, it is not parcelled out into wards, but is divided into convenient chambers, each of which has all the comforts of a very comfortable home. The principal medical attendant resides under the same roof; and were the patients members of his own family, they could not be better cared for, or attended with greater gentleness and consideration. The weekly charge in this establishment for each female patient is three dollars, or twelve shillings English; but no girl employed by any of the corporations is ever excluded for want of the means of payment. That they do not very often want the means may be gathered from the fact, that in July, 1841, no fewer than nine hundred and seventy-eight of these girls were depositors in the Lowell Savings Bank: the amount of whose joint savings was estimated at one hundred thousand dollars, or twenty thousand English pounds.

I am now going to state three facts, which will startle a large class of readers on this side of the Atlantic very much.

Firstly, there is a joint-stock piano in a great many of the boarding-houses. Secondly, nearly all these young ladies subscribe to circulating libraries. Thirdly, they have got up among themselves a periodical called THE LOWELL OFFERING, "a repository of original articles, written exclusively by females actively employed in the mills,"—which is duly printed, published, and sold; and whereof I brought away from Lowell four hundred good solid pages, which I have read from beginning to end.

The large class of readers, startled by these facts, will exclaim, with one voice, "How very preposterous!" On my deferentially inquiring why, they will answer, "These things are above their station." In reply to that objection, I would beg to ask what their station is.

It is their station to work. And they *do* work. They labor in these mills, upon an average, twelve hours a day, which is unquestionably work, and pretty tight work too. Perhaps it is above their station to indulge in such amusements on any terms. Are we quite sure that we in England have not formed our ideas of the "station" of working-people from accustoming ourselves to the contemplation of that class as they are, and not as they might be? I think that, if we examine our own feelings, we shall find that the pianos, and the circulating libraries, and even the Lowell Offering, startle us by their novelty, and not by their bearing upon any abstract question of right or wrong.

For myself, I know no station in which, the occupation of to-day cheerfully done and the occupation of to-morrow cheerfully looked to, any one of these pursuits is not most humanizing and laudable. I know no station which is rendered more endurable to the person in it, or more safe to the person out of it, by having ignorance for its associate. I know no station which has a right to monopolize the means of mutual instruction, improvement, and rational entertainment; or which has ever continued to be a station very long after seeking to do so.

Of the merits of the Lowell Offering as a literary production I will only observe, putting entirely out of sight the fact of the articles having been written by these girls after the arduous labors of the day, that it will compare advantageously with a great many English Annuals. It is pleasant to find that many of its Tales are of the Mills, and of those who work in them; that they inculcate habits of self-denial and contentment, and teach good doctrines of enlarged benevolence. A strong feeling for the beauties of nature, as displayed in the solitudes the writers have left at home, breathes through its pages like wholesome village air; and though a circulating library is a favorable school for the study of such topics, it has very scant allusion to fine clothes, fine marriages, fine houses, or fine life. Some persons might object to the papers being signed occasionally with rather fine names, but this is an American fashion. One of the provinces of the State Legislature of Massachusetts is to alter ugly names into pretty ones, as the children improve upon the tastes of their parents. These changes costing little or nothing, scores of Mary Annes are solemnly converted into Bevelinas every session.

It is said that on the occasion of a visit from General Jackson or General Harrison to this town (I forget which, but it is not to the purpose), he walked through three miles and a half of these young ladies, all dressed out with parasols and silk stockings. But, as I am not aware that any worse consequence ensued than a sudden looking-up of all the parasols and silk stockings in the market; and perhaps the Bankruptcy of some speculative New Englander who bought them all up at any price, in expectation of a demand that never came; I set no great store by the circumstance.

In this brief account of Lowell, and inadequate expression of the gratification it yielded me, and cannot fail to afford to any foreigner to whom the condition of such people at home is a subject of interest and anxious speculation, I have carefully abstained from drawing a comparison between these factories and those of our own land. Many of the circumstances whose strong influence has been at work for years in our manufacturing towns have not arisen here; and there is no manufacturing population in Lowell, so to speak: for these girls (often the daughters of small farmers) come from other States, remain a few years in the mills, and then go home for good.

The contrast would be a strong one, for it would be between the Good and Evil, the living light and deepest shadow. I abstain from it, because I deem it just to do so. But I only the more earnestly adjure all those whose eyes may rest on these pages, to pause and reflect upon the difference between this town and those great haunts of desperate misery: to call to mind, if they can in the midst of party strife and squabble, the efforts that must be made to purge them of their suffering and danger: and last, and foremost, to remember how the precious Time is rushing by.

I returned at night by the same railroad, and in the same kind of car. One of the passengers being exceedingly anxious to expound at great length to my companion (not to me, of course) the true principles on which books of travel in America should be written by Englishmen, I feigned to fall asleep. But, glancing all the way out at window from the corners of my eyes, I found abundance of entertainment for the rest of the ride in watching the effects of the wood fire, which had been invisible in the morning, but were now brought out in full relief by the darkness; for we were travelling in a whirlwind of bright sparks, which showered about us like a storm of fiery snow.

CHAPTER 5

Worcester. The Connecticut River. Hartford. New Haven to New York.

LEAVING Boston on the afternoon of Saturday, the fifth of February, we proceeded by another railroad to Worcester: a pretty New England town, where we had arranged to remain under the hospitable roof of the Governor of the State until Monday morning.

These towns and cities of New England (many of which would be villages in Old England) are as favorable specimens of rural America as their people are of rural Americans. The well-trimmed lawns and green meadows of home are not there; and the grass, compared with our ornamental plots and pastures, is rank, and rough, and wild: but delicate slopes of land, gently swelling hills, wooded valleys, and slender streams abound. Every little colony of houses has its church and schoolhouse peeping from among the white roofs and shady trees; every house is the whitest of the white; every Venetian blind the greenest of the green; every fine day's sky the bluest of the blue. A sharp dry wind and a slight frost had so hardened the roads when we alighted at Worcester, that their furrowed tracks were like ridges of granite. There was the usual aspect of newness on every object, of course. All the buildings looked as if they had been built and painted that morning, and could be taken down on Monday with very little trouble. In the keen evening air, every sharp outline looked a hundred times sharper than ever. The clean cardboard colonnades had no more perspective than a Chinese bridge on a teacup, and appeared equally well calculated for use. The razor-like edges of the detached cottages seemed to cut the very wind as it whistled against them, and to send it smarting on its way with a shriller cry than before. Those slightly built wooden dwellings, behind which the sun was setting with a brilliant lustre, could be so looked through and through, that the idea of any inhabitant being able to hide himself from the public gaze, or to have any secrets from the public eye, was not entertainable for a moment. Even where a blazing fire shone through the uncurtained windows of some distant house, it had the air of being newly lighted, and of lacking warmth; and instead of awakening thoughts of a snug chamber, bright with faces that first saw the light round that same hearth, and ruddy with warm hangings, it came upon one suggestive of the smell of new mortar and damp walls.

So I thought, at least, that evening. Next morning, when the sun was shining brightly, and the clear church bells were ringing, and sedate people in their best clothes enlivened the pathway near at hand, and dotted the distant thread of road, there was a pleasant Sabbath peacefulness on everything which it was good to feel. It would have been the better for an old church; better still for some old graves; but, as it was, a wholesome repose and tranquillity pervaded the scene, which, after the restless ocean and the hurried city, had a doubly grateful influence on the spirits.

We went on next morning, still by railroad, to Springfield. From that place to Hartford, whither we were bound, is a distance of only five and twenty miles, but at that time of the year the roads were so bad that the journey would probably have occupied ten or twelve hours. Fortunately, however, the winter having been unusually mild, the Connecticut River was "open," or, in other words, not frozen. The captain of a small steamboat was going to make his first trip for the season that day (the second February trip, I believe, within the memory of man), and only waited for us to go on board. Accordingly, we went on board with as little delay as might be. He was as good as his word, and started directly.

It certainly was not called a small steamboat without reason. I omitted to ask the question, but I should think it must have been of about half a pony power. Mr. Paap, the celebrated Dwarf, might have lived and died happily in the cabin, which was fitted with common sash-windows like an ordinary dwelling-house. These windows had bright red curtains, too, hung on slack strings across the lower panes; so that it looked like the parlor of a Lilliputian public-house, which had got afloat in a flood or some other water accident, and was drifting nobody knew where. But even in this chamber there was a rocking-chair. It would be impossible to get on anywhere, in America, without a rocking-chair.

I am afraid to tell how many feet short this vessel was, or how many feet narrow; to apply the words length and width to such measurement would be a contradiction in terms. But I may state that we all kept the middle of the deck, lest the boat should unexpectedly tip over: and that the machinery, by some surprising process of condensation, worked between it and the keel: the whole forming a warm sandwich, about three feet thick.

It rained all day, as I once thought it never did rain anywhere but in the Highlands of Scotland. The river was full of floating blocks of ice, which were constantly crunching and cracking under us; and the depth of water, in the course we took to avoid the larger masses, carried down the middle of the river by the current, did not exceed a few inches. Nevertheless, we moved onward dexterously; and, being well wrapped up, bade defiance to the weather, and enjoyed the journey. The Connecticut River is a fine stream; and the banks in summer-time are, I have no doubt, beautiful: at all events, I was told so by a young lady in the cabin; and she should be a judge of beauty, if the possession of a quality include the appreciation of it, for a more beautiful creature I never looked upon.

After two hours and a half of this odd travelling (including a stoppage at a small town, where we were saluted by a gun considerably bigger than our own chimney), we reached Hartford, and straight-way repaired to an extremely comfortable hotel: except, as usual, in the article of bedrooms, which, in almost every place we visited, were very conducive to early rising.

We tarried here four days. The town is beautifully situated in a basin of green hills; the soil is rich, well wooded, and carefully improved. It is the seat of the local legislature of Connecticut, which sage body enacted, in bygone times, the renowned code of "Blue Laws," in virtue whereof, among other enlightened provisions, any citizen who could be proved to have kissed his wife on Sunday was punishable, I believe, with the stocks. Too much of the old Puritan spirit exists in these parts to the present hour; but its influence has not tended, that I know, to make the people less hard in their bargains, or more equal in their dealings. As I never heard of its working that effect anywhere else, I infer that it never will here. Indeed, I am accustomed, with reference to great professions and severe faces, to judge of the goods of the other world pretty much as I judge of the goods of this; and whenever I see a dealer in such commodities with too great a display of them in his window, I doubt the quality of the article within.

In Hartford stands the famous oak in which the charter of King Charles was hidden. It is now enclosed in a gentleman's garden. In the State House is the charter itself. I found the courts of law here just the same as at Boston; the public Institutions almost as good. The Insane Asylum is admirably conducted, and so is the Institution for the Deaf and Dumb.

I very much questioned within myself, as I walked through the Insane Asylum, whether I should have known the attendants from the patients, but for the few words which passed between the former and the Doctor, in reference to the persons under their charge. Of course I limit this remark merely to their looks; for the conversation of the mad people was mad enough.

There was one little prim old lady, of very smiling and good-humored appearance, who came sidling up to me from the end of a long passage, and, with a courtesy of inexpressible condescension, propounded this unaccountable inquiry:

"Does Pontefract still flourish, sir, upon the soil of England?"

"He does, ma'am," I rejoined.

"When you last saw him, sir, he was—"

"Well, ma'am," said I, "extremely well. He begged me to present his compliments. I never saw him looking better."

At this the old lady was very much delighted. After glancing at me for a moment, as if to be quite sure that

I was serious in my respectful air, she sidled back some paces; sidled forward again; made a sudden skip (at which I precipitately retreated a step or two); and said,—

"*I* am an antediluvian, sir."

I thought the best thing to say was, that I had suspected as much from the first. Therefore I said so.

"It is an extremely proud and pleasant thing, sir, to be an antediluvian," said the old lady.

"I should think it was, ma'am," I rejoined.

The old lady kissed her hand, gave another skip, smirked, and sidled down the gallery in a most extraordinary manner, and ambled gracefully into her own bedchamber.

In another part of the building there was a male patient in bed; very much flushed and heated.

"Well!" said he, starting up, and pulling off his nightcap: "it's all settled at last. I have arranged it with Queen Victoria."

"Arranged what?" asked the Doctor.

"Why, that business," passing his hand wearily across his forehead, "about the siege of New York."

"Oh!" said I, like a man suddenly enlightened. For he looked at me for an answer.

"Yes. Every house without a signal will be fired upon by the British troops. No harm will be done to the others. No harm at all. Those that want to be safe must hoist flags. That's all they'll have to do. They must hoist flags."

Even while he was speaking he seemed, I thought, to have some faint idea that his talk was incoherent. Directly he had said these words, he lay down again; gave a kind of groan; and covered his hot head with the blankets.

There was another: a young man whose madness was love and music. After playing on the accordion a march he had composed, he was very anxious that I should walk into his chamber, which I immediately did.

By way of being very knowing, and humoring him to the top of his bent, I went to the window, which commanded a beautiful prospect, and remarked, with an address upon which I greatly plumed myself,—

"What a delicious country you have about these lodgings of yours!"

"Poh!" said he, moving his fingers carelessly over the

notes of his instrument. *"Well enough for such an Institution as this!"*

I don't think I was ever so taken aback in all my life. "I come here just for a whim," he said coolly. "That's all."

"Oh! That's all!" said I.

"Yes. That's all. The Doctor's a smart man. He quite enters into it. It's a joke of mine. I like it for a time. You needn't mention it, but I think I shall go out next Tuesday!"

I assured him that I would consider our interview perfectly confidential: and rejoined the Doctor. As we were passing through a gallery on our way out, a well-dressed lady, of quiet and composed manners, came up, and, proffering a slip of paper and a pen, begged that I would oblige her with an autograph. I complied, and we parted.

"I think I remember having had a few interviews like that with ladies out of doors. I hope *she* is not mad?"

"Yes."

"On what subject? Autographs?"

"No. She hears voices in the air."

"Well!" thought I, "it would be well if we could shut up a few false prophets of these later times, who have professed to do the same; and I should like to try the experiment on a Mormonist or two to begin with."

In this place there is the best Jail for untried offenders in the world. There is also a very well-ordered State prison, arranged upon the same plan as that at Boston, except that here there is always a sentry on the wall with a loaded gun. It contained at that time about two hundred prisoners. A spot was shown me in the sleeping ward, where a watchman was murdered some years since in the dead of night, in a desperate attempt to escape made by a prisoner who had broken from his cell. A woman, too, was pointed out to me, who, for the murder of her husband, had been a close prisoner for sixteen years.

"Do you think," I asked of my conductor, "that after so very long an imprisonment, she has any thought or hope of ever regaining her liberty?"

"Oh dear yes!" he answered. "To be sure she has."

"She has no chance of obtaining it, I suppose?"

"Well, I don't know:" which, by the by, is a national answer. "Her friends mistrust her."

"What have *they* to do with it?" I naturally inquired.

"Well, they won't petition."

"But if they did, they couldn't get her out, I suppose?"

"Well, not the first time, perhaps, nor yet the second, but tiring and wearying for a few years might do it."

"Does that ever do it?"

"Why, yes, that'll do it sometimes. Political friends 'll do it sometimes. It's pretty often done, one way or another."

I shall always entertain a very pleasant and grateful recollection of Hartford. It is a lovely place, and I had many friends there, whom I never can remember with indifference. We left it with no little regret on the evening of Friday the 11th, and travelled that night by railroad to New Haven. Upon the way, the guard and I were formally introduced to each other (as we usually were on such occasions), and exchanged a variety of small talk. We reached New Haven at about eight o'clock, after a journey of three hours, and put up for the night at the best inn.

New Haven, known also as the City of Elms, is a fine town. Many of its streets (as its *alias* sufficiently imports) are planted with rows of grand old elm-trees; and the same natural ornaments surround Yale College, an establishment of considerable eminence and reputation. The various departments of this Institution are erected in a kind of park or common in the middle of the town, where they are dimly visible among the shadowing trees. The effect is very like that of an old cathedral yard in England; and, when their branches are in full leaf, must be extremely picturesque. Even in the winter-time, these groups of well-grown trees, clustering among the busy streets and houses of a thriving city, have a very quaint appearance: seeming to bring about a kind of compromise between town and country; as if each had met the other half-way, and shaken hands upon it; which is at once novel and pleasant.

After a night's rest, we rose early, and in good time went down to the wharf, and on board the packet New York *for* New York. This was the first American steamboat of any size that I had seen: and certainly, to an English eye, it was infinitely less like a steamboat than a huge floating bath. I could hardly persuade myself, indeed, but that the bathing establishment of Westminster Bridge, which I left a baby, had suddenly grown to an enormous size; run away from home; and set up in foreign parts as a steamer. Being in America, too, which our vagabonds do so particularly favor, it seemed the more probable.

The great difference in appearance between these packets and ours is, that there is so much of them out of the water: the main deck being enclosed on all sides, and filled with casks and goods, like any second or third floor in a stack of warehouses; and the promenade or hurricane deck being atop of that again. A part of the machinery is always above this deck; where the connecting-rod, in a strong and lofty frame, is seen working away like an iron top-sawyer. There is seldom any mast or tackle: nothing aloft but two tall black chimneys. The man at the helm is shut up in a little house in the fore part of the boat (the wheel being connected with the rudder by iron chains, working the whole length of the deck); and the passengers, unless the weather be very fine indeed, usually congregate below. Directly you have left the wharf, all the life, and stir, and bustle of a packet cease. You wonder for a long time how she goes on, for there seems to be nobody in charge of her; and when another of these dull machines comes splashing by, you feel quite indignant with it, as a sullen, cumbrous, ungraceful, unshiplike leviathan: quite forgetting that the vessel you are on board of is its very counterpart.

There is always a clerk's office on the lower deck, where you pay your fare; a ladies' cabin; baggage and stowage rooms; engineer's room; and, in short, a great variety of perplexities which render the discovery of the gentlemen's cabin a matter of some difficulty. It often occupies the whole length of the boat (as it did in this case), and has three or four tiers of berths on each side. When I first descended into the cabin of the New York, it looked, in my unaccustomed eyes, about as long as the Burlington Arcade.

The Sound, which has to be crossed on this passage, is not always a very safe or pleasant navigation, and has been the scene of some unfortunate accidents. It was a wet morning, and very misty, and we soon lost sight of land. The day was calm, however, and brightened towards noon. After exhausting (with good help from a friend) the larder, and the stock of bottled beer, I lay down to sleep: being very much tired with the fatigues of yesterday. But

I awoke from my nap in time to hurry up, and see Hell Gate, the Hog's Back, the Frying Pan, and other notorious localities, attractive to all readers of famous Diedrich Knickerbocker's History. We were now in a narrow channel, with sloping banks on either side, besprinkled with pleasant villas, and made refreshing to the sight by turf and trees. Soon we shot, in quick succession, past a lighthouse: a madhouse (how the lunatics flung up their caps and roared in sympathy with the head-long engine and the driving tide!) ; a jail; and other buildings: and so emerged into a noble bay, whose waters sparkled in the now cloudless sunshine like Nature's eyes turned up to Heaven.

Then there lay stretched out before us, to the right, confused heaps of buildings, with here and there a spire or steeple, looking down upon the herd below; and here and there, again, a cloud of lazy smoke; and in the foreground a forest of ships, masts, cheery with flapping sails and waving flags. Crossing from among them to the opposite shore, were steam ferry-boats laden with people, coaches, horses, wagons, baskets, boxes: crossed and recrossed by other ferry-boats: all travelling to and fro: and never idle. Stately among these restless Insects were two or three large ships, moving with slow majestic pace, as creatures of a prouder kind, disdainful of their puny journeys, and making for the broad sea. Beyond were shining heights, and islands in the glancing river, and a distance scarcely less blue and bright than the sky it seemed to meet. The city's hum and buzz, the clinking of capstans, the ringing of bells, the barking of dogs, the clattering of wheels, tingled in the listening ear. All of which life and stir, coming across the stirring water, caught new life and animation from its free companionship; and, sympathizing with its buoyant spirits, glistened as it seemed in sport upon its surface, and hemmed the vessel round, and plashed the water high about her sides, and, floating her gallantly into the dock, flew off again to welcome other comers, and speed before them to the busy port.

CHAPTER 6

New York.

THE beautiful metropolis of America is by no means so
clean a city as Boston, but many of its streets have the
same characteristics; except that the houses are not quite
so fresh-colored, the sign-boards are not quite so gaudy,
the gilded letters not quite so golden, the bricks not
quite so red, the stone not quite so white, the blinds and
area railings not quite so green, the knobs and plates upon
the street-doors not quite so bright and twinkling. There
are many by-streets, almost as neutral in clean colors, and
positive in dirty ones, as by-streets in London; and there is
one quarter, commonly called the Five Points, which, in
respect of filth and wretchedness, may be safely backed
against Seven Dials, or any other part of famed St. Giles's.

The great promenade and thoroughfare, as most people
know, is Broadway; a wide and bustling street, which,
from the Battery Gardens to its opposite termination in a
country road, may be four miles long. Shall we sit down in
an upper floor of the Carlton House Hotel (situated in the
best part of this main artery of New York), and, when we
are tired of looking down upon the life below, sally forth
arm in arm, and mingle with the stream?

Warm weather! The sun strikes upon our heads, at
this open window, as though its rays were concentrated
through a burning-glass; but the day is in its zenith, and
the season an unusual one. Was there ever such a sunny
street as this Broadway? The pavement stones are polished
with the tread of feet until they shine again; the red bricks
of the houses might be yet in the dry, hot kilns; and the

99

roofs of those omnibuses look as though, if water were poured on them, they would hiss and smoke, and smell like half-quenched fires. No stint of omnibuses here! Half a dozen have gone by within as many minutes. Plenty of hackney cabs and coaches, too; gigs, phaetons, large-wheeled tilburies, and private carriages—rather of a clumsy make, and not very different from the public vehicles, but built for the heavy roads beyond the city pavement. Negro coachmen and white; in straw hats, black hats, white hats, glazed caps, fur caps; in coats of drab, black, brown, green, blue, nankeen, striped jean and linen; and there, in that one instance (look while it passes, or it will be too late), in suits of livery. Some Southern republican that, who puts his blacks in uniform, and swells with Sultan pomp and power. Yonder, where that phaeton with the well-clipped pair of grays has stopped—standing at their heads now—is a Yorkshire groom, who has not been very long in these parts, and looks sorrowfully round for a companion pair of top-boots, which he may traverse the city half a year without meeting. Heaven save the ladies, how they dress! We have seen more colors in these ten minutes than we should have seen elsewhere in as many days. What various parasols! what rainbow silks and satins! what pinking of thin stockings, and pinching of thin shoes, and fluttering of ribbons and silk tassels, and display of rich cloaks with gaudy hoods and linings! The young gentlemen are fond, you see, of turning down their shirt collars and cultivating their whiskers, especially under the chin; but they cannot approach the ladies in their dress or bearing, being, to say the truth, humanity of quite another sort. Byrons of the desk and counter, pass on, and let us see what kind of men those are behind ye: those two laborers in holiday clothes, of whom one carries in his hand a crumpled scrap of paper from which he tries to spell out a hard name, while the other looks about for it on all the doors and windows.

Irishmen both! You might know them, if they were masked, by their long-tailed blue coats and bright buttons, and their drab trousers, which they wear like men well used to working dresses, who are easy in no others. It would be hard to keep your model republics going without the countrymen and countrywomen of those two laborers.

For who else would dig, and delve, and drudge, and do
domestic work, and make canals and roads, and execute
great lines of Internal Improvement? Irishmen both,
and sorely puzzled, too, to find out what they seek. Let us
go down, and help them, for the love of home, and that
spirit of liberty which admits of honest service to honest
men, and honest work for honest bread, no matter what it
be.

That's well! We have got at the right address at last,
though it is written in strange characters truly, and might
have been scrawled with the blunt handle of the spade the
writer better knows the use of than a pen. Their way lies
yonder, but what business takes them there? They carry
savings: to hoard up? No. They are brothers, those men.
One crossed the sea alone, and working very hard for
one half year, and living harder, saved funds enough to
bring the other out. That done, they worked together side
by side, contentedly sharing hard labor and hard living
for another term, and then their sisters came, and then
another brother, and lastly, their old mother. And what
now? Why, the poor old crone is restless in a strange land,
and yearns to lay her bones, she says, among her people
in the old graveyard at home: and so they go to pay her
passage back: and God help her and them, and every
simple heart, and all who turn to the Jerusalem of their
younger days, and have an altar-fire upon the cold hearth
of their fathers!

This narrow thoroughfare, baking and blistering in the
sun, is Wall Street: the Stock Exchange and Lombard
Street of New York. Many a rapid fortune has been made
in this street, and many a no less rapid ruin. Some of these
very merchants whom you see hanging about here now,
have locked up money in their strong-boxes, like the man
in the Arabian Nights, and opening them again, have
found but withered leaves. Below, here by the water-side,
where the bowsprits of ships stretch across the footway,
and almost thrust themselves into the windows, lie the
noble American vessels which have made their Packet
Service the finest in the world. They have brought hither
the foreigners who abound in all the streets: not, perhaps,
that there are more here than in other commercial cities;
but elsewhere they have particular haunts, and you must
find them out; here they pervade the town.

We must cross Broadway again; gaining some refreshment from the heat in the sight of the great blocks of clean ice which are being carried into shops and bar-rooms; and the pine-apples and water-melons profusely displayed for sale. Fine streets of spacious houses here, you see!— Wall Street has furnished and dismantled many of them very often—and here a deep green leafy square. Be sure that is a hospitable house, with inmates to be affectionately remembered always, where they have the open door and pretty show of plants within, and where the child with laughing eyes is peeping out of window at the little dog below. You wonder what may be the use of this tall flagstaff in the by-street, with something like Liberty's head-dress on its top: so do I. But there is a passion for tall flagstaffs hereabout, and you may see its twin brother in five minutes, if you have a mind.

Again across Broadway, and so—passing from the many-colored crowd and glittering shops—into another long main street, the Bowery. A railroad yonder, see, where two stout horses trot along, drawing a score or two of people and a great wooden ark with ease. The stores are poorer here, the passengers less gay. Clothes ready made, and meat ready cooked, are to be bought in these parts; and the lively whirl of carriages is exchanged for the deep rumble of carts and wagons. These signs which are so plentiful, in shape like river buoys, or small balloons, hoisted by cords to poles, and dangling there, announce, as you may see by looking up, "OYSTERS IN EVERY STYLE." They tempt the hungry most at night, for then dull candles, glimmering inside, illuminate these dainty words, and make the mouths of idlers water as they read and linger.

What is this dismal-fronted pile of bastard Egyptian, like an enchanter's palace in a melodrama?—A famous prison, called The Tombs. Shall we go in?

So. A long, narrow, lofty building, stove-heated as usual, with four galleries, one above the other, going round it, and communicating by stairs. Between the two sides of each gallery, and in its centre, a bridge, for the greater convenience of crossing. On each of these bridges sits a man: dozing or reading, or talking to an idle companion. On each tier are two opposite rows of small iron doors. They look like furnace doors, but are cold and black, as though the fires within had all gone out. Some two or three are open, and women, with drooping heads bent down, are talking to the inmates. The whole is lighted by a skylight, but it is fast closed; and from the roof there dangle, limp and drooping, two useless wind-sails.

A man with keys appears, to show us round. A good-looking fellow, and, in his way, civil and obliging.

"Are those black doors the cells?"

"Yes."

"Are they all full?"

"Well, they're pretty nigh full, and that's a fact, and no two ways about it."

"Those at the bottom are unwholesome, surely?"

"Why, we *do* only put colored people in 'em. That's the truth."

"When do the prisoners take exercise?"

"Well, they do without it pretty much."

"Do they never walk in the yard?"

"Considerable seldom."

"Sometimes, I suppose?"

"Well, it's rare they do. They keep pretty bright without it."

"But suppose a man were here for a twelve-month. I know this is only a prison for criminals who are charged with grave offences, while they are awaiting their trial, or are under remand, but the law here affords criminals many means of delay. What with motions for new trial, and in arrest of judgment, and what not, a prisoner might be here for twelve months, I take it, might he not?"

"Well, I guess he might."

"Do you mean to say that in all that time he would never come out at that little iron door for exercise?"

"He might walk some, perhaps—not much."

"Will you open one of the doors?"

"All, if you like."

The fastenings jar and rattle, and one of the doors turns slowly on its hinges. Let us look in. A small bare cell, into which the light enters through a high chink in the wall. There is a rude means of washing, a table, and a bedstead. Upon the latter sits a man of sixty; reading. He looks up for a moment; gives an impatient dogged shake; and fixes his eyes upon his book again. As we withdraw our heads, the door closes on him, and is fastened as before. This man has murdered his wife, and will probably be hanged.

"How long has he been here?"

"A month."

"When will he be tried?"

"Next term."

"When is that?"

"Next month."

"In England, if a man be under a sentence of death even, he has air and exercise at certain periods of the day."

"Possible?"

With what stupendous and untranslatable coolness he says this, and how loungingly he leads on to the women's side: making, as he goes, a kind of iron castanet of the key and the stair-rail!

Each cell door on this side has a square aperture in it. Some of the women peep anxiously through it at the sound of footsteps; others shrink away in shame.—For what offence can that lonely child, of ten or twelve years old, be shut up here? Oh! that boy? He is the son of a prisoner we saw just now; is a witness against his father; and is detained here for safe keeping until the trial; that's all.

But it is a dreadful place for a child to pass the long days and nights in. This is rather hard treatment for a young witness, is it not?—What says our conductor?

"Well, it ain't a very rowdy life, and *that's* a fact!"

Again he clinks his metal castanet, and leads us leisurely away. I have a question to ask him as we go.

"Pray, why do they call this place The Tombs?"

"Well, it's the cant name."

"I know it is. Why?"

"Some suicides happened here when it was first built. I expect it come about from that."

"I saw, just now, that that man's clothes were scattered about the floor of his cell. Don't you oblige the prisoners to be orderly, and put such things away?"

"Where should they put 'em?"

"Not on the ground, surely. What do you say to hanging them up?"

He stops and looks round to emphasize his answer:

"Why, I say that's just it. When they had hooks they

would hang themselves, so they're taken out of every cell, and there's only the marks left where they used to be!"

The prison yard, in which he pauses now, has been the scene of terrible performances. Into this narrow, grave-like place men are brought out to die. The wretched creature stands beneath the gibbet on the ground; the rope about his neck; and when the sign is given, a weight at its other end comes running down, and swings him up into the air—a corpse.

The law requires that there be present at this dismal spectacle the judge, the jury, and citizens to the amount of twenty-five. From the community it is hidden. To the dissolute and bad, the thing remains a frightful mystery. Between the criminal and them, the prison wall is interposed as a thick gloomy veil. It is the curtain to his bed of death, his winding-sheet, and grave. From him it shuts out life, and all the motives to unrepenting hardihood in that last hour, which its mere sight and presence is often all-sufficient to sustain. There are no bold eyes to make him bold; no ruffians to uphold a ruffian's name before. All beyond the pitiless stone wall is unknown space.

Let us go forth again into the cheerful streets.

Once more in Broadway! Here are the same ladies in bright colors, walking to and fro, in pairs and singly; yonder the very same light blue parasol which passed and repassed the hotel window twenty times while we were sitting there. We are going to cross here. Take care of the pigs. Two portly sows are trotting up behind this carriage, and a select party of half a dozen gentlemen hogs have just now turned the corner.

Here is a solitary swine lounging homeward by himself. He has only one ear; having parted with the other to vagrant dogs in the course of his city rambles. But he gets on very well without it; and leads a roving, gentlemanly, vagabond kind of life, somewhat answering to that of our club men at home. He leaves his lodgings every morning at a certain hour, throws himself upon the town, gets through his day in some manner quite satisfactory to himself, and regularly appears at the door of his own house again at night, like the mysterious master of Gil Blas. He is a free-and-easy, careless, indifferent kind of pig, having a very large acquaintance among other pigs of the same character, whom he rather knows by sight than conversation, as he seldom troubles himself to stop and exchange civilities, but goes grunting down the kennel, turning up the news and small-talk of the city in the shape of cabbage-stalks and offal, and bearing no tails but his own: which is a very short one, for his old enemies, the dogs, have been at that too, and have left him hardly enough to swear by. He is in every respect a republican pig, going wherever he pleases, and mingling with the best society, on an equal, if not superior footing, for every one makes way when he appears, and the haughtiest give him the wall, if he prefer it. He is a great philosopher, and seldom moved, unless by the dogs before mentioned. Sometimes, indeed, you may see his small eyes twinkling on a slaughtered friend, whose carcass garnishes a butcher's door-post, but he grunts out, "Such is life: all flesh is pork!" buries his nose in the mire again, and waddles down the gutter: comforting himself with the reflection that there is one snout the less to anticipate stray cabbage-stalks, at any rate.

They are the city scavengers, these pigs. Ugly brutes they are; having, for the most part, scanty, brown backs, like the lids of old horsehair trunks: spotted with unwholesome black blotches. They have long, gaunt legs, too, and such peaked snouts, that if one of them could be persuaded to sit for his profile, nobody would recognize it for a pig's likeness. They are never attended upon, or fed, or driven, or caught, but are thrown upon their own resources in early life, and become preternaturally knowing in consequence. Every pig knows where he lives, much better than anybody could tell him. At this hour, just as evening is closing in, you will see them roaming towards bed by scores, eating their way to the last. Occasionally, some youth among them who has over-eaten himself, or has been much worried by dogs, trots shrinkingly homeward, like a prodigal son; but this is a rare case: perfect self-possession and self-reliance, and immovable composure, being their foremost attributes.

The streets and shops are lighted now; and as the eye travels down the long thoroughfare, dotted with bright jets of gas, it is reminded of Oxford Street or Piccadilly. Here and there a flight of broad stone cellar steps appears, and a painted lamp directs you to the Bowling Saloon, or Ten-Pin alley: Ten-Pins being a game of mingled chance and skill, invented when the legislature passed an act forbidding Nine-Pins. At other downward flights of steps are other lamps, marking the whereabouts of oyster cellars—pleasant retreats, say I: not only by reason of their wonderful cookery of oysters, pretty nigh as large as cheese-plates (or for thy dear sake, heartiest of Greek Professors!) but because, of all kinds of eaters of fish, or flesh, or fowl, in these latitudes, the swallowers of oysters alone are not gregarious; but subduing themselves, as it were, to the nature of what they work in, and copying the coyness of the thing they eat, do sit apart in curtained boxes, and consort by twos, not by two hundreds.

But how quiet the streets are! Are there no itinerant bands; no wind or stringed instruments? No, not one. By day, are there no Punches, Fantoccini, Dancing Dogs, Jugglers, Conjurers, Orchestrinas, or even Barrel-organs? No, not one. Yes, I remember one. One barrel-organ and a dancing monkey—sportive by nature, but fast fading into a dull, lumpish monkey, of the Utilitarian school. Beyond that, nothing lively; no, not so much as a white mouse in a twirling cage.

Are there no amusements? Yes, there is a lecture-room across the way, from which that glare of light proceeds, and there may be evening service for the ladies thrice a week, or oftener. For the young gentlemen there is the counting-house, the store, the bar-room; the latter, as you may see through these windows, pretty full. Hark! to the clinking sound of hammers breaking lumps of ice, and to the cool gurgling of the pounded bits, as, in the process of mixing, they are poured from glass to glass! No amusements? What are these suckers of cigars and swallowers of strong drinks, whose hats and legs we see in every possible variety of twist, doing, but amusing themselves? What are the fifty newspapers, which those precocious urchins are bawling down the street, and which are kept filed within, what are they but amusements? Not vapid, waterish amusements, but good strong stuff; dealing in round abuse and blackguard names; pulling off the roofs of private houses, as the Halting Devil did in Spain; pimping and pandering for all degrees of vicious taste, and gorging with coined lies the most voracious maw; imputing to every man in public life the coarsest and the vilest motives; scaring away from the stabbed and prostrate body politic every Samaritan of clear conscience and good deeds; and setting on, with yell and whistle, and the clapping of foul hands, the vilest vermin and worst birds of prey.—No amusements!

Let us go on again; and passing this wilderness of an hotel with stores about its base, like some Continental theatre, or the London Opera House shorn of its colonnade, plunge into the Five Points. But it is needful, first, that we take as our escort these two heads of the police, whom you would know for sharp and well-trained officers if you met them in the Great Desert. So true it is that certain pursuits, wherever carried on, will stamp men with the same character. These two might have been begotten, born, and bred in Bow Street.

We have seen no beggars in the streets by night or day; but of other kinds of strollers plenty. Poverty, wretchedness, and vice are rife enough where we are going now.

This is the place, these narrow ways, diverting to the right and left, and reeking everywhere with dirt and filth. Such lives as are led here, bear the same fruits here as elsewhere. The coarse and bloated faces at the doors have counterparts at home, and all the wide world over. Debauchery has made the very houses prematurely old. See how the rotten beams are tumbling down, and how the patched and broken windows seem to scowl dimly, like eyes that have been hurt in drunken frays. Many of those pigs live here. Do they ever wonder why their masters walk upright in lieu of going on all-fours? and why they talk instead of grunting?

So far, nearly every house is a low tavern; and on the bar-room walls are colored prints of Washington, and Queen Victoria of England, and the American Eagle. Among the pigeon-holes that hold the bottles are pieces of plate glass and colored paper, for there is, in some sort, a taste for decoration even here. And, as seamen frequent these haunts, there are maritime pictures by the dozen: of partings between sailors and their lady loves, portraits of William of the ballad, and his Black-Eyed Susan; of Will Watch, the Bold Smuggler; of Paul Jones the Pirate, and the like: on which the painted eyes of Queen Victoria, and of Washington to boot, rest in as

strange companionship as on most of the scenes that are
enacted in their wondering presence.

What place is this, to which the squalid street conducts
us? A kind of square of leprous houses, some of which
are attainable only by crazy wooden stairs without. What
lies beyond this tottering flight of steps, that creak beneath our tread?—A miserable room, lighted by one dim
candle, and destitute of all comfort, save that which may
be hidden in a wretched bed. Beside it sits a man: his
elbows on his knees: his forehead hidden in his hands.
"What ails that man?" asks the foremost officer. "Fever,"
he sullenly replies, without looking up. Conceive the fancies of a fevered brain in such a place as this!

Ascend these pitch-dark stairs, heedful of a false footing on the trembling boards, and grope your way with
me into this wolfish den, where neither ray of light nor
breath of air appears to come. A Negro lad, startled
from his sleep by the officer's voice—he knows it well—
but comforted by his assurance that he has not come on
business, officiously bestirs himself to light a candle. The
match flickers for a moment, and shows great mounds of
dusky rags upon the ground; then dies away and leaves a
denser darkness than before, if there can be degrees in
such extremes. He stumbles down the stairs, and presently
comes back shading a flaring taper with his hand. Then
the mounds of rags are seen to be astir, and rise slowly
up, and the floor is covered with heaps of Negro women,
waking from their sleep: their white teeth chattering,
and their bright eyes glistening and winking on all sides
with surprise and fear, like the countless repetition of one
astonished African face in some strange mirror.

Mount up these other stairs with no less caution (there
are traps and pitfalls here for those who are not so well
escorted as ourselves) into the housetop; where the bare
beams and rafters meet overhead, and calm night looks
down through the crevices in the roof. Open the door of
one of these cramped hutches full of sleeping Negroes.
Pah! They have a charcoal fire within; there is a smell of
singeing clothes, or flesh, so close they gather round the
brazier; and vapors issue forth that blind and suffocate.
From every corner, as you glance about you in these dark
retreats, some figure crawls half awakened, as if the judgment hour were near at hand, and every obscene grave

were giving up its dead. Where dogs would howl to lie, women, and men, and boys slink off to sleep, forcing the dislodged rats to move away in quest of better lodgings.

Here, too, are lanes and alleys, paved with mud knee-deep: underground chambers, where they dance and game; the walls bedecked with rough designs of ships, and forts, and flags, and American Eagles out of number: ruined houses, open to the street, whence, through wide gaps in the walls, other ruins loom upon the eye, as though the world of vice and misery had nothing else to show: hideous tenements which take their name from robbery and murder; all that is loathsome, drooping, and decayed is here.

Our leader has his hand upon the latch of "Almack's," and calls to us from the bottom of the steps; for the assembly-room of the Five-Point fashionables is approached by a descent. Shall we go in? It is but a moment.

Heyday! the landlady of Almack's thrives! A buxom fat mulatto woman, with sparkling eyes, whose head is daintily ornamented with a handkerchief of many colors. Nor is the landlord much behind her in his finery, being attired in a smart blue jacket, like a ship's steward, with a thick gold ring upon his little finger, and round his neck a gleaming golden watch-guard. How glad he is to see us! What will we please to call for? A dance? It shall be done directly, sir: "a regular break-down."

The corpulent black fiddler, and his friend who plays the tambourine, stamp upon the boarding of the small raised orchestra in which they sit, and play a lively measure. Five or six couples come upon the floor, marshalled by a lively young Negro, who is the wit of the assembly, and the greatest dancer known. He never leaves off making queer faces, and is the delight of all the rest, who grin from ear to ear incessantly. Among the dancers are two young mulatto girls, with large, black, drooping eyes, and headgear after the fashion of the hostess, who are as shy, or feign to be, as though they never danced before, and so look down before the visitors, that their partners can see nothing but the long fringed lashes.

But the dance commences. Every gentleman sets as long as he likes to the opposite lady, and the opposite lady to him, and all are so long about it that the sport begins to languish, when suddenly the lively hero dashes in to the

WHEN SUDDENLY THE LIVELY HERO DASHES IN TO THE RESCUE.

rescue. Instantly the fiddler grins, and goes at it tooth and nail; there is new energy in the tambourine; new laughter in the dancers; new smiles in the landlady; new confidence in the landlord; new brightness in the very candles. Single shuffle, double shuffle, cut and cross-cut: snapping his fingers, rolling his eyes, turning in his knees, presenting the backs of his legs in front, spinning about on his toes and heels like nothing but the man's fingers on the tambourine; dancing with two left legs, two right legs, two wooden legs, two wire legs, two spring legs—all sorts of legs and no legs—what is this to him? And in what walk of life, or dance of life, does man ever get such stimulating applause as thunders about him, when, having danced his partner off her feet, and himself too, he finishes by leaping gloriously on the bar-counter, and calling for something to drink, with the chuckle of a million of counterfeit Jim Crows, in one inimitable sound?

The air, even in these distempered parts, is fresh after the stifling atmosphere of the houses; and now, as we emerge into a broader street, it blows upon us with a purer breath, and the stars look bright again. Here are The Tombs once more. The city watch-house is a part of the building. It follows naturally on the sights we have just left. Let us see that, and then to bed.

What! do you thrust your common offenders against the police discipline of the town into such holes as these? Do men and women, against whom no crime is proved, lie here all night in perfect darkness, surrounded by the noisome vapors which encircle that flagging lamp you light us with, and breathing this filthy and offensive stench? Why, such indecent and disgusting dungeons as these cells would bring disgrace upon the most despotic empire in the world! Look at them, man—you, who see them every night, and keep the keys. Do you see what they are? Do you know how drains are made below the streets, and wherein these human sewers differ, except in being always stagnant?

Well, he don't know. He has had five and twenty young women locked up in this very cell at one time, and you'd hardly realize what handsome faces there were among 'em.

In God's name! shut the door upon the wretched creature who is in it now, and put its screen before a place quite unsurpassed in all the vice, neglect, and devilry of the worst old town in Europe.

Are people really left all night, untried, in those black sties?—Every night. The watch is set at seven in the evening. The magistrate opens his court at five in the morning. That is the earliest hour at which the first prisoner can be released; and if an officer appear against him, he is not taken out till nine o'clock or ten.—But if any one among them die in the interval, as one man did not long ago? Then he is half eaten by the rats in an hour's time, as that man was; and there an end.

What is this intolerable tolling of great bells, and crashing of wheels, and shouting in the distance? A fire. And what that deep red light in the opposite direction? Another fire. And what these charred and blackened walls we stand before? A dwelling where a fire has been. It was more than hinted, in an official report, not long ago, that some of these conflagrations were not wholly accidental, and that speculation and enterprise found a field of exertion, even in flames: but, be this as it may, there was a fire last night, there are two to-night, and you may lay an even wager there will be at least one to-morrow. So, carrying that with us for our comfort, let us say, Good-night, and climb upstairs to bed.

One day, during my stay in New York, I paid a visit to the different public institutions on Long Island, or Rhode Island: I forget which. One of them is a Lunatic Asylum. The building is handsome; and is remarkable for a spacious and elegant staircase. The whole structure is not yet finished, but it is already one of considerable size and extent, and is capable of accommodating a very large number of patients.

I cannot say that I derived much comfort from the inspection of this charity. The different wards might have been cleaner and better ordered; I saw nothing of that salutary system which had impressed me so favorably elsewhere; and everything had a lounging, listless, madhouse air, which was very painful. The moping idiot, cowering down with long dishevelled hair; the gibbering maniac, with his hideous laugh and pointed finger; the vacant eye, the fierce wild face, the gloomy picking of the hands and lips, and munching of the nails: there they were all, without disguise, in naked ugliness and horror. In the dining-room, a bare, dull, dreary place, with nothing for the eye to rest on but the empty walls, a woman was locked up alone. She was bent, they told me, on committing suicide. If anything could have strengthened her in her resolution, it would certainly have been the insupportable monotony of such an existence.

The terrible crowd with which these halls and galleries were filled so shocked me, that I abridged my stay within the shortest limits, and declined to see that portion of the building in which the refractory and violent were under closer restraint. I have no doubt that the gentleman who presided over this establishment at the time I write of, was competent to manage it, and had done all in his power to promote its usefulness: but will it be believed that the miserable strife of Party feeling is carried even into this sad refuge of afflicted and degraded humanity? Will it be believed that the eyes which are to watch over and control the wanderings of minds on which the most dreadful visitation to which our nature is exposed has fallen, must wear the glasses of some wretched side in Politics? Will it be believed that the governor of such a house as this is appointed, and deposed, and changed perpetually, as Parties fluctuate and vary, and as their despicable weather-cocks are blown this way or that? A hundred times in every week, some new most paltry exhibition of that narrow-minded and injurious Party Spirit which is the Simoom of America, sickening and blighting everything of wholesome life within its reach, was forced upon my notice; but I never turned my back upon it with feelings of such deep disgust and measureless contempt as when I crossed the threshold of this madhouse.

At a short distance from this building is another called the Alms House, that is to say, the workhouse of New York. This is a large institution also: lodging, I believe, when I was there, nearly a thousand poor. It was badly ventilated, and badly lighted; was not too clean; and impressed me, on the whole, very uncomfortably. But it must be remembered that New York, as a great emporium of commerce, and as a place of general resort, not only from all parts of the States, but from most parts of the world, has always a large pauper population to provide for; and labors, therefore, under peculiar difficulties in this respect. Nor must it be forgotten that New York is a large town, and that in all large towns a vast amount of good and evil is intermixed and jumbled up together.

In the same neighborhood is the Farm, where young orphans are nursed and bred. I did not see it, but I believe it is well conducted; and I can the more easily credit it, from knowing how mindful they usually are, in America, of that beautiful passage in the Litany which remembers all sick persons and young children.

I was taken to these Institutions by water, in a boat belonging to the Island Jail, and rowed by a crew of prisoners, who were dressed in a striped uniform of black and buff, in which they looked like faded tigers. They took me, by the same conveyance, to the Jail itself.

It is an old prison, and quite a pioneer establishment, on the plan I have already described. I was glad to hear this, for it is unquestionably a very indifferent one. The most is made, however, of the means it possesses, and it is as well regulated as such a place can be.

The women worked in covered sheds erected for that purpose. If I remember right, there are no shops for the men; but, be that as it may, the greater part of them labor in certain stone quarries near at hand. The day being very wet indeed, this labor was suspended, and the prisoners were in their cells. Imagine these cells, some two or three hundred in number, and in every one a man locked up; this one at his door for air, with his hands thrust through the grate; this one in bed (in the middle of the day, remember); and this one flung down in a heap upon the ground, with his head against the bars, like a wild beast. Make the rain pour down, outside, in torrents. Put the everlasting stove in the midst; hot, and suffocating, and vaporous as a witch's caldron. Add a collection of gentle odors, such as would arise from a thousand mildewed umbrellas, wet through, and a thousand buckbaskets, full of half-washed linen—and there is the prison as it was that day.

The prison for the State at Sing Sing is, on the other hand, a model jail. That, and Auburn, are, I believe, the largest and best examples of the silent system.

In another part of the city is the Refuge for the Destitute: an Institution whose object is to reclaim youthful offenders, male and female, black and white, without distinction; to teach them useful trades, apprentice them to respectable masters, and make them worthy members of society. Its design, it will be seen, is similar to that at Boston; and it is a no less meritorious and admirable establishment. A suspicion crossed my mind during my inspection of this noble charity, whether the superintendent had quite sufficient knowledge of the world and worldly characters; and whether he did not commit a great mistake in treating some young girls, who were to all intents and purposes, by their years and their past lives, women, as though they were little children; which certainly had a ludicrous effect in my eyes, and, or I am much mistaken, in theirs also. As the Institution, however, is always under the vigilant examination of a body of gentlemen of great intelligence and experience, it cannot fail to be well conducted; and whether I am right or wrong in this slight particular is unimportant to its deserts and character, which it would be difficult to estimate too highly.

In addition to these establishments, there are, in New York, excellent hospitals and schools, literary institutions and libraries; an admirable fire department (as, indeed, it should þe, having constant practice), and charities of every sort and kind. In the suburbs there is a spacious cemetery; unfinished yet, but every day improving. The saddest tomb I saw there was "The Strangers' Grave. Dedicated to the different hotels in this city."

There are three principal theatres. Two of them, the Park and the Bowery, are large, elegant, and handsome buildings, and are, I grieve to write it, generally deserted. The third, the Olympic, is a tiny show-box for vaudevilles and burlesques. It is singularly well conducted by Mr. Mitchell, a comic actor of great quiet humor and originality, who is well remembered and esteemed by London play-goers. I am happy to report of this deserving gentleman, that his benches are usually well filled, and that his theatre rings with merriment every night. I had almost forgotten a small summer theatre, called Niblo's, with gardens and open-air amusements attached; but I believe it is not exempt from the general depression under which Theatrical Property, or what is humorously called by that name, unfortunately labors.

The country around New York is surpassingly and exquisitely picturesque. The climate, as I have already intimated, is somewhat of the warmest. What it would be without the sea-breezes which come from its beautiful Bay in the evening-time, I will not throw myself or my readers into a fever by inquiring.

The tone of the best society in this city is like that of Boston; here and there, it may be, with a greater infusion of the mercantile spirit, but generally polished and refined, and always most hospitable. The houses and tables are elegant; the hours later and more rakish; and there is, perhaps, a greater spirit of contention in reference to appearances, and the display of wealth and costly living. The ladies are singularly beautiful.

Before I left New York I made arrangements for securing a passage home in the George Washington packet-ship, which was advertised to sail in June; that being the month in which I had determined, if prevented by no accident in the course of my ramblings, to leave America.

I never thought that going back to England, returning to all who are dear to me, and to pursuits that have insensibly grown to be part of my nature, I could have felt so much sorrow as I endured when I parted at last, on board this ship, with the friends who had accompanied me from this city. I never thought the name of any place so far away, and so lately known, could ever associate itself in my mind with the crowd of affectionate remembrances that now cluster about it. There are those in this city who would brighten, to me, the darkest winter day that ever glimmered and went out in Lapland; and before whose presence even Home grew dim, when they and I exchanged that painful word which mingles with our every thought and deed; which haunts our cradle-heads in infancy, and closes up the vista of our lives in age.

CHAPTER 7

Philadelphia, and Its Solitary Prison.

THE journey from New York to Philadelphia is made by railroad, and two ferries; and usually occupies between five and six hours. It was a fine evening when we were passengers in the train: and watching the bright sunset from a little window near the door by which we sat, my attention was attracted to a remarkable appearance issuing from the windows of the gentlemen's car immediately in front of us, which I supposed for some time was occasioned by a number of industrious persons inside ripping open feather beds, and giving the feathers to the wind. At length it occurred to me that they were only spitting, which was indeed the case; though how any number of passengers which it was possible for that car to contain could have maintained such a playful and incessant shower of expectoration, I am still at a loss to understand: notwithstanding the experience in all salivatory phenomena which I afterwards acquired.

I made acquaintance, on this journey, with a mild and modest young Quaker, who opened the discourse by informing me, in a grave whisper, that his grandfather was the inventor of cold-drawn castor oil. I mention the circumstance here, thinking it probable that this is the first occasion on which the valuable medicine in question was ever used as a conversational aperient.

We reached the city late that night. Looking out of my chamber window before going to bed, I saw, on the opposite side of the way, a handsome building of white marble, which had a mournful, ghost-like aspect, dreary to behold. I attributed this to the sombre influence of the night, and, on rising in the morning, looked out again, expecting to see its steps and portico thronged with groups of people passing in and out. The door was still tight shut, however; the same cold, cheerless air prevailed; and the building looked as if the marble statue of Don Guzman could alone have any business to transact within its gloomy walls. I hastened to inquire its name and purpose, and then my surprise vanished. It was the Tomb of many fortunes; the Great Catacomb of investment; the memorable United States Bank.

The stoppage of this bank, with all its ruinous consequences, had cast (as I was told on every side) a gloom on Philadelphia, under the depressing effect of which it yet labored. It certainly did seem rather dull and out of spirits.

It is a handsome city, but distractingly regular. After walking about it for an hour or two, I felt that I would have given the world for a crooked street. The collar of my coat appeared to stiffen, and the brim of my hat to expand, beneath its Quakerly influence. My hair shrunk into a sleek short crop, my hands folded themselves upon my breast of their own calm accord, and thoughts of taking lodgings in Mark Lane over against the Market-place, and of making a large fortune by speculations in corn, came over me involuntarily.

Philadelphia is most bountifully provided with fresh water, which is showered and jerked about, and turned on, and poured off everywhere. The Water-works, which are on a height near the city, are no less ornamental than useful, being tastefully laid out as a public garden, and kept in the best and neatest order. The river is dammed at this point, and forced by its own power into certain high tanks or reservoirs, whence the whole city, to the top stories of the houses, is supplied at a very trifling expense.

There are various public institutions. Among them a most excellent Hospital—a Quaker establishment, but not sectarian in the great benefits it confers; a quiet, quaint old Library, named after Franklin; a handsome Exchange and Post Office; and so forth. In connection with the Quaker Hospital there is a picture by West, which is exhibited for the benefit of the funds of the Institution. The subject is our Saviour healing the sick, and it is, perhaps,

as favorable a specimen of the master as can be seen
anywhere. Whether this be high or low praise, depends
upon the reader's taste.

In the same room there is a very characteristic and life-
like portrait by Mr. Sully, a distinguished American artist.

My stay in Philadelphia was very short, but what
I saw of its society I greatly liked. Treating of its general
characteristics, I should be disposed to say that it is more
provincial than Boston or New York, and that there is
afloat in the fair city an assumption of taste and criticism,
savoring rather of those genteel discussions upon the
same themes, in connection with Shakespeare and the Musical Glasses, of which we read in the Vicar of Wakefield.
Near the city is a most splendid unfinished marble structure for the Girard College, founded by a deceased gentleman of that name, and of enormous wealth, which, if
completed according to the original design, will be perhaps the richest edifice of modern times. But the bequest
is involved in legal disputes, and pending them the work
has stopped; so that, like many other great undertakings
in America, even this is rather going to be done one of
these days than doing now.

In the outskirts stands a great prison, called the Eastern
Penitentiary: conducted on a plan peculiar to the State
of Pennsylvania. The system here is rigid, strict, and
hopeless solitary confinement. I believe it, in its effects, to
be cruel and wrong.

In its intention I am well convinced that it is kind,
humane, and meant for reformation; but I am persuaded
that those who devised this system of Prison Discipline, and
those benevolent gentlemen who carry it into execution,
do not know what it is that they are doing. I believe
that very few men are capable of estimating the immense
amount of torture and agony which this dreadful punishment, prolonged for years, inflicts upon the sufferers; and
in guessing at it myself, and in reasoning from what I have
seen written upon their faces, and what to my certain
knowledge they feel within, I am only the more convinced
that there is a depth of terrible endurance in it which
none but the sufferers themselves can fathom, and which
no man has a right to inflict upon his fellow-creature. I
hold this slow and daily tampering with the mysteries of
the brain to be immeasurably worse than any torture of

the body; and because its ghastly signs and tokens are not so palpable to the eye and sense of touch as scars upon the flesh; because its wounds are not upon the surface, and it extorts few cries that human ears can hear; therefore I the more denounce it, as a secret punishment which slumbering humanity is not roused up to stay. I hesitated once, debating with myself whether, if I had the power of saying "Yes" or "No," I would allow it to be tried in certain cases, where the terms of imprisonment were short; but now I solemnly declare, that with no rewards or honors could I walk a happy man beneath the open sky by day, or lay me down upon my bed at night, with the consciousness that one human creature, for any length of time, no matter what, lay suffering this unknown punishment in his silent cell, and I the cause, or I consenting to it in the least degree.

I was accompanied to this prison by two gentlemen officially connected with its management, and passed the day in going from cell to cell, and talking with the inmates. Every facility was afforded me that the utmost courtesy could suggest. Nothing was concealed or hidden from my view, and every piece of information that I sought was openly and frankly given. The perfect order of the building cannot be praised too highly, and of the excellent motives of all who are immediately concerned in the administration of the system there can be no kind of question.

Between the body of the prison and the outer wall there is a spacious garden. Entering it by a wicket in the massive gate, we pursued the path before us to its other termination, and passed into a large chamber, from which seven long passages radiate. On either side of each is a long, long row of low cell doors, with a certain number over every one. Above, a gallery of cells like those below, except that they have no narrow yard attached (as those in the ground tier have), and are somewhat smaller. The possession of two of these is supposed to compensate for the absence of so much air and exercise as can be had in the dull strip attached to each of the others, in an hour's time every day; and therefore every prisoner in this upper story has two cells, adjoining, and communicating with, each other.

Standing at the central point, and looking down these dreary passages, the dull repose and quiet that prevails is awful. Occasionally there is a drowsy sound from some lone weaver's shuttle, or shoemaker's last, but it is stifled by the thick walls and heavy dungeon door, and only serves to make the general stillness more profound. Over the head and face of every prisoner who comes into this melancholy house a black hood is drawn; and in this dark shroud, an emblem of the curtain dropped between him and the living world, he is led to the cell from which he never again comes forth until his whole term of imprisonment has expired. He never hears of wife or children; home or friends; the life or death of any single creature. He sees the prison officers, but, with that exception, he never looks upon a human countenance, or hears a human voice. He is a man buried alive; to be dug out in the slow round of years; and in the meantime dead to everything but torturing anxieties and horrible despair.

His name, and crime, and term of suffering are unknown, even to the officer who delivers him his daily food. There is a number over his cell door, and in a book of which the governor of the prison has one copy, and the moral instructor another: this is the index to his history. Beyond these pages the prison has no record of his existence: and though he live to be in the same cell ten weary years, he has no means of knowing, down to the very last hour, in what part of the building it is situated; what kind of men there are about him; whether in the long winter nights there are living people near, or he is in some lonely corner of the great jail, with walls, and passages, and iron doors between him and the nearest sharer in its solitary horrors.

Every cell has double doors: the outer one of sturdy oak, the other of grated iron, wherein there is a trap through which his food is handed. He has a Bible, and a slate and pencil, and, under certain restrictions, has sometimes other books, provided for the purpose, and pen and ink and paper. His razor, plate, and can, and basin hang upon the wall, or shine upon the little shelf. Fresh water is laid on in every cell, and he can draw it at his pleasure. During the day, his bedstead turns up against the wall, and leaves more space for him to work in. His loom, or bench, or wheel is there; and there he labors, sleeps and wakes, and counts the seasons as they change, and grows old.

The first man I saw was seated at his loom, at work.

He had been there six years, and was to remain, I think, three more. He had been convicted as a receiver of stolen goods, but even after this long imprisonment denied his guilt, and said he had been hardly dealt by. It was his second offence.

He stopped his work when we went in, took off his spectacles, and answered freely to everything that was said to him, but always with a strange kind of pause first, and in a low, thoughtful voice. He wore a paper hat of his own making, and was pleased to have it noticed and commended. He had very ingeniously manufactured a sort of Dutch clock from some disregarded odds and ends; and his vinegar bottle served for the pendulum. Seeing me interested in this contrivance, he looked up at it with a great deal of pride, and said that he had been thinking of improving it, and that he hoped the hammer and a little piece of broken glass beside it "would play music before long." He had extracted some colors from the yarn with which he worked, and painted a few poor figures on the wall. One, of a female, over the door, he called "The Lady of the Lake."

He smiled as I looked at these contrivances to while away the time; but, when I looked from them to him, I saw that his lip trembled, and could have counted the beating of his heart. I forget how it came about, but some allusion was made to his having a wife. He shook his head at the word, turned aside, and covered his face with his hands.

"But you are resigned now?" said one of the gentlemen after a short pause, during which he had resumed his former manner. He answered with a sigh that seemed quite reckless in its hopelessness, "Oh, yes! oh, yes! I am resigned to it." "And are a better man, you think?" "Well, I hope so: I'm sure I hope I may be." "And time goes pretty quickly?" "Time is very long, gentlemen, within these four walls!"

He gazed about him—Heaven only knows how wearily! —as he said these words; and, in the act of doing so, fell into a strange stare as if he had forgotten something. A moment afterwards he sighed heavily, put on his spectacles, and went about his work again.

In another cell there was a German, sentenced to five years' imprisonment for larceny, two of which had just expired. With colors procured in the same manner, he had painted every inch of the walls and ceiling quite beautifully. He had laid out the few feet of ground behind with exquisite neatness, and had made a little bed in the centre, that looked, by the by, like a grave. The taste and ingenuity he had displayed in everything were most extraordinary; and yet a more dejected, heart-broken, wretched creature it would be difficult to imagine. I never saw such a picture of forlorn affliction and distress of mind. My heart bled for him; and when the tears ran down his cheeks, and he took one of the visitors aside, to ask, with his trembling hands nervously clutching at his coat to detain him, whether there was no hope of his dismal sentence being commuted, the spectacle was really too painful to witness. I never saw or heard of any kind of misery that impressed me more than the wretchedness of this man.

In a third cell was a tall, strong black, a burglar, working at his proper trade of making screws and the like. His time was nearly out. He was not only a very dexterous thief, but was notorious for his boldness and hardihood, and for the number of his previous convictions. He entertained us with a long account of his achievements, which he narrated with such infinite relish, that he actually seemed to lick his lips as he told us racy anecdotes of stolen plate, and of old ladies whom he had watched as they sat at windows in silver spectacles (he had plainly had an eye to their metal, even from the other side of the street), and had afterwards robbed. This fellow, upon the slightest encouragement, would have mingled with his professional recollections the most detestable cant; but I am very much mistaken if he could have surpassed the unmitigated hypocrisy with which he declared that he blessed the day on which he came into that prison, and that he never would commit another robbery as long as he lived.

There was one man who was allowed, as an indulgence, to keep rabbits. His room having rather a close smell in consequence, they called to him at the door to come out into the passage. He complied, of course, and stood shading his haggard face in the unwonted sunlight of the great window, looking as wan and unearthly as if he had been summoned from the grave. He had a white rabbit in his breast; and when the little creature, getting down upon the ground, stole back into the cell, and he, being dismissed, crept timidly after it, I thought it would have been very hard to say in what respect the man was the nobler animal of the two.

There was an English thief, who had been there but a few days out of seven years: a villainous, low-browed, thin-lipped fellow, with a white face; who had as yet no relish for visitors, and who, but for the additional penalty, would have gladly stabbed me with his shoemaker's knife. There was another German who had entered the jail but yesterday, and who started from his bed when we looked in, and pleaded, in his broken English, very hard for work. There was a poet, who, after doing two days' work in every four and twenty hours, one for himself and one for the prison, wrote verses about ships (he was by trade a mariner), and the "maddening wine-cup," and his friends at home. There were very many of them. Some reddened at the sight of visitors, and some turned very pale. Some two or three had prisoner nurses with them, for they were very sick, and one, a fat old Negro, whose leg had been taken off within the jail, had for his attendant a classical scholar and an accomplished surgeon, himself a prisoner likewise. Sitting upon the stairs, engaged in some slight work, was a pretty colored boy. "Is there no refuge for young criminals in Philadelphia, then?" said I. "Yes, but only for white children." Noble aristocracy in crime!

There was a sailor who had been there upwards of eleven years, and who in a few months' time would be free. Eleven years of solitary confinement!

"I am very glad to hear your time is nearly out." What does he say? Nothing. Why does he stare at his hands, and pick the flesh upon his fingers, and raise his eyes for an instant, every now and then, to those bare walls which have seen his head turn gray? It is a way he has sometimes.

Does he never look men in the face, and does he always pluck at those hands of his, as though he were bent on parting skin and bone? It is his humor: nothing more.

It is his humor, too, to say that he does not look forward to going out; that he is not glad the time is drawing near; that he did look forward to it once, but that was very long ago; that he has lost all care for everything. It is his humor to be a helpless, crushed, and broken man. And, Heaven be his witness that he has his humor thoroughly gratified!

There were three young women in adjoining cells, all convicted at the same time of a conspiracy to rob their prosecutor. In the silence and solitude of their lives they had grown to be quite beautiful. Their looks were very sad, and might have moved the sternest visitor to tears, but not to that kind of sorrow which the contemplation of the men awakens. One was a young girl; not twenty, as I recollect; whose snow-white room was hung with the work of some former prisoner, and upon whose downcast face the sun in all its splendor shone down through the high chink in the wall, where one narrow strip of bright blue sky was visible. She was very penitent and quiet; had come to be resigned, she said (and I believe her); and had a mind at peace. "In a word, you are happy here?" said one of my companions. She struggled— she did struggle very hard—to answer, Yes: but raising her eyes, and meeting that glimpse of freedom overhead, she burst into tears, and said, "She tried to be; she uttered no complaint; but it was natural that she should sometimes long to go out of that one cell: she could not help *that*," she sobbed, poor thing!

I went from cell to cell that day; and every face I saw, or word I heard, or incident I noted, is present to my mind in all its painfulness. But let me pass them by, for one, more pleasant, glance of a prison on the same plan which I afterwards saw at Pittsburg.

When I had gone over that in the same manner, I asked the governor if he had any person in his charge who was shortly going out. He had one, he said, whose time was up next day; but he had only been a prisoner two years.

Two years! I looked back through two years in my own life—out of jail, prosperous, happy, surrounded by blessings, comforts, and good fortune—and thought how wide a gap it was, and how long those two years passed in solitary captivity would have been. I have the face of this man, who was going to be released next day, before me now. It is almost more memorable in its happiness than the other faces in their misery. How easy and how natural it was for him to say that the system was a good one; and that the time went "pretty quick—considering;" and that when a man once felt he had offended the law, and must satisfy it, "he got along somehow;" and so forth!

"What did he call you back to say to you, in that strange flutter?" I asked of my conductor, when he had locked the door and joined me in the passage.

"Oh! That he was afraid the soles of his boots were not fit for walking, as they were a good deal worn when he came in; and that he would thank me very much to have them mended ready."

Those boots had been taken off his feet, and put away with the rest of his clothes, two years before!

I took that opportunity of inquiring how they conducted themselves immediately before going out; adding that I presumed they trembled very much.

"Well, it's not so much a trembling," was the answer —"though they do quiver—as a complete derangement of the nervous system. They can't sign their names to the book; sometimes can't even hold the pen; look about 'em without appearing to know why, or where they are; and sometimes get up and sit down again twenty times in a minute. This is when they're in the office, where they are taken with the hood on as they were brought in. When they get outside the gate, they stop, and look first one way and then the other: not knowing which to take. Sometimes they stagger as if they were drunk, and sometimes are forced to lean against the fence, they're so bad:— but they clear off in course of time."

As I walked among these solitary cells, and looked at the faces of the men within them, I tried to picture to myself the thoughts and feelings natural to their condition. I imagined the hood just taken off, and the scene of their captivity disclosed to them in all its dismal monotony.

At first the man is stunned. His confinement is a hideous vision; and his old life a reality. He throws himself upon his bed, and lies there abandoned to despair. By degrees the insupportable solitude and barrenness of the place rouses him from this stupor, and when the trap in his grated door is opened, he humbly begs and prays for work. "Give me some work to do, or I shall go raving mad!"

He has it; and by fits and starts applies himself to

labor; but every now and then there comes upon him a burning sense of the years that must be wasted in that stone coffin, and an agony so piercing in the recollection of those who are hidden from his view and knowledge, that he starts from his seat, and, striding up and down the narrow room with both hands clasped on his uplifted head, hears spirits tempting him to beat his brains out on the wall.

Again he falls upon his bed, and lies there moaning. Suddenly he starts up, wondering whether any other man is near; whether there is another cell like that on either side of him; and listens keenly.

There is no sound, but other prisoners may be near for all that. He remembers to have heard once, when he little thought of coming here himself, that the cells were so constructed that the prisoners could not hear each other, though the officers could hear them. Where is the nearest man—upon the right, or on the left? or is there one in both directions? Where is he sitting now—with his face to the light? or is he walking to and fro? How is he dressed? Has he been here long? Is he much worn away? Is he very white and spectre-like? Does *he* think of his neighbor too?

Scarcely venturing to breathe, and listening while he thinks, he conjures up a figure with his back towards him, and imagines it moving about in this next cell. He has no idea of the face, but he is certain of the dark form of a stooping man. In the cell upon the other side he puts another figure, whose face is hidden from him also. Day after day, and often when he wakes up in the middle of the night, he thinks of these two men until he is almost distracted. He never changes them. There they are always as he first imagined them—an old man on the right; a younger man upon the left—whose hidden features torture him to death, and have a mystery that makes him tremble.

The weary days pass on with solemn pace, like mourners at a funeral; and slowly he begins to feel that the white walls of the cell have something dreadful in them: that their color is horrible: that their smooth surface chills his blood: that there is one hateful corner which torments him. Every morning, when he wakes, he hides his head beneath the coverlet, and shudders to see the

ghastly ceiling looking down upon him. The blessed light
of day itself peeps in, an ugly phantom face, through the
unchangeable crevice which is his prison window.

By slow but sure degrees, the terrors of that hateful
corner swell until they beset him at all times; invade his
rest, make his dreams hideous, and his nights dreadful.
At first he took a strange dislike to it: feeling as though
it gave birth in his brain to something of corresponding
shape, which ought not to be there, and racked his head
with pains. Then he began to fear it, then to dream of
it, and of men whispering its name and pointing to it.
Then he could not bear to look at it, nor yet to turn his
back upon it. Now, it is every night the lurking-place of
a ghost: a shadow:—a silent something, horrible to see,
but whether bird, or beast, or muffled human shape, he
cannot tell.

When he is in his cell by day, he fears the little yard
without. When he is in the yard, he dreads to re-enter
the cell. When night comes, there stands the phantom in
the corner. If he have the courage to stand in its place,
and drive it out (he had once: being desperate), it
broods upon his bed. In the twilight, and always at the
same hour, a voice calls to him by name; as the darkness
thickens, his Loom begins to live; and even that, his comfort, is a hideous figure, watching him till daybreak.

Again, by slow degrees, these horrible fancies depart
from him one by one; returning sometimes unexpectedly,
but at longer intervals, and in less alarming shapes. He
has talked upon religious matters with the gentleman who
visits him, and has read his Bible, and has written a
prayer upon his slate, and hung it up as a kind of protection, and an assurance of Heavenly companionship. He
dreams now, sometimes, of his children or his wife, but
is sure that they are dead, or have deserted him. He is
easily moved to tears; is gentle, submissive, and broken-
spirited. Occasionally the old agony comes back: a very
little thing will revive it: even a familiar sound, or the
scent of summer flowers in the air; but it does not last
long now: for the world without has come to be the
vision, and this solitary life the sad reality.

If his term of imprisonment be short—I mean comparatively, for short it cannot be—the last half-year is
almost worse than all; for then he thinks the prison

will take fire, and he be burnt in the ruins, or that he
is doomed to die within the walls, or that he will be detained on some false charge, and sentenced for another
term: or that something, no matter what, must happen
to prevent his going at large. And this is natural, and impossible to be reasoned against, because, after his long
separation from human life, and his great suffering, any
event will appear to him more probable in the contemplation than the being restored to liberty and his fellow-
creatures.

If his period of confinement has been very long, the
prospect of release bewilders and confuses him. His broken heart may flutter for a moment, when he thinks of
the world outside, and what it might have been to him in
all those lonely years, but that is all. The cell door has
been closed too long on all its hopes and cares. Better to
have hanged him in the beginning than bring him to this
pass, and send him forth to mingle with his kind, who
are his kind no more.

On the haggard face of every man among these prisoners the same expression sat. I know not what to liken
it to. It had something of that strained attention which
we see upon the faces of the blind and deaf, mingled with
a kind of horror, as though they had all been secretly
terrified. In every little chamber that I entered, and at
every grate through which I looked, I seemed to see the
same appalling countenance. It lives in my memory, with
the fascination of a remarkable picture. Parade before my
eyes a hundred men, with one among them newly released
from this solitary suffering, and I would point him out.

The faces of the women, as I have said, it humanizes
and refines. Whether this be because of their better nature, which is elicited in solitude, or because of their
being gentler creatures, of greater patience and longer
suffering, I do not know; but so it is. That the punishment is nevertheless, to my thinking, fully as cruel and as
wrong in their case as in that of the men, I need scarcely
add.

My firm conviction is that, independent of the mental
anguish it occasions—an anguish so acute and so tremendous, that all imagination of it must fall far short of the
reality—it wears the mind into a morbid state, which
renders it unfit for the rough contact and busy action of

the world. It is my fixed opinion that those who have undergone this punishment MUST pass into society again morally unhealthy and diseased. There are many instances on record of men who have chosen, or have been condemned, to lives of perfect solitude, but I scarcely remember one, even among sages of strong and vigorous intellect, where its effect has not become apparent, in some disordered train of thought, or some gloomy hallucination. What monstrous phantoms, bred of despondency and doubt, and born and reared in solitude, have stalked upon the earth, making creation ugly, and darkening the face of Heaven!

Suicides are rare among these prisoners: are almost, indeed, unknown. But no argument in favor of the system can reasonably be deduced from this circumstance, although it is very often urged. All men who have made diseases of the mind their study, know perfectly well that such extreme depression and despair as will change the whole character, and beat down all its powers of elasticity and self-resistance, may be at work within a man, and yet stop short of self-destruction. This is a common case.

That it makes the senses dull, and by degrees impairs the bodily faculties, I am quite sure. I remarked to those who were with me in this very establishment at Philadelphia, that the criminals who had been there long were deaf. They, who were in the habit of seeing these men constantly, were perfectly amazed at the idea, which they regarded as groundless and fanciful. And yet the very first prisoner to whom they appealed—one of their own selection—confirmed my impression (which was unknown to him) instantly, and said, with a genuine air it was impossible to doubt, that he couldn't think how it happened, but he *was* growing very dull of hearing.

That it is a singularly unequal punishment, and affects the worst man least, there is no doubt. In its superior efficiency as a means of reformation, compared with that other code of regulations which allows the prisoners to work in company without communicating together, I have not the smallest faith. All the instances of reformation that were mentioned to me were of a kind that might have been—and I have no doubt whatever, in my own mind, would have been—equally well brought about by the Silent System. With regard to such men as the Negro burglar and the English thief, even the most enthusiastic have scarcely any hope of their conversion.

It seems to me that the objection that nothing wholesome or good has ever had its growth in such unnatural solitude, and that even a dog, or any of the more intelligent among beasts, would pine, and mope, and rust away beneath its influence, would be in itself a sufficient argument against this system. But when we recollect, in addition, how very cruel and severe it is, and that a solitary life is always liable to peculiar and distinct objections of a most deplorable nature, which have arisen here; and call to mind, moreover, that the choice is not between this system and a bad or ill-considered one, but between it and another which has worked well, and is, in its whole design and practice, excellent; there is surely more than sufficient reason for abandoning a mode of punishment attended by so little hope or promise, and fraught, beyond dispute, with such a host of evils.

As a relief to its contemplation, I will close this chapter with a curious story, arising out of the same theme, which was related to me, on the occasion of this visit, by some of the gentlemen concerned.

At one of the periodical meetings of the inspectors of this prison, a working-man of Philadelphia presented himself before the Board, and earnestly requested to be placed in solitary confinement. On being asked what motive could possibly prompt him to make this strange demand, he answered that he had an irresistible propensity to get drunk; that he was constantly indulging in it, to his great misery and ruin; that he had no power of resistance; that he wished to be put beyond the reach of temptation; and that he could think of no better way than this. It was pointed out to him, in reply, that the prison was for criminals who had been tried and sentenced by the law, and could not be made available for any such fanciful purposes; he was exhorted to abstain from intoxicating drinks, as he surely might if he would; and received other very good advice, with which he retired, exceedingly dissatisfied with the result of his application.

He came again, and again, and again, and was so very earnest and importunate, that at last they took counsel together, and said, "He will certainly qualify himself for admission, if we reject him any more. Let us shut him up.

He will soon be glad to go away, and then we shall get rid of him." So they made him sign a statement which would prevent his ever sustaining an action for false imprisonment, to the effect that his incarceration was voluntary, and of his own seeking; they requested him to take notice that the officer in attendance had orders to release him at any hour of the day or night, when he might knock upon his door for that purpose; but desired him to understand, that once going out, he would not be admitted any more. These conditions agreed upon, and he still remaining in the same mind, he was conducted to the prison, and shut up in one of the cells.

In this cell, the man who had not the firmness to leave a glass of liquor standing untasted on a table before him —in this cell, in solitary confinement, and working every day at his trade of shoemaking, this man remained nearly two years. His health beginning to fail at the expiration of that time, the surgeon recommended that he should work occasionally in the garden; and, as he liked the notion very much, he went about this new occupation with great cheerfulness.

He was digging here, one summer day, very industriously, when the wicket in the outer gate chanced to be left open; showing, beyond, the well-remembered dusty road and sunburnt fields. The way was as free to him as to any man living, but he no sooner raised his head and caught sight of it, all shining in the light, than, with the involuntary instinct of a prisoner, he cast away his spade, scampered off as fast as his legs would carry him, and never once looked back.

CHAPTER 8

Washington. The Legislature. And the President's House.

WE left Philadelphia by steamboat, at six o'clock one very cold morning, and turned our faces towards Washington.

In the course of this day's journey, as on subsequent occasions, we encountered some Englishmen (small farmers, perhaps, or country publicans at home) who were settled in America, and were travelling on their own affairs. Of all grades and kinds of men that jostle one in the public conveyances of the States, these are often the most intolerable and the most insufferable companions. United to every disagreeable characteristic that the worst kind of American travellers possess, these countrymen of ours display an amount of insolent conceit and cool assumption of superiority quite monstrous to behold. In the coarse familiarity of their approach, and the effrontery of their inquisitiveness (which they are in great haste to assert, as if they panted to revenge themselves upon the decent old restraints of home), they surpass any native specimens that came within my range of observation: and I often grew so patriotic when I saw and heard them, that I would cheerfully have submitted to a reasonable fine, if I could have given any other country in the whole world the honor of claiming them for its children.

As Washington may be called the headquarters of tobacco-tinctured saliva, the time is come when I must confess, without any disguise, that the prevalence of those two odious practices of chewing and expectorating began about this time to be anything but agreeable, and soon became most offensive and sickening. In all the public places of America this filthy custom is recognized. In the courts of law the judge has his spittoon, the crier his, the witness his, and the prisoner his; while the jurymen and spectators are provided for, as so many men who in the course of nature must desire to spit incessantly. In the hospitals the students of medicine are requested, by notices upon the wall, to eject their tobacco juice into the boxes provided for that purpose, and not to discolor the stairs. In public buildings visitors are implored, through the same agency, to squirt the essence of their quids, or "plugs," as I have heard them called by gentlemen learned in this kind of sweetmeat, into the national spittoons, and not about the bases of the marble columns. But in some parts this custom is inseparably mixed up with every meal and morning call, and with all the transactions of social life. The stranger, who follows in the track I took myself, will find it in its full bloom and glory, luxuriant in all its alarming recklessness, at Washington. And let him not persuade himself (as I once did, to my shame) that previous tourists have exaggerated its extent. The thing itself is an exaggeration of nastiness, which cannot be outdone.

On board this steamboat there were two young gentlemen, with shirt collars reversed as usual, and armed with very big walking-sticks; who planted two seats in the middle of the deck, at a distance of some four paces apart; took out their tobacco boxes; and sat down opposite each other to chew. In less than a quarter of an hour's time, these hopeful youths had shed about them, on the clean boards, a copious shower of yellow rain; clearing, by that means, a kind of magic circle, within whose limits no intruders dared to come, and which they never failed to refresh and re-refresh before a spot was dry. This being before breakfast, rather disposed me, I confess, to nausea; but looking attentively at one of the expectorators, I plainly saw that he was young in chewing, and felt inwardly uneasy himself. A glow of delight came over me at this discovery; and, as I marked his face turn paler and paler, and saw the ball of tobacco in his left cheek quiver with his suppressed agony, while yet he spat, and chewed, and spat again, in emulation of his older friend, I could have fallen on his neck and implored him to go on for hours.

We all sat down to a comfortable breakfast in the cabin below, where there was no more hurry or confusion than at such a meal in England, and where there was certainly greater politeness exhibited than at most of our stage-coach banquets. At about nine o'clock we arrived at the railroad station, and went on by the cars. At noon we turned out again, to cross a wide river in another steamboat; landed at a continuation of the railroad on the opposite shore; and went on by other cars; in which, in the course of the next hour or so, we crossed by wooden bridges, each a mile in length, two creeks, called respectively Great and Little Gunpowder. The water in both was blackened with flights of canvas-backed ducks, which are most delicious eating, and abound hereabouts at that season of the year.

These bridges are of wood, have no parapet, and are only just wide enough for the passage of the trains; which, in the event of the smallest accident, would inevitably be plunged into the river. They are startling contrivances, and are most agreeable when passed.

We stopped to dine at Baltimore, and, being now in Maryland, were waited on, for the first time, by slaves. The sensation of exacting any service from human creatures who are bought and sold, and being, for the time, a party, as it were, to their condition, is not an enviable one. The institution exists, perhaps, in its least repulsive and most mitigated form in such a town as this; but it *is* slavery; and though I was, with respect to it, an innocent man, its presence filled me with a sense of shame and self-reproach.

After dinner we went down to the railroad again, and took our seats in the cars for Washington. Being rather early, those men and boys who happened to have nothing particular to do, and were curious in foreigners, came (according to custom) round the carriage in which I sat; let down all the windows; thrust in their heads and shoulders; hooked themselves on conveniently by their elbows; and fell to comparing notes on the subject of my personal appearance, with as much indifference as if I were a stuffed figure. I never gained so much uncompromising information with reference to my own nose and eyes, the various impressions wrought by my mouth and chin on different minds, and how my head looks when it is viewed from be-

hind, as on these occasions. Some gentlemen were only
satisfied by exercising their sense of touch; and the
boys (who are surprisingly precocious in America) were
seldom satisfied even by that, but would return to the
charge over and over again. Many a budding president
has walked into my room with his cap on his head and his
hands in his pockets, and stared at me for two whole
hours: occasionally refreshing himself with a tweak at his
nose, or a draught from the water jug; or by walking to
the windows, and inviting other boys in the street below
to come up and do likewise: crying, "Here he is!" "Come
on!" "Bring all your brothers!" with other hospitable
entreaties of that nature.

We reached Washington at about half-past six that
evening, and had upon the way a beautiful view of the
Capitol, which is a fine building of the Corinthian order,
placed upon a noble and commanding eminence. Arrived
at the hotel, I saw no more of the place that night; being
very tired, and glad to get to bed.

Breakfast over next morning, I walk about the streets
for an hour or two, and, coming home, throw up the window in the front and back, and look out. Here is Washington, fresh in my mind and under my eye.

Take the worst parts of the City Road and Pentonville, or the straggling outskirts of Paris, where the houses
are smallest, preserving all their oddities, but especially
the small shops and dwellings occupied in Pentonville (but
not in Washington) by furniture brokers, keepers of poor
eating-houses, and fanciers of birds. Burn the whole
down; build it up again in wood and plaster; widen it a
little; throw in part of St. John's Wood; put green blinds
outside all the private houses, with a red curtain and a
white one in every window; plough up all the roads; plant
a great deal of coarse turf in every place where it ought
not to be; erect three handsome buildings in stone and
marble anywhere, but the more entirely out of everybody's way the better; call one the Post Office, one the
Patent Office, and one the Treasury; make it scorching
hot in the morning, and freezing cold in the afternoon,
with an occasional tornado of wind and dust; leave a brick-
field, without the bricks, in all central places where a
street may naturally be expected; and that's Washington.

The hotel in which we live is a long row of small houses

fronting on the street, and opening at the back upon a common yard, in which hangs a great triangle. Whenever a servant is wanted, somebody beats on this triangle from one stroke up to seven, according to the number of the house in which his presence is required; and as all the servants are always being wanted, and none of them ever come, this enlivening engine is in full performance the whole day through. Clothes are drying in this same yard; female slaves, with cotton handkerchiefs twisted round their heads, are running to and fro on the hotel business; black waiters cross and recross with dishes in their hands; two great dogs are playing upon a mound of loose bricks in the centre of the little square; a pig is turning up his stomach to the sun, and grunting "That's comfortable!" and neither the men, nor the women, nor the dogs, nor the pig, nor any created creature takes the smallest notice of the triangle, which is tingling madly all the time.

I walk to the front window, and look across the road upon a long, straggling row of houses, one story high, terminating, nearly opposite, but a little to the left, in a melancholy piece of waste ground with frowzy grass, which looks like a small piece of country that has taken to drinking, and has quite lost itself. Standing anyhow and all wrong, upon this open space, like something meteoric that has fallen down from the moon, is an odd, lop-sided, one-eyed kind of wooden building, that looks like a church, with a flagstaff as long as itself sticking out of a steeple something larger than a tea-chest. Under the window is a small stand of coaches, whose slave drivers are sunning themselves on the steps of our door, and talking idly together. The three most obtrusive houses near at hand are the three meanest. On one—a shop, which never has anything in the window, and never has the door open—is painted in large characters, "THE CITY LUNCH." At another, which looks like the back-way to somewhere else, but is an independent building in itself, oysters are procurable in every style. At the third, which is a very, very little tailor's shop, pants are fixed to order; or, in other words, pantaloons are made to measure. And that is our street in Washington.

It is sometimes called the City of Magnificent Distances, but it might with greater propriety be termed the City of Magnificent Intentions; for it is only on taking a bird's-eye view of it from the top of the Capitol that one can at all comprehend the vast designs of its projector, an aspiring Frenchman. Spacious avenues that begin in nothing, and lead nowhere; streets, mile long, that only want houses, roads, and inhabitants; public buildings that need but a public to be complete; and ornaments of great thoroughfares, which only lack great thoroughfares to ornament—are its leading features. One might fancy the season over, and most of the houses gone out of town forever with their masters. To the admirers of cities it is a Barmecide Feast; a pleasant field for the imagination to rove in; a monument raised to a deceased project, with not even a legible inscription to record its departed greatness.

Such as it is, it is likely to remain. It was originally chosen for the seat of Government, as a means of averting the conflicting jealousies and interests of the different States; and very probably, too, as being remote from mobs: a consideration not to be slighted, even in America. It has no trade or commerce of its own: having little or no population beyond the President and his establishment: the members of the legislature, who reside there during the session; the Government clerks and officers employed in the various departments; the keepers of the hotels and boarding-houses; and the tradesmen who supply their tables. It is very unhealthy. Few people would live in Washington, I take it, who were not obliged to reside there; and the tides of emigration and speculation, those rapid and regardless currents, are little likely to flow at any time towards such dull and sluggish water.

The principal features of the Capitol are, of course, the two Houses of Assembly. But there is, besides, in the centre of the building, a fine rotunda, ninety-six feet in diameter, and ninety-six high, whose circular wall is divided into compartments, ornamented by historical pictures. Four of these have for their subjects prominent events in the revolutionary struggle. They were painted by Colonel Trumbull, himself a member of Washington's staff at the time of their occurrence; from which circumstance they derive a peculiar interest of their own. In this same hall Mr. Greenough's large statue of Washington has been lately placed. It has great merits, of course, but it struck me as being rather strained and violent for its subject. I could wish, however, to have seen it in a better light than it can ever be viewed in where it stands.

There is a very pleasant and commodious library in the Capitol; and from a balcony in front, the bird's-eye view, of which I have just spoken, may be had, together with a beautiful prospect of the adjacent country. In one of the ornamented portions of the building there is a figure of Justice; whereunto, the Guide Book says, "the artist at first contemplated giving more of nudity, but he was warned that the public sentiment in this country would not admit of it, and in his caution he has gone, perhaps, into the opposite extreme." Poor Justice! she has been made to wear much stranger garments in America than those she pines in in the Capitol. Let us hope that she has changed her dressmaker since they were fashioned, and that the public sentiment of the country did not cut out the clothes she hides her lovely figure in just now.

The House of Representatives is a beautiful and spacious hall of semicircular shape, supported by handsome pillars. One part of the gallery is appropriated to the ladies, and there they sit in front rows, and come in, and go out, as at a play or concert. The chair is canopied, and raised considerably above the floor of the House; and every member has an easy-chair and a writing-desk to himself: which is denounced by some people out of doors as a most unfortunate and injudicious arrangement, tending to long sittings and prosaic speeches. It is an elegant chamber to look at, but a singularly bad one for all purposes of hearing. The Senate, which is smaller, is free from this objection, and is exceedingly well adapted to the uses for which it is designed. The sittings, I need hardly add, take place in the day; and the parliamentary forms are modelled on those of the old country.

I was sometimes asked, in my progress through other places, whether I had not been very much impressed by the _heads_ of the law-makers at Washington; meaning not their chiefs and leaders, but literally their individual and personal heads, whereon their hair grew, and whereby the phrenological character of each legislator was expressed; and I almost as often struck my questioner dumb with indignant consternation by answering, "No, that I didn't remember being at all overcome." As I must, at whatever hazard, repeat the avowal here, I will follow it up by relating my impressions on this subject in as few words as possible.

In the first place—it may be from some imperfect development of my organ of veneration—I do not remember having ever fainted away, or having even been moved to tears of joyful pride, at sight of any legislative body. I have borne the House of Commons like a man, and have yielded to no weakness, but slumber, in the House of Lords. I have seen elections for borough and county, and have never been impelled (no matter which party won) to damage my hat by throwing it up into the air in triumph, or to crack my voice by shouting forth any reference to our Glorious Constitution, to the noble purity of our independent voters, or the unimpeachable integrity of our independent members. Having withstood such strong attacks upon my fortitude, it is possible that I may be of a cold and insensible temperament, amounting to iciness, in such matters; and therefore my impressions of the live pillars of the Capitol at Washington must be received with such grains of allowance as this free confession may seem to demand.

Did I see in this public body an assemblage of men, bound together in the sacred names of Liberty and Freedom, and so asserting the chaste dignity of those twin goddesses, in all their discussions, as to exalt at once the Eternal Principles to which their names are given, and their own character, and the character of their countrymen, in the admiring eyes of the whole world?

It was but a week since an aged, gray-haired man, a lasting honor to the land that gave him birth, who has done good service to his country, as his forefathers did, and who will be remembered scores upon scores of years after the worms bred in its corruption are but so many grains of dust—it was but a week since this old man had stood for days upon his trial before this very body, charged with having dared to assert the infamy of that traffic which has for its accursed merchandise men and women, and their unborn children. Yes. And publicly exhibited in the same city all the while; gilded, framed, and glazed; hung up for general admiration; shown to strangers, not with shame, but pride; its face not turned towards the wall, itself not taken down and burned; is the Unanimous Declaration of The Thirteen United

States of America, which solemnly declares that All Men are created Equal; and are endowed by their Creator with the Inalienable Rights of Life, Liberty, and the Pursuit of Happiness!

It was not a month since this same body had sat calmly by, and heard a man, one of themselves, with oaths which beggars in their drink reject, threaten to cut another's throat from ear to ear. There he sat among them; not crushed by the general feeling of the assembly, but as good a man as any.

There was but a week to come, and another of that body, for doing his duty to those who sent him there; for claiming in a Republic the Liberty and Freedom of expressing their sentiments, and making known their prayer; would be tried, found guilty, and have strong censure passed upon him by the rest. His was a grave offence indeed; for, years before, he had risen up and said, "A gang of male and female slaves for sale, warranted to breed like cattle, linked to each other by iron fetters, are passing now along the open street beneath the windows of your Temple of Equality! Look!" But there are many kinds of hunters engaged in the Pursuit of Happiness, and they go variously armed. It is the Inalienable Right of some among them to take the field after *their* Happiness, equipped with cat and cart-whip, stocks, and iron collar, and to shout their view halloa (always in praise of Liberty) to the music of clanking chains and bloody stripes.

Where sat the many legislators of coarse threats; of words and blows such as coalheavers deal upon each other, when they forget their breeding? On every side. Every session had its anecdotes of that kind, and the actors were all there.

Did I recognize in this assembly a body of men who, applying themselves in a new world to correct some of the falsehoods and vices of the old, purified the avenues to Public Life, paved the dirty ways to Place and Power, debated and made laws for the Common Good, and had no party but their Country?

I saw in them the wheels that move the meanest perversion of virtuous Political Machinery that the worst tools ever wrought. Despicable trickery at elections; underhanded tamperings with public officers; cowardly attacks upon opponents, with scurrilous newspapers for shields, and hired pens for daggers; shameful trucklings to mercenary knaves, whose claim to be considered is, that every day and week they sow new crops of ruin with their venal types, which are the dragon's teeth of yore, in everything but sharpness; aidings and abettings of every bad inclination in the popular mind, and artful suppressions of all its good influences: such things as these, and, in a word, Dishonest Faction in its most depraved and most unblushing form, stared out from every corner of the crowded hall. Did I see among them the intelligence and refinement: the true, honest, patriotic heart of America? Here and there were drops of its blood and life, but they scarcely colored the stream of desperate adventurers which sets that way for profit and for pay. It is the game of these men, and of their profligate organs, to make the strife of politics so fierce and brutal, and so destructive of all self-respect in worthy men, that sensitive and delicate-minded persons shall be kept aloof, and they, and such as they, be left to battle out their selfish views unchecked. And thus this lowest of all scrambling fights goes on, and they who in other countries would, from their intelligence and station, most aspire to make the laws, do here recoil the farthest from that degradation.

That there are, among the representatives of the people in both Houses, and among all parties, some men of high character and great abilities, I need not say. The foremost among those politicians who are known in Europe have been already described, and I see no reason to depart from the rule I have laid down for my guidance, of abstaining from all mention of individuals. It will be sufficient to add that, to the most favorable accounts that have been written of them, I more than fully and most heartily subscribe; and that personal intercourse and free communication have bred within me, not the result predicted in the very doubtful proverb, but increased admiration and respect. They are striking men to look at, hard to deceive, prompt to act, lions in energy, Crichtons in varied accomplishments, Indians in fire of eye and gesture, Americans in strong and generous impulse; and they as well represent the honor and wisdom of their country at home, as the distinguished gentleman who is now its minister at the British Court sustains its highest character abroad.

I visited both Houses nearly every day during my stay in Washington. On my initiatory visit to the House of Representatives, they divided against a decision of the chair; but the chair won. The second time I went, the member who was speaking, being interrupted by a laugh, mimicked it, as one child would in quarrelling with another, and added "that he would make honorable gentlemen opposite sing out a little more on the other side of their mouths presently." But interruptions are rare; the speaker being usually heard in silence. There are more quarrels than with us, and more threatenings than gentlemen are accustomed to exchange in any civilized society of which we have record: but farmyard imitations have not as yet been imported from the Parliament of the United Kingdom. The feature in oratory which appears to be most practised, and most relished, is the constant repetition of the same idea, or shadow of an idea, in fresh words; and the inquiry out of doors is not, "What did he say?" but, "How long did he speak?" These, however, are but enlargements of a principle which prevails elsewhere.

The Senate is a dignified and decorous body, and its proceedings are conducted with much gravity and order. Both Houses are handsomely carpeted; but the state to which these carpets are reduced by the universal disregard of the spittoon with which every honorable member is accommodated, and the extraordinary improvements on the pattern which are squirted and dabbled upon it in every direction, do not admit of being described. I will merely observe, that I strongly recommend all strangers not to look at the floor; and if they happen to drop anything, though it be their purse, not to pick it up with an ungloved hand on any account.

It is somewhat remarkable too, at first, to say the least, to see so many honorable members with swelled faces; and it is scarcely less remarkable to discover that this appearance is caused by the quantity of tobacco they contrive to stow within the hollow of the cheek. It is strange enough, too, to see an honorable gentleman leaning back in his tilted chair, with his legs on the desk before him, shaping a convenient "plug" with his penknife, and, when it is quite ready for use, shooting the old one from his mouth as from a pop-gun, and clapping the new one in its place.

I was surprised to observe that even steady old chewers

of great experience are not always good marksmen, which has rather inclined me to doubt that general proficiency with the rifle, of which we have heard so much in England. Several gentlemen called upon me who, in the course of conversation, frequently missed the spittoon at five paces; and one (but he was certainly short-sighted) mistook the closed sash for the open window at three. On another occasion, when I dined out, and was sitting with two ladies and some gentlemen round a fire before dinner, one of the company fell short of the fireplace six distinct times. I am disposed to think, however, that this was occasioned by his not aiming at that object; as there was a white marble hearth before the fender, which was more convenient, and may have suited his purpose better.

The Patent Office at Washington furnishes an extraordinary example of American enterprise and ingenuity; for the immense number of models it contains are the accumulated inventions of only five years: the whole of the previous collection having been destroyed by fire. The elegant structure in which they are arranged is one of design rather than execution, for there is but one side erected out of four, though the works are stopped. The Post Office is a very compact and very beautiful building. In one of the departments, among a collection of rare and curious articles, are deposited the presents which have been made from time to time to the American ambassadors at foreign courts by the various potentates to whom they were the accredited agents of the Republic: gifts which, by the law, they are not permitted to retain. I confess that I looked upon this as a very painful exhibition, and one by no means flattering to the national standard of honesty and honor. That can scarcely be a high state of moral feeling which imagines a gentleman of repute and station likely to be corrupted, in the discharge of his duty, by the present of a snuff-box, or a richly mounted sword, or an Eastern shawl; and surely the Nation who reposes confidence in her appointed servants is likely to be better served than she who makes them the subject of such very mean and paltry suspicions.

At George Town, in the suburbs, there is a Jesuit College; delightfully situated, and, so far as I had an opportunity of seeing, well managed. Many persons who are not members of the Romish church avail themselves, I believe,

of these institutions, and of the advantageous opportunities
they afford for the education of their children. The
heights in this neighborhood, above the Potomac River,
are very picturesque; and are free, I should conceive,
from some of the insalubrities of Washington. The air, at
that elevation, was quite cool and refreshing, when in the
city it was burning hot.

The President's mansion is more like an English club-
house, both within and without, than any other kind of
establishment with which I can compare it. The ornamental ground about it has been laid out in garden walks;
they are pretty, and agreeable to the eye; though they
have that uncomfortable air of having been made yesterday, which is far from favorable to the display of such
beauties.

My first visit to this house was on the morning after
my arrival, when I was carried thither by an official
gentleman, who was so kind as to charge himself with my
presentation to the President.

We entered a large hall, and, having twice or thrice
rung a bell which nobody answered, walked without further ceremony through the rooms on the ground-floor, as
divers other gentlemen (mostly with their hats on, and
their hands in their pockets) were doing very leisurely.
Some of these had ladies with them, to whom they were
showing the premises; others were lounging on the chairs
and sofas; others, in a perfect state of exhaustion from list-
lessness, were yawning drearily. The greater portion of
this assemblage were rather asserting their supremacy
than doing anything else, as they had no particular business
there, that anybody knew of. A few were closely eying
the movables, as if to make quite sure that the President
(who was far from popular) had not made away with
any of the furniture, or sold the fixtures for his private
benefit.

After glancing at these loungers; who were scattered
over a pretty drawing-room, opening upon a terrace which
commanded a beautiful prospect of the river and the
adjacent country, and who were sauntering, too, about a
larger state-room called the Eastern Drawing-room, we
went upstairs into another chamber, where were certain
visitors waiting for audiences. At sight of my conductor, a
black in plain clothes and yellow slippers who was gliding

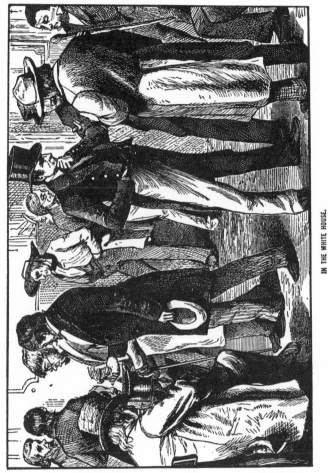

IN THE WHITE HOUSE.

noiselessly about, and whispering messages in the ears of the more impatient, made a sign of recognition, and glided off to announce him.

We had previously looked into another chamber fitted all round with a great bare wooden desk or counter, whereon lay files of newspapers, to which sundry gentlemen were referring. But there were no such means of beguiling the time in this apartment, which was as unpromising and tiresome as any waiting-room in one of our public establishments, or any physician's dining-room during his hours of consultation at home.

There were some fifteen or twenty persons in the room. One, a tall, wiry, muscular old man, from the west; sunburnt and swarthy; with a brown-white hat on his knees, and a giant umbrella resting between his legs; who sat bolt-upright in his chair, frowning steadily at the carpet, and twitching the hard lines about his mouth, as if he had made up his mind "to fix" the President on what he had to say, and wouldn't bate him a grain. Another, a Kentucky farmer, six feet six in height, with his hat on, and his hands under his coat-tails, who leaned against the wall and kicked the floor with his heel, as though he had Time's head under his shoe, and were literally "killing" him. A third, an oval-faced, bilious-looking man, with sleek black hair cropped close, and whiskers and beard shaved down to blue dots, who sucked the head of a thick stick, and from time to time took it out of his mouth to see how it was getting on. A fourth did nothing but whistle. A fifth did nothing but spit. And, indeed, all these gentlemen were so very persevering and energetic in this latter particular, and bestowed their favors so abundantly upon the carpet, that I take it for granted the Presidential housemaids have high wages, or, to speak more genteelly, an ample amount of "compensation:" which is the American word for salary in the case of all public servants.

We had not waited in this room many minutes before the black messenger returned, and conducted us into another of smaller dimensions, where, at a business-like table covered with papers, sat the President himself. He looked somewhat worn and anxious,—and well he might: being at war with everybody,—but the expression of his face was mild and pleasant, and his manner was remarkably unaffected, gentlemanly, and agreeable. I thought that, in his whole carriage and demeanor, he became his station singularly well.

Being advised that the sensible etiquette of the republican court admitted of a traveller, like myself, declining, without any impropriety, an invitation to dinner, which did not reach me until I had concluded my arrangements for leaving Washington some days before that to which it referred, I only returned to this house once. It was on the occasion of one of those general assemblies which are held on certain nights, between the hours of nine and twelve o'clock, and are called, rather oddly, Levees.

I went, with my wife, at about ten. There was a pretty dense crowd of carriages and people in the courtyard, and, so far as I could make out, there were no very clear regulations for the taking up or setting down of company. There were certainly no policemen to soothe startled horses, either by sawing at their bridles or flourishing truncheons in their eyes; and I am ready to make oath that no inoffensive persons were knocked violently on the head, or poked acutely in their backs or stomachs; or brought to a stand-still by any such gentle means, and then taken into custody for not moving on. But there was no confusion or disorder. Our carriage reached the porch in its turn, without any blustering, swearing, shouting, backing, or other disturbance: and we dismounted with as much ease and comfort as though we had been escorted by the whole Metropolitan Force, from A to Z inclusive.

The suite of rooms on the ground-floor were lighted up; and a military band was playing in the hall. In the smaller drawing-room, the centre of a circle of company, were the President and his daughter-in-law, who acted as the lady of the mansion: and a very interesting, graceful, and accomplished lady too. One gentleman who stood among this group appeared to take upon himself the functions of a master of the ceremonies. I saw no other officers or attendants, and none were needed.

The great drawing-room which I have already mentioned, and the other chambers on the ground-floor, were crowded to excess. The company was not, in our sense of the term, select, for it comprehended persons of very many grades and classes; **nor** was there any great display of costly attire: indeed, some of the costumes may have been, for aught I know, grotesque enough. But the decorum

and propriety of behavior which prevailed were unbroken by any rude or disagreeable incident; and every
man, even among the miscellaneous crowd in the hall who
were admitted without any orders or tickets to look on,
appeared to feel that he was a part of the Institution,
and was responsible for its preserving a becoming character, and appearing to the best advantage.

That these visitors, too, whatever their station, were
not without some refinement of taste and appreciation of
intellectual gifts, and gratitude to those men who, by the
peaceful exercise of great abilities, shed new charms and
associations upon the homes of their countrymen, and
elevate their character in other lands, was most earnestly testified by their reception of Washington Irving, my
dear friend, who had recently been appointed Minister at
the Court of Spain, and who was among them that night,
in his new character, for the first and last time before
going abroad. I sincerely believe that, in all the madness of
American politics, few public men would have been so
earnestly, devotedly, and affectionately caressed as this
most charming writer: and I have seldom respected a
public assembly more than I did this eager throng, when
I saw them turning with one mind from noisy orators and
officers of state, and flocking with a generous and honest
impulse round the man of quiet pursuits: proud in his
promotion, as reflecting back upon their country: and
grateful to him with their whole hearts for the store of
graceful fancies he had poured out among them. Long
may he dispense such treasures with unsparing hand; and
long may they remember him as worthily!

The term we had assigned for the duration of our stay
in Washington was now at an end, and we were to begin
to travel; for the railroad distances we had traversed
yet, in journeying among these older towns, are on that
great continent looked upon as nothing.

I had at first intended going South—to Charleston.
But when I came to consider the length of time which this
journey would occupy, and the premature heat of the
season, which even at Washington had been often very trying; and weighed, moreover, in my mind, the pain of living in the constant contemplation of slavery, against the
more than doubtful chances of my ever seeing it, in the

time I had to spare, stripped of the disguises in which it would certainly be dressed, and so adding any item to the host of facts already heaped together on the subject; I began to listen to old whisperings which had often been present to me at home in England, when I little thought of ever being here; and to dream again of cities growing up, like palaces in fairy tales, among the wilds and forests of the west.

The advice I received in most quarters, when I began to yield to my desire of travelling towards that point of the compass, was, according to custom, sufficiently cheerless: my companion being threatened with more perils, dangers, and discomforts than I can remember, or would catalogue if I could; but of which it will be sufficient to remark that blowings-up in steamboats and breakings-down in coaches were among the least. But, having a western route sketched out for me by the best and kindest authority to which I could have resorted, and putting no great faith in these discouragements, I soon determined on my plan of action.

This was to travel south only to Richmond in Virginia; and then to turn, and shape our course for the Far West; whither I beseech the reader's company in a new chapter.

CHAPTER 9

*A Night Steamer on the Potomac River.
Virginia Road, and a Black Driver.
Richmond. Baltimore. The Harrisburg
Mail, and a Glimpse of the City.
A Canal Boat.*

WE were to proceed in the first instance by steamboat: and
as it is usual to sleep on board, in consequence of the starting hour being four o'clock in the morning, we went down
to where she lay, at that very uncomfortable time for
such expeditions when slippers are most valuable, and a
familiar bed, in the perspective of an hour or two, looks
uncommonly pleasant.

It is ten o'clock at night: say half-past ten: moonlight,
warm, and dull enough. The steamer (not unlike a
child's Noah's ark in form, with the machinery on the top
of the roof) is riding lazily up and down, and bumping
clumsily against the wooden pier, as the ripple of the river
trifles with its unwieldy carcass. The wharf is some distance from the city. There is nobody down here; and one
or two dull lamps upon the steamer's decks are the only
signs of life remaining, when our coach has driven away.
As soon as our footsteps are heard upon the planks, a fat
Negress, particularly favored by nature in respect of
bustle, emerges from some dark stairs, and marshals my
wife towards the ladies' cabin, to which retreat she goes,
followed by a mighty bale of cloaks and great-coats. I
valiantly resolve not to go to bed at all, but to walk up and
down the pier till morning.

I begin my promenade—thinking of all kinds of distant things and persons, and of nothing near—and pace up and down for half an hour. Then I go on board again: and, getting into the light of one of the lamps, look at my watch, and think it must have stopped; and wonder what has become of the faithful secretary whom I brought along with me from Boston. He is supping with our late landlord (a Field Marshal at least, no doubt) in honor of our departure, and may be two hours longer. I walk again, but it gets duller and duller: the moon goes down: next June seems farther off in the dark, and the echoes of my footsteps make me nervous. It has turned cold, too; and walking up and down without any companion in such lonely circumstances is but poor amusement. So I break my stanch resolution, and think it may be, perhaps, as well to go to bed.

I go on board again; open the door of the gentlemen's cabin; and walk in. Somehow or other—from its being so quiet, I suppose—I have taken it into my head that there is nobody there. To my horror and amazement it is full of sleepers in every stage, shape, attitude, and variety of slumber: in the berths, on the chairs, on the floors, on the tables, and particularly round the stove, my detested enemy. I take another step forward, and slip upon the shining face of a black steward, who lies rolled in a blanket on the floor. He jumps up, grins, half in pain and half in hospitality; whispers my own name in my ear; and, groping among the sleepers, leads me to my berth. Standing beside it, I count these slumbering passengers, and get past forty. There is no use in going further, so I begin to undress. As the chairs are all occupied, and there is nothing else to put my clothes on, I deposit them upon the ground: not without soiling my hands, for it is in the same condition as the carpets in the Capitol, and from the same cause. Having but partially undressed, I clamber on my shelf, and hold the curtain open for a few minutes while I look round on all my fellow-travellers again. That done, I let it fall on them, and on the world: turn round: and go to sleep.

I wake, of course, when we get under way, for there is a good deal of noise. The day is then just breaking. Everybody wakes at the same time. Some are self-possessed directly, and some are much perplexed to make out where they are until they have rubbed their eyes, and, leaning on one elbow, looked about them. Some yawn, some groan, nearly all spit, and a few get up. I am among the risers: for it is easy to feel, without going into fresh air, that the atmosphere of the cabin is vile in the last degree. I huddle on my clothes, go down into the fore-cabin, get shaved by the barber, and wash myself. The washing and dressing apparatus, for the passengers generally, consists of two jack-towels, three small wooden basins, a keg of water and a ladle to serve it out with, six square inches of looking-glass, two ditto ditto of yellow soap, a comb and brush for the head, and nothing for the teeth. Everybody uses the comb and brush, except myself. Everybody stares to see me using my own; and two or three gentlemen are strongly disposed to banter me on my prejudices, but don't. When I have made my toilet, I go upon the hurricane deck, and set in for two hours of hard walking up and down. The sun is rising brilliantly; we are passing Mount Vernon, where Washington lies buried; the river is wide and rapid; and its banks are beautiful. All the glory and splendor of the day are coming on, and growing brighter every minute.

At eight o'clock we breakfast in the cabin where I passed the night, but the windows and doors are all thrown open, and now it is fresh enough. There is no hurry or greediness apparent in the despatch of the meal. It is longer than a travelling breakfast with us; more orderly; and more polite.

Soon after nine o'clock we come to Potomac Creek, where we are to land; and then comes the oddest part of the journey. Seven stage-coaches are preparing to carry us on. Some of them are ready, some of them are not ready. Some of the drivers are blacks, some whites. There are four horses to each coach, and all the horses, harnessed or unharnessed, are there. The passengers are getting out of the steamboat, and into the coaches; the luggage is being transferred in noisy wheelbarrows; the horses are frightened, and impatient to start; the black drivers are chattering to them like so many monkeys; and the white ones whooping like so many drovers: for the main thing to be done, in all kinds of hostlering here, is to make as much noise as possible. The coaches are something like the French coaches, but not nearly so good. In lieu of springs, they are hung on bands of the strongest leather. There is very little choice or difference between them; and they may be likened to the car portion of the swings at an English fair, roofed, put upon axletrees and wheels, and curtained with painted canvas. They are covered with mud from the roof to the wheel-tire, and have never been cleaned since they were first built.

The tickets we have received on board the steamboat are marked No. 1, so we belong to coach No. 1. I throw my coat on the box, and hoist my wife and her maid into the inside. It has only one step, and that, being about a yard from the ground, is usually approached by a chair: when there is no chair, ladies trust in Providence. The coach holds nine inside, having a seat across from door to door, where we in England put our legs; so that there is only one feat more difficult in the performance than getting in, and that is getting out again. There is only one outside passenger, and he sits upon the box. As I am that one, I climb up; and while they are strapping the luggage on the roof, and heaping it into a kind of tray behind, have a good opportunity of looking at the driver.

He is a Negro—very black indeed. He is dressed in a coarse pepper-and-salt suit excessively patched and darned (particularly at the knees), gray stockings, enormous unblacked high-low shoes, and very short trousers. He has two odd gloves: one of party-colored worsted, and one of leather. He has a very short whip, broken in the middle, and bandaged up with string. And yet he wears a low-crowned, broad-brimmed, black hat: faintly shadowing forth a kind of insane imitation of an English coachman! But somebody in authority cries "Go ahead!" as I am making these observations. The mail takes the lead in a four-horse wagon, and all the coaches follow in procession: headed by No. 1.

By the way, whenever an Englishman would cry "All right!" an American cries "Go ahead!" which is somewhat expressive of the national character of the two countries.

The first half-mile of the road is over bridges made of loose planks laid across two parallel poles, which tilt up as the wheels roll over them; and in the river. The river has a clayey bottom, and is full of holes, so that half a horse is constantly disappearing unexpectedly, and can't be found again for some time.

But we get past even this, and come to the road itself, which is a series of alternate swamps and gravel-pits. A tremendous place is close before us, the black driver rolls his eyes, screws his mouth up very round, and looks straight between the two leaders, as if he were saying to himself, "We have done this often before, but *now* I think we shall have a crash." He takes a rein in each hand; jerks and pulls at both; and dances on the splash-board with both feet (keeping his seat, of course) like the late lamented Ducrow on two of his fiery coursers. We come to the spot, sink down in the mire nearly to the coach windows, tilt on one side at an angle of forty-five degrees, and stick there. The insides scream dismally; the coach stops; the horses flounder; all the other six coaches stop; and their four and twenty horses flounder likewise: but merely for company, and in sympathy with ours. Then the following circumstances occur.

BLACK DRIVER (to the horses). "Hi!"
Nothing happens. Insides scream again.
BLACK DRIVER (to the horses). "Ho!"
Horses plunge, and splash the black driver.
GENTLEMAN INSIDE (looking out). "Why, what on airth—"
Gentleman receives a variety of splashes, and draws his head in again, without finishing his question or waiting for an answer.
BLACK DRIVER (still to the horses). "Jiddy! Jiddy!"
Horses pull violently, drag the coach out of the hole, and draw it up a bank; so steep that the black driver's legs fly up into the air, and he goes back among the luggage on the roof. But he immediately recovers himself, and cries (still to the horses),
"Pill!"
No effect. On the contrary, the coach begins to roll back upon No. 2, which rolls back upon No. 3, which rolls back upon No. 4, and so on, until No. 7 is heard to curse and swear nearly a quarter of a mile behind.
BLACK DRIVER (louder than before). "Pill!"
Horses make another struggle to get up the bank, and again the coach rolls backward.
BLACK DRIVER (louder than before). "Pe-e-e-ill!"
Horses make a desperate struggle.

BLACK DRIVER (recovering spirits). "Hi! Jiddy, Jiddy, Pill!"

Horses make another effort.

BLACK DRIVER (with great vigor). "Ally Loo! Hi. Jiddy, Jiddy. Pill. Ally Loo!"

Horses almost do it.

BLACK DRIVER (with his eyes starting out of his head). "Lee, den. Lee, dere. Hi. Jiddy, Jiddy. Pill. Ally Loo. Lee-e-e-e-e!"

They run up the bank, and go down again on the other side at a fearful pace. It is impossible to stop them, and at the bottom there is a deep hollow, full of water. The coach rolls frightfully. The insides scream. The mud and water fly about us. The black driver dances like a madman. Suddenly we are all right by some extraordinary means, and stop to breathe.

A black friend of the black driver is sitting on a fence. The black driver recognizes him by twirling his head round and round like a harlequin, rolling his eyes, shrugging his shoulders, and grinning from ear to ear. He stops short, turns to me, and says,—

"We shall get you through, sa, like a fiddle, and hope a please you when we get you through, sa. Old 'ooman at home, sa:" chuckling very much. "Outside gentleman, sa, he often remember old 'ooman at home, sa," grinning again.

"Ay, ay, we'll take care of the old woman. Don't be afraid."

The black driver grins again, but there is another hole, and, beyond that, another bank, close before us. So he stops short: cries (to the horses again) "Easy. Easy den. Ease. Steady. Hi. Jiddy. Pill. Ally. Loo," but never "Lee!" until we are reduced to the very last extremity, and are in the midst of difficulties, extrication from which appears to be all but impossible.

And so we do the ten miles or thereabouts in two hours and a half; breaking no bones, though bruising a great many; and, in short, getting through the distance "like a fiddle."

This singular kind of coaching terminates at Fredericksburg, whence there is a railway to Richmond. The tract of country through which it takes its course was once productive: but the soil has been exhausted by the system of employing a great amount of slave labor in forcing crops, without strengthening the land: and it is now little better than a sandy desert overgrown with trees. Dreary and uninteresting as its aspect is, I was glad to the heart to find anything on which one of the curses of this horrible institution has fallen; and had greater pleasure in contemplating the withered ground than the richest and most thriving cultivation in the same place could possibly have afforded me.

In this district, as in all others where slavery sits brooding (I have frequently heard this admitted, even by those who are its warmest advocates), there is an air of ruin and decay abroad, which is inseparable from the system. The barns and outhouses are mouldering away; the sheds are patched and half roofless; the log-cabins (built in Virginia with external chimneys made of clay or wood) are squalid in the last degree. There is no look of decent comfort anywhere. The miserable stations by the railway side; the great wild woodyards, whence the engine is supplied with fuel; the Negro children rolling on the ground before the cabin doors, with dogs and pigs; the biped beasts of burden slinking past: gloom and dejection are upon them all.

In the Negro car belonging to the train in which we made this journey were a mother and her children who had just been purchased; the husband and father being left behind with their old owner. The children cried the whole way, and the mother was misery's picture. The champion of Life, Liberty, and the Pursuit of Happiness, who had bought them, rode in the same train; and, every time we stopped, got down to see that they were safe. The black in Sinbad's Travels, with one eye in the middle of his forehead which shone like a burning coal, was nature's aristocrat compared with this white gentleman.

It was between six and seven o'clock in the evening when we drove to the hotel: in front of which, and on the top of the broad flight of steps leading to the door, two or three citizens were balancing themselves on rocking-chairs, and smoking cigars. We found it a very large and elegant establishment, and were as well entertained as travellers need desire to be. The climate being a thirsty one, there was never, at any hour of the day, a scarcity of loungers in the spacious bar, or a cessation of the mixing of cool liquors: but they were a merrier people here, and had musical instruments playing to them o' nights, which it was a treat to hear again.

The next day, and the next, we rode and walked about the town, which is delightfully situated on eight hills overhanging James River; a sparkling stream, studded here and there with bright islands, or brawling over broken rocks. Although it was yet but the middle of March, the weather in this southern temperature was extremely warm; the peach-trees and magnolias were in full bloom; and the trees were green. In a low ground among the hills is a valley known as "Bloody Run," from a terrible conflict with the Indians which once occurred there. It is a good place for such a struggle, and, like every other spot I saw associated with any legend of that wild people now so rapidly fading from the earth, interested me very much.

The city is the seat of the local Parliament of Virginia; and, in its shady legislative halls, some orators were drowsily holding forth to the hot noonday. By dint of constant repetition, however, these constitutional sights had very little more interest for me than so many parochial vestries; and I was glad to exchange this one for a lounge in a well-arranged public library of some ten thousand volumes, and a visit to a tobacco manufactory, where the workmen were all slaves.

I saw in this place the whole process of picking, rolling, pressing, drying, packing in casks, and branding. All the tobacco thus dealt with was in course of manufacture for chewing; and one would have supposed there was enough in that one storehouse to have filled even the comprehensive jaws of America. In this form the weed looks like the oil-cake on which we fatten cattle; and, even without reference to its consequences, is sufficiently uninviting.

Many of the workmen appeared to be strong men, and it is hardly necessary to add that they were all laboring quietly then. After two o'clock in the day they are allowed to sing, a certain number at a time. The hour striking while I was there, some twenty sang a hymn in parts, and sang it by no means ill; pursuing their work meanwhile. A bell rang as I was about to leave, and they all poured forth into a building on the opposite side of the street to dinner. I said several times that I should like to see them at their meal; but, as the gentleman to whom I mentioned this desire appeared to be suddenly taken rather deaf, I did not pursue the request. Of their appearance I shall have something to say presently.

On the following day I visited a plantation or farm, of about twelve hundred acres, on the opposite bank of the river. Here again, although I went down with the owner of the estate, to "the quarter," as that part of it in which the slaves live is called, I was not invited to enter into any of their huts. All I saw of them was, that they were very crazy, wretched cabins, near to which groups of half-naked children basked in the sun, or wallowed on the dusty ground. But I believe that this gentleman is a considerate and excellent master, who inherited his fifty slaves, and is neither a buyer nor a seller of human stock; and I am sure, from my own observation and conviction, that he is a kind-hearted, worthy man.

The planter's house was an airy, rustic dwelling, that brought Defoe's description of such places strongly to my recollection. The day was very warm, but the blinds being all closed, and the windows and doors set wide open, a shady coolness rustled through the rooms, which was exquisitely refreshing after the glare and heat without. Before the windows was an open piazza, where, in what they call the hot weather—whatever that may be—they sling hammocks, and drink and doze luxuriously. I do not know how their cool refections may taste within the hammocks, but, having experience, I can report that, out of them, the mounds of ices and the bowls of mint-julep and sherry-cobbler they make in these latitudes, are refreshments never to be thought of afterwards, in summer, by those who would preserve contented minds.

There are two bridges across the river: one belongs to the railroad, and the other, which is a very crazy affair, is the private property of some old lady in the neighborhood, who levies tolls upon the townspeople. Crossing this bridge on my way back, I saw a notice painted on the gate, cautioning all persons to drive slowly: under a penalty, if the offender were a white man, of five dollars; if a Negro, fifteen stripes.

The same decay and gloom that overhang the way by which it is approached, hover above the town of Richmond. There are pretty villas and cheerful houses in its streets, and Nature smiles upon the country round; but jostling its handsome residences, like slavery itself going hand in hand with many lofty virtues, are deplorable tenements, fences unrepaired, walls crumbling into ruinous heaps. Hinting gloomily at things below the surface, these, and many other tokens of the same description, force themselves upon the notice, and are remembered with depressing influence, when livelier features are forgotten.

To those who are happily unaccustomed to them, the countenances in the streets and laboring places, too, are shocking. All men who know that there are laws against instructing slaves, of which the pains and penalties greatly exceed in their amount the fines imposed on those who maim and torture them, must be prepared to find their faces very low in the scale of intellectual expression. But the darkness—not of skin, but mind—which meets the stranger's eye at every turn; the brutalizing and blotting out of all fairer characters traced by Nature's hand; immeasurably outdo his worst belief. That travelled creation of the great satirist's brain, who, fresh from living among horses, peered from a high casement down upon his own kind with trembling horror, was scarcely more repelled and daunted by the sight than those who look upon some of these faces for the first time must surely be.

I left the last of them behind me in the person of a wretched drudge, who, after running to and fro all day till midnight, and moping in his stealthy winks of sleep upon the stairs between-whiles, was washing the dark passages at four o'clock in the morning; and went upon my way with a grateful heart that I was not doomed to live where slavery was, and had never had my senses blunted to its wrongs and horrors in a slave-rocked cradle.

It had been my intention to proceed by James River and Chesapeake Bay to Baltimore; but one of the steamboats being absent from her station through some accident, and the means of conveyance being consequently rendered uncertain, we returned to Washington by the way we had come (there were two constables on board the steamboat, in pursuit of runaway slaves), and, halting there again for one night, went on to Baltimore next afternoon.

The most comfortable of all the hotels of which I had any experience in the United States, and they were not a

few, is Barnum's, in that city: where the English traveller
will find curtains to his bed, for the first and probably the
last time in America (this is a disinterested remark, for
I never use them); and where he will be likely to have
enough water for washing himself, which is not at all a
common case.

This capital of the State of Maryland is a bustling, busy
town, with a great deal of traffic of various kinds, and in
particular of water commerce. That portion of the town
which it most favors is none of the cleanest, it is true; but
the upper part is of a very different character, and has
many agreeable streets and public buildings. The Washington Monument, which is a handsome pillar with a statue
on its summit; the Medical College; and the Battle Monument in memory of an engagement with the British at
North Point; are the most conspicuous among them.

There is a very good prison in this city, and the State
Penitentiary is also among its institutions. In this latter
establishment there were two curious cases.

One was that of a young man who had been tried for
the murder of his father. The evidence was entirely cir-
cumstantial, and was very conflicting and doubtful; nor
was it possible to assign any motive which could have
tempted him to the commission of so tremendous a crime.
He had been tried twice; and, on the second occasion, the
jury felt so much hesitation in convicting him, that they
found a verdict of manslaughter, or murder in the second
degree; which it could not possibly be, as there had, beyond
all doubt, been no quarrel or provocation, and if he were
guilty at all, he was unquestionably guilty of murder in its
broadest and worst signification.

The remarkable feature in the case was, that if the unfortunate deceased were not really murdered by this own
son of his, he must have been murdered by his own
brother. The evidence lay, in a most remarkable manner, between those two. On all the suspicious points, the
dead man's brother was the witness; all the explanations
for the prisoner (some of them extremely plausible) went,
by construction and inference, to inculpate him as plotting
to fix the guilt upon his nephew. It must have been one
of them; and the jury had to decide between two sets of
suspicions, almost equally unnatural, unaccountable,
and strange.

The other case was that of a man who once went to a certain distiller's, and stole a copper measure containing a quantity of liquor. He was pursued and taken with the property in his possession, and was sentenced to two years' imprisonment. On coming out of the jail at the expiration of that term, he went back to the same distiller's, and stole the same copper measure, containing the same quantity of liquor. There was not the slightest reason to suppose that the man wished to return to prison: indeed, everything, but the commission of the offence, made directly against that assumption. There are only two ways of accounting for this extraordinary proceeding. One is that, after undergoing so much for this copper measure, he conceived he had established a sort of claim and right to it. The other that, by dint of long thinking about, it had become a monomania with him, and had acquired a fascination which he found it impossible to resist: swelling from an Earthly Copper Gallon into an Ethereal Golden Vat.

After remaining here a couple of days, I bound myself to a rigid adherence to the plan I had laid down so recently, and resolved to set forward on our western journey without any more delay. Accordingly, having reduced the luggage within the smallest possible compass (by sending back to New York, to be afterwards forwarded to us in Canada, so much of it as was not absolutely wanted); and having procured the necessary credentials to banking-houses on the way; and having, moreover, looked for two evenings at the setting sun, with as well-defined an idea of the country before us as if we had been going to travel into the very centre of that planet; we left Baltimore by another railway at half-past eight in the morning, and reached the town of York, some sixty miles off, by the early dinner-time of the hotel which was the starting-place of the four-horse coach wherein we were to proceed to Harrisburg.

This conveyance, the box of which I was fortunate enough to secure, had come down to meet us at the railroad station, and was as muddy and cumbersome as usual. As more passengers were waiting for us at the inn door, the coachman observed under his breath, in the usual self-communicative voice, looking the while at his mouldy harness as if it were to that he was addressing himself,—

"I expect we shall want *the big* coach."

I could not help wondering within myself what the size of this big coach might be, and how many persons it might be designed to hold; for the vehicle which was too small for our purpose was something larger than two English heavy night coaches, and might have been the twin brother of a French Diligence. My speculations were speedily set at rest, however, for, as soon as we had dined, there came rumbling up the street, shaking its sides like a corpulent giant, a kind of barge on wheels. After much blundering and backing, it stopped at the door: rolling heavily from side to side, when its other motion had ceased, as if it had taken cold in its damp stable, and between that, and the having been required in its dropsical old age to move at any faster pace than a walk, was distressed by shortness of wind.

"If here ain't the Harrisburg mail at last, and dreadful bright and smart to look at too," cried an elderly gentleman in some excitement, "darn my mother!"

I don't know what the sensation of being darned may be, or whether a man's mother has a keener relish or disrelish of the process than anybody else; but if the endurance of this mysterious ceremony by the old lady in question had depended on the accuracy of her son's vision in respect to the abstract brightness and smartness of the Harrisburg mail, she would certainly have undergone its infliction. However, they booked twelve people inside; and the luggage (including such trifles as a large rocking-chair and a good-sized dining-table) being at length made fast upon the roof, we started off in great state.

At the door of another hotel there was another passenger to be taken up.

"Any room, sir?" cries the new passenger to the coachman.

"Well, there's room enough," replies the coachman, without getting down, or even looking at him.

"There ain't no room at all, sir," bawls a gentleman inside. Which another gentleman (also inside) confirms, by predicting that the attempt to introduce any more passengers "won't fit nohow."

The new passenger, without any expression of anxiety, looks into the coach, and then looks up at the coachman. "Now, how do you mean to fix it?" says he after a pause: "for I *must* go."

The coachman employs himself in twisting the lash of his whip into a knot, and takes no more notice of the question: clearly signifying that it is anybody's business but his, and that the passengers would do well to fix it among themselves. In this state of things, matters seem to be approximating to a fix of another kind, when another inside passenger in a corner, who is nearly suffocated, cries faintly,—

"I'll get out."

This is no matter of relief or self-congratulation to the driver, for his immovable philosophy is perfectly undisturbed by anything that happens in the coach. Of all things in the world, the coach would seem to be the very last upon his mind. The exchange is made, however, and then the passenger who has given up his seat makes a third upon the box, seating himself in what he calls the middle: that is, with half his person on my legs, and the other half on the driver's.

"Go ahead, cap'en," cries the colonel, who directs.

"Go-lang!" cries the cap'en to his company, the horses, and away we go.

We took up at a rural bar-room, after we had gone a few miles, an intoxicated gentleman who climbed upon the roof among the luggage, and subsequently slipping off without hurting himself, was seen in the distant perspective reeling back to the grog-shop where we had found him. We also parted with more of our freight at different times, so that when we came to change horses, I was again alone outside.

The coachmen always change with the horses, and are usually as dirty as the coach. The first was dressed like a very shabby English baker; the second like a Russian peasant: for he wore a loose purple camlet robe with a fur collar, tied round his waist with a party-colored worsted sash; gray trousers; light blue gloves; and a cap of bearskin. It had by this time come on to rain very heavily, and there was a cold damp mist besides, which penetrated to the skin. I was very glad to take advantage of a stoppage, and get down to stretch my legs, shake the water off my great-coat, and swallow the usual anti-temperance recipe for keeping out the cold.

When I mounted to my seat again, I observed a new parcel lying on the coach roof, which I took to be a rather large fiddle in a brown bag. In the course of a few miles, however, I discovered that it had a glazed cap at one end and a pair of muddy shoes at the other; and further observation demonstrated it to be a small boy in a snuff-colored coat, with his arms quite pinioned to his sides, by deep forcing into his pockets. He was, I presume, a relative or friend of the coachman's, as he lay atop of the luggage, with his face towards the rain; and, except when a change of position brought his shoes in contact with my hat, he appeared to be asleep. At last, on some occasion of our stopping, this thing slowly upreared itself to the height of three feet six, and, fixing its eyes on me, observed in piping accents, with a complaisant yawn, half quenched in an obliging air of friendly patronage, "Well now, stranger, I guess you find this a'most like an English arternoon, hey?"

The scenery, which had been tame enough at first, was, for the last ten or twelve miles, beautiful. Our road wound through the pleasant valley of the Susquehanna; the river, dotted with innumerable green islands, lay upon our right; and on the left, a steep ascent, craggy with broken rock, and dark with pine-trees. The mist, wreathing itself into a hundred fantastic shapes, moved solemnly upon the water; and the gloom of evening gave to all an air of mystery and silence which greatly enhanced its natural interest.

We crossed this river by a wooden bridge, roofed and covered in on all sides, and nearly a mile in length. It was profoundly dark; perplexed, with great beams crossing and recrossing it at every possible angle; and through the broad chinks and crevices of the floor the rapid river gleamed, far down below, like a legion of eyes. We had no lamps; and as the horses stumbled and floundered through this place, towards the distant speck of dying light, it seemed interminable. I really could not at first persuade myself, as we rumbled heavily on, filling the bridge with hollow noises, and I held down my head to save it from the rafters above, but that I was in a painful dream; for I have often dreamed of toiling through such places, and as often argued, even at the time, "this cannot be reality."

At length, however, we emerged upon the streets of Harrisburg, whose feeble lights, reflected dismally from the wet ground, did not shine out upon a very cheerful city.

We were soon established in a snug hotel, which, though smaller and far less splendid than many we put up at, is raised above them all in my remembrance, by having for its landlord the most obliging, considerate, and gentlemanly person I ever had to deal with.

As we were not to proceed upon our journey until the afternoon, I walked out, after breakfast the next morning, to look about me; and was duly shown a model prison on the solitary system, just erected, and as yet without an inmate; the trunk of an old tree to which Harris, the first settler here (afterwards buried under it), was tied by hostile Indians, with his funeral pile about him, when he was saved by the timely appearance of a friendly party on the opposite shore of the river; the local legislature (for there was another of those bodies here, again, in full debate); and the other curiosities of the town.

I was very much interested in looking over a number of treaties made from time to time with the poor Indians, signed by the different chiefs at the period of their ratification, and preserved in the office of the Secretary to the Commonwealth. These signatures, traced of course by their own hands, are rough drawings of the creatures or weapons they were called after. Thus, the Great Turtle makes a crooked pen-and-ink outline of a great turtle; the Buffalo sketches a buffalo; the War Hatchet sets a rough image of that weapon for his mark. So with the Arrow, the Fish, the Scalp, the Big Canoe, and all of them.

I could not but think—as I looked at these feeble and tremulous productions of hands which could draw the longest arrow to the head in a stout elk-horn bow, or split a bead or feather with a rifle ball—of Crabbe's musings over the Parish Register, and the irregular scratches made with a pen by men who would plough a lengthy furrow straight from end to end. Nor could I help bestowing many sorrowful thoughts upon the simple warriors whose hands and hearts were set there in all truth and honesty; and who only learned in course of time from white men how to break their faith, and quibble out of forms and bonds. I wondered, too, how many times the credulous Big Turtle, or trusting Little Hatchet, had put his mark to treaties which were falsely read to him; and had signed away, he knew not what, until it went and cast him loose upon the new possessors of the land, a savage indeed.

Our host announced, before our early dinner, that some members of the legislative body proposed to do us the honor of calling. He had kindly yielded up to us his wife's own little parlor, and when I begged that he would show them in, I saw him look with painful apprehension at its pretty carpet; though, being otherwise occupied at the time, the cause of his uneasiness did not occur to me.

It certainly would have been more pleasant to all parties concerned, and would not, I think, have compromised their independence in any material degree, if some of these gentlemen had not only yielded to the prejudice in favor of spittoons, but had abandoned themselves, for the moment, even to the conventional absurdity of pocket-handkerchiefs.

It still continued to rain heavily, and when we went down to the Canal Boat (for that was the mode of conveyance by which we were to proceed) after dinner, the weather was as unpromising and obstinately wet as one would desire to see. Nor was the sight of this canal boat, in which we were to spend three or four days, by any means a cheerful one; as it involved some uneasy speculations concerning the disposal of the passengers at night, and opened a wide field of inquiry touching the other domestic arrangements of the establishment, which was sufficiently disconcerting.

However, there it was—a barge with a little house in it, viewed from the outside; and a caravan at a fair, viewed from within: the gentlemen being accommodated as the spectators usually are in one of those locomotive museums of penny wonders; and the ladies being partitioned off by a red curtain, after the manner of the dwarfs and giants in the same establishments, whose private lives are passed in rather close exclusiveness.

We sat here, looking silently at the row of little tables which extended down both sides of the cabin, and listening to the rain as it dripped and pattered on the boat, and plashed with a dismal merriment in the water, until the arrival of the railway train, for whose final contribution to our stock of passengers our departure was alone deferred. It brought a great many boxes, which were bumped and tossed upon the roof, almost as painfully as if they had been deposited on one's own head, without the intervention of a porter's knot; and several damp gentlemen, whose clothes, on their drawing round the stove, began to steam again. No doubt it would have been a thought more comfortable if the driving rain, which now poured down more soakingly than ever, had admitted of a window being opened, or if our number had been something less than thirty; but there was scarcely time to think as much, when a train of three horses was attached to the tow-rope, the boy upon the leader smacked his whip, the rudder creaked and groaned complainingly, and we had begun our journey.

CHAPTER 10

Some Further Account of the Canal Boat, Its Domestic Economy, and Its Passengers. Journey to Pittsburg Across the Alleghany Mountains. Pittsburg.

As it continued to rain most perseveringly, we all remained below: the damp gentlemen round the stove gradually becoming mildewed by the action of the fire: and the dry gentlemen lying at full length upon the seats, or slumbering uneasily with their faces on the tables, or walking up and down the cabin, which it was barely possible for a man of the middle height to do without making bald places on his head by scraping it against the roof. At about six o'clock all the small tables were put together to form one long table, and everybody sat down to tea, coffee, bread, butter, salmon, shad, liver, steak, potatoes, pickles, ham, chops, black puddings, and sausages.

"Will you try," said my opposite neighbor, handing me a dish of potatoes broken up in milk and butter, "will you try some of these fixings?"

There are few words which perform such various duties as this word "fix." It is the Caleb Quotem of the American vocabulary. You call upon a gentleman in a country town, and his help informs you that he is "fixing himself" just now, but will be down directly: by which you are to understand that he is dressing. You inquire, on board a steamboat, of a fellow-passenger, whether breakfast will be ready soon, and he tells you he should think so, for, when he was last below, they were "fixing the tables:" in other words, laying the cloth. You beg a porter to collect your luggage, and he entreats you not to be uneasy, for he'll "fix it presently:" and if you complain of indisposition, you are advised to have recourse to Doctor So-and-so, who will "fix you" in no time.

One night I ordered a bottle of mulled wine at an hotel where I was staying, and waited a long time for it; at length it was put upon the table, with an apology from the landlord that he feared it wasn't "fixed properly." And I recollect once, at a stage-coach dinner, overhearing a very stern gentleman demand of a waiter who presented him with a plate of under-done roast beef, "whether he called *that* fixing God A'mighty's vittles?"

There is no doubt that the meal, at which the invitation was tendered to me which has occasioned this digression, was disposed of somewhat ravenously; and that the gentlemen thrust the broad-bladed knives and the two-pronged forks further down their throats than I ever saw the same weapons go before, except in the hands of a skilful juggler: but no man sat down until the ladies were seated; or omitted any little act of politeness which could contribute to their comfort. Nor did I ever once, on any occasion, anywhere, during my rambles in America, see a woman exposed to the slightest act of rudeness, incivility, or even inattention.

By the time the meal was over, the rain, which seemed to have worn itself out by coming down so fast, was nearly over too; and it became feasible to go on deck: which was a great relief, notwithstanding its being a very small deck, and being rendered still smaller by the luggage, which was heaped together in the middle under a tarpaulin covering; leaving, on either side, a path so narrow, that it became a science to walk to and fro without tumbling overboard into the canal. It was somewhat embarrassing at first, too, to have to duck nimbly every five minutes whenever the man at the helm cried "Bridge!" and sometimes, when the cry was "Low Bridge," to lie down nearly flat. But custom familiarizes one to anything, and there were so many bridges that it took a very short time to get used to this.

As night came on, and we drew in sight of the first range of hills, which are the outposts of the Alleghany Mountains, the scenery, which had been uninteresting hitherto, became more bold and striking. The wet ground reeked and smoked after the heavy fall of rain; and the croaking of the frogs (whose noise in these parts is almost incredible) sounded as though a million of fairy teams with bells were travelling through the air, and keeping pace with us. The night was cloudy yet, but moonlight too: and when we crossed the Susquehanna River—over which there is an extraordinary wooden bridge with two galleries, one above the other, so that, even there, two boat-teams meeting may pass without confusion—it was wild and grand.

I have mentioned my having been in some uncertainty and doubt, at first, relative to the sleeping arrangements on board this boat. I remained in the same vague state of mind until ten o'clock or thereabouts, when, going below, I found suspended, on either side of the cabin, three long tiers of hanging book-shelves, designed apparently for volumes of the small octavo size. Looking with greater attention at these contrivances (wondering to find such literary preparations in such a place), I descried on each shelf a sort of microscopic sheet and blanket; then I began dimly to comprehend that the passengers were the library, and that they were to be arranged edgewise on these shelves till morning.

I was assisted to this conclusion by seeing some of them gather round the master of the boat at one of the tables, drawing lots with all the anxieties and passions of gamesters depicted in their countenances; while others, with small pieces of cardboard in their hands, were groping among the shelves in search of numbers corresponding with those they had drawn. As soon as any gentleman found his number, he took possession of it by immediately undressing himself and crawling into bed. The rapidity with which an agitated gambler subsided into a snoring slumberer was one of the most singular effects I have ever witnessed. As to the ladies, they were already abed, behind the red curtain, which was carefully drawn and pinned up the centre; though as every cough, or sneeze, or whisper, behind this curtain, was perfectly audible before it, we had still a lively consciousness of their society.

The politeness of the person in authority had secured to me a shelf in a nook near this red curtain, in some degree removed from the great body of sleepers: to which place I retired, with many acknowledgments to him for his attention. I found it, on after-measurement, just the width of an ordinary sheet of Bath post letter-paper; and I was at first in some uncertainty as to the best means of getting into it. But the shelf being a bottom one, I finally determined on lying upon the floor, rolling gently in, stopping immediately I touched the mattress, and remaining for the night with that side uppermost, whatever it might be. Luckily, I came upon my back at exactly the right moment. I was much alarmed, on looking upward, to see, by the shape of his half yard of sacking (which his weight had bent into an exceedingly tight bag), that there was a very heavy gentleman above me, whom the slender cords seemed quite incapable of holding; and I could not help reflecting upon the grief of my wife and family in the event of his coming down in the night. But, as I could not have got up again without a severe bodily struggle, which might have alarmed the ladies; and as I had nowhere to go to even if I had; I shut my eyes upon the danger, and remained there.

One of two remarkable circumstances is indisputably a fact, with reference to that class of society who travel in these boats. Either they carry their restlessness to such a pitch that they never sleep at all; or they expectorate in dreams, which would be a remarkable mingling of the real and ideal. All night long, and every night, on this canal, there was a perfect storm and tempest of spitting; and once my coat, being in the very centre of a hurricane sustained by five gentlemen (which moved vertically, strictly carrying out Reid's Theory of the Law of Storms), I was fain the next morning to lay it on the deck, and rub it down with fair water before it was in a condition to be worn again.

Between five and six o'clock in the morning we got up, and some of us went on deck, to give them an opportunity of taking the shelves down; while others, the morning being very cold, crowded round the rusty stove, cherishing the newly kindled fire, and filling the grate with those voluntary contributions of which they had been so liberal all night. The washing accommodations were primitive. There was a tin ladle chained to the deck, with which every gentleman who thought it necessary to cleanse himself (many were superior to this weakness) fished the dirty water out of the canal, and poured it into a tin basin, secured in like manner. There was also a jack-towel. And, hanging up before a little looking-glass in the bar, in the immediate vicinity of the bread and cheese and biscuits, were a public comb and brush.

At eight o'clock, the shelves being taken down and put away, and the tables joined together, everybody sat down to the tea, coffee, bread, butter, salmon, shad, liver, steak, potatoes, pickles, ham, chops, black puddings, and sausages, all over again. Some were fond of compounding this variety, and having it all on their plates at once. As each gentleman got through his own personal amount of tea, coffee, bread, butter, salmon, shad, liver, steak, potatoes, pickles, ham, chops, black puddings, and sausages, he rose up and walked off. When everybody had done with everything, the fragments were cleared away: and one of the waiters, appearing anew in the character of a barber, shaved such of the company as desired to be shaved; while the remainder looked on, or yawned over their newspapers. Dinner was breakfast again, without the tea and coffee; and supper and breakfast were identical.

There was a man on board this boat with a light, fresh-colored face, and a pepper-and-salt suit of clothes, who was the most inquisitive fellow that can possibly be imagined. He never spoke otherwise than interrogatively. He was an embodied inquiry. Sitting down or standing up, still or moving, walking the deck or taking his meals, there he was, with a great note of interrogation in each eye, two in his cocked ears, two more in his turned-up nose and chin, at least half a dozen more about the corners of his mouth, and the largest one of all in his hair, which was brushed pertly off his forehead in a flaxen clump. Every button in his clothes said, "Eh? What's that? Did you speak? Say that again, will you?" He was always wide awake, like the enchanted bride who drove her husband frantic; always restless; always thirsting for answers; perpetually seeking and never finding. There never was such a curious man.

I wore a fur great-coat at that time, and before we were well clear of the wharf, he questioned me concerning it, and its price, and where I bought it, and when, and what fur it was, and what it weighed, and what it cost.

Then he took notice of my watch, and asked what *that* cost, and whether it was a French watch, and where I got it, and how I got it, and whether I bought it or had it given me, and how it went, and where the keyhole was, and when I wound it, every night or every morning, and whether I ever forgot to wind it at all, and if I did, what then? Where had I been to last, and where was I going next, and where was I going after that, and had I seen the President, and what did he say, and what did I say, and what did he say when I had said that? Eh? Lor, now! do tell!

Finding that nothing would satisfy him, I evaded his questions after the first score or two, and in particular pleaded ignorance respecting the name of the fur whereof the coat was made. I am unable to say whether this was the reason, but that coat fascinated him ever afterwards; he usually kept close behind me as I walked, and moved as I moved, that he might look at it the better; and he frequently dived into narrow places after me at the risk of his life, that he might have the satisfaction of passing his hand up the back, and rubbing it the wrong way.

We had another odd specimen on board of a different kind. This was a thin-faced, spare-figured man of middle age and stature, dressed in a dusty drabbish-colored suit, such as I never saw before. He was perfectly quiet during the first part of the journey: indeed, I don't remember having so much as seen him until he was brought out by circumstances, as great men often are. The conjunction of events which made him famous happened, briefly, thus.

The canal extends to the foot of the mountain, and there, of course, it stops; the passengers being conveyed across it by land carriage, and taken on afterwards by another canal boat, the counterpart of the first, which awaits them on the other side. There are two canal lines of passage boats; one is called the Express, and one (a cheaper one) the Pioneer. The Pioneer gets first to the mountain, and waits for the Express people to come up; both sets of passengers being conveyed across it at the same time. We were the Express company; but when we had crossed the mountain, and had come to the second boat, the proprietors took it into their heads to draft all the Pioneers into it likewise, so that we were five and forty at least, and the accession of passengers was not at all of that kind which improved the prospect of sleeping at night. Our people grumbled at this, as people do in such cases; but suffered the boat to be towed off with the whole freight aboard nevertheless; and away we went down the canal. At home I should have protested lustily, but, being a foreigner here, I held my peace. Not so this passenger. He cleft a path among the people on deck (we were nearly all on deck), and, without addressing anybody whomsoever, soliloquized as follows:—

"This may suit *you*, this may, but it don't suit *me*. This may be all very well with Down Easters, and men of Boston raising, but it won't suit my figure nohow; and no two ways about *that;* and so I tell you. Now! I'm from the brown forests of the Mississippi, *I* am, and when the sun shines on me, it does shine—a little. It don't glimmer where *I* live, the sun don't. No. I'm a brown forester, I am. I ain't a Johnny Cake. There are no smooth skins where I live. We're rough men there. Rather. If Down Easters and men of Boston raising like this, I'm glad of it, but I'm none of that raising nor of that breed. No. This company wants a little fixing, *it* does. I'm the wrong sort of man for 'em, *I* am. They won't like me, *they* won't. This is piling of it up a little too moũntaĩnoũs, this is." At the end of every one of these short sentences he turned upon his heel, and walked the other way; checking himself abruptly when he had finished another short sentence, and turning back again.

It is impossible for me to say what terrific meaning was hidden in the words of this brown forester, but I know that the other passengers looked on in a sort of admiring horror, and that presently the boat was put back to the wharf, and as many of the Pioneers as could be coaxed or bullied into going away were got rid of.

When we started again, some of the boldest spirits on board made bold to say to the obvious occasion of this improvement in our prospects, "Much obliged to you, sir:" whereunto the brown forester (waving his hand, and still walking up and down as before), replied, "No, you ain't. You're none o' my raising. You may act for yourselves, *you* may. I have pinted out the way. Down Easters and Johnny Cakes can follow if they please. I ain't a Johnny Cake, *I* ain't. I am from the brown forests of the Mississippi, *I* am"—and so on, as before. He was unanimously voted one of the tables for his bed at night —there is a great contest for the tables—in consideration of his public services: and he had the warmest corner by the stove throughout the rest of the journey. But I never could find out that he did anything except sit there; nor did I hear him speak again until, in the midst of the bustle and turmoil of getting the luggage ashore in the dark at Pittsburg, I stumbled over him as he sat smoking a cigar on the cabin steps, and heard him muttering to himself, with a short laugh of defiance, "I ain't a Johnny Cake, *I* ain't. I'm from the brown forests of the Mississippi, *I* am, damme!" I am inclined to argue, from this, that he had never left off saying so; but I could not make affidavit of that part of the story, if required to do so by my Queen and Country.

As we have not reached Pittsburg yet, however, in the order of our narrative, I may go on to remark that breakfast was perhaps the least desirable meal of the day, as, in addition to the many savory odors arising from the eatables already mentioned, there were whiffs of gin, whiskey, brandy, and rum from the little bar hard by, and a decided seasoning of stale tobacco. Many of the gentlemen passengers were far from particular in respect of their linen, which was in some cases as yellow as the little rivulets that had trickled from the corners of their mouths in chewing, and dried there. Nor was the atmosphere quite free from zephyr whisperings of the thirty beds which had just been cleared away, and of which we were further and more pressingly reminded by the occasional appearance on the tablecloth of a kind of Game not mentioned in the Bill of Fare.

And yet despite these oddities—and even they had, for me at least, a humor of their own—there was much in this mode of travelling which I heartily enjoyed at the time, and look back upon with great pleasure. Even the running up, bare-necked, at five o'clock in the morning, from the tainted cabin to the dirty deck; scooping up the icy water, plunging one's head into it, and drawing it out all fresh and glowing with the cold; was a good thing. The fast, brisk walk upon the towing-path, between that time and breakfast, when every vein and artery seemed to tingle with health; the exquisite beauty of the opening day, when light came gleaming off from everything; the lazy motion of the boat, when one lay idly on the deck, looking through, rather than at, the deep blue sky; the gliding on at night, so noiselessly, past frowning hills, sullen with dark trees, and sometimes angry in one red burning spot high up, where unseen men lay crouching round a fire; the shining out of the bright stars, undisturbed by noise of wheels or steam, or any other sound than the liquid rippling of the water as the boat went on: all these were pure delights.

Then, there were new settlements and detached log-cabins and frame-houses, full of interest for strangers from an old country: cabins with simple ovens, outside, made of clay; and lodgings for the pigs nearly as good as many of the human quarters; broken windows, patched with worn-out hats, old clothes, old boards, fragments of blankets and paper; and home-made dressers standing in the open air without the door, whereon was ranged the household store, not hard to count, of earthen jars and pots. The eye was pained to see the stumps of great trees thickly strewn in every field of wheat, and seldom to lose the eternal swamp and dull morass, with hundreds of rotten trunks and twisted branches steeped in its unwholesome water. It was quite sad and oppressive to come upon great tracts where settlers had been burning down the trees, and where their wounded bodies lay about like those of murdered creatures, while here and there some charred and blackened giant reared aloft two withered arms, and seemed to call down curses on his foes. Sometimes, at night, the way wound through some lonely gorge, like a mountain pass in Scotland, shining and coldly glittering in the light of the moon, and so closed in by high steep hills all round, that there seemed to be no egress save through the narrower path by which we had come, until one rugged hillside seemed to open, and, shutting out the moonlight as we passed into its gloomy throat, wrapped our new course in shade and darkness.

We had left Harrisburg on Friday. On Sunday morning we arrived at the foot of the mountain, which is crossed by railroad. There are ten inclined planes; five *a*scending, and five *de*scending; the carriages are dragged up the former, and let slowly down the latter, by means of stationary engines; the comparatively level spaces between being traversed, sometimes by horse, and sometimes by engine power, as the case demands. Occasionally the rails are laid upon the extreme verge of a giddy precipice; and looking from the carriage window, the traveller gazes sheer down, without a stone or scrap of fence between, into the mountain depths below. The journey is very carefully made, however; only two carriages travelling together; and, while proper precautions are taken, is not to be dreaded for its dangers.

It was very pretty, travelling thus at a rapid pace along the heights of the mountain in a keen wind, to look down into a valley full of light and softness; catching glimpses, through the tree-tops, of scattered cabins; children running to the doors; dogs bursting out to bark, whom we could see without hearing; terrified pigs scampering homewards; families sitting out in their rude gardens; cows gazing upward with a stupid indifference; men in their shirtsleeves, looking on at their unfinished houses, planning out to-morrow's work; and we riding onward, high above them, like a whirlwind. It was amusing, too, when we had dined, and rattled down a steep pass, having no other moving power than the weight of the carriages themselves, to see the engine, released long after us, come buzzing down alone, like a great insect, its back of green and gold so shining in the sun, that if it had spread a pair of wings and soared away, no one would have had occasion, as I fancied, for the least surprise. But it stopped short of us in a very business-like manner when we reached the canal; and, before we left the wharf, went panting up this hill again, with the passengers who had waited our arrival for the means of traversing the road by which we had come.

On the Monday evening, furnace fires and clanking hammers on the banks of the canal warned us that we approached the termination of this part of our journey. After going through another dreamy place—a long aqueduct across the Alleghany River, which was stranger than the bridge at Harrisburg, being a vast, low, wooden chamber full of water—we emerged upon that ugly confusion of backs of buildings, and crazy galleries and stairs, which always abuts on water, whether it be river, sea, canal, or ditch: and were at Pittsburg.

Pittsburg is like Birmingham in England; at least, its

townspeople say so. Setting aside the streets, the shops, the houses, wagons, factories, public buildings, and population, perhaps it may be. It certainly has a great quantity of smoke hanging about it, and is famous for its ironworks. Besides the prison to which I have already referred, this town contains a pretty arsenal and other institutions. It is very beautifully situated on the Alleghany River, over which there are two bridges; and the villas of the wealthier citizens, sprinkled about the high grounds in the neighborhood, are pretty enough. We lodged at a most excellent hotel, and were admirably served. As usual, it was full of boarders, was very large, and had a broad colonnade to every story of the house.

We tarried here three days. Our next point was Cincinnati: and as this was a steamboat journey, and western steamboats usually blow up one or two a week in the season, it was advisable to collect opinions in reference to the comparative safety of the vessels bound that way, then lying in the river. One called the Messenger was the best recommended. She had been advertised to start positively every day for a fortnight or so, and had not gone yet, nor did her captain seem to have any fixed intention on the subject. But this is the custom: for if the law were to bind down a free and independent citizen to keep his word with the public, what would become of the liberty of the subject? Besides, it is in the way of trade. And if passengers be decoyed in the way of trade, and people be inconvenienced in the way of trade, what man, who is a sharp tradesman himself, shall say, "We must put a stop to this"?

Impressed by the deep solemnity of the public announcement, I (being then ignorant of these usages) was for hurrying on board in a breathless state immediately; but receiving private and confidential information that the boat would certainly not start until Friday, April the First, we made ourselves very comfortable in the meanwhile, and went on board at noon that day.

CHAPTER 11

From Pittsburg to Cincinnati in a Western Steamboat. Cincinnati.

THE Messenger was one among a crowd of high-pressure steamboats clustered together by the wharf-side, which, looked down upon from the rising ground that forms the landing-place, and backed by the lofty bank on the opposite side of the river, appeared no larger than so many floating models. She had some forty passengers on board, exclusive of the poorer persons on the lower deck; and in half an hour, or less, proceeded on her way.

We had, for ourselves, a tiny stateroom with two berths in it, opening out of the ladies' cabin. There was, undoubtedly, something satisfactory in this "location," inasmuch as it was in the stern, and we had been a great many times very gravely recommended to keep as far aft as possible, "because the steamboats generally blew up forward." Nor was this an unnecessary caution, as the occurrence and circumstances of more than one such fatality during our stay sufficiently testified. Apart from this source of self-congratulation, it was an unspeakable relief to have any place, no matter how confined, where one could be alone: and as the row of little chambers, of which this was one, had each a second glass door besides that in the ladies' cabin, which opened on a narrow gallery outside the vessel, where the other passengers seldom came, and where one could sit in peace and gaze upon the shifting prospect, we took possession of our new quarters with much pleasure.

If the native packets I have already described be unlike

anything we are in the habit of seeing on water, these western vessels are still more foreign to all the ideas we are accustomed to entertain of boats. I hardly know what to liken them to, or how to describe them.

In the first place, they have no mast, cordage, tackle, rigging, or other such boat-like gear; nor have they anything in their shape at all calculated to remind one of a boat's head, stern, sides, or keel. Except that they are in the water, and display a couple of paddle-boxes, they might be intended, for anything that appears to the contrary, to perform some unknown service, high and dry, upon a mountain-top. There is no visible deck even: nothing but a long, black, ugly roof, covered with burnt-out feathery sparks; above which tower two iron chimneys, and a hoarse escape valve, and a glass steerage house. Then, in order as the eye descends towards the water, are the sides, and doors, and windows of the staterooms, jumbled as oddly together as though they formed a small street, built by the varying tastes of a dozen men: the whole is supported on beams and pillars resting on a dirty barge, but a few inches above the water's edge: and in the narrow space between this upper structure and this barge's deck are the furnace fires and machinery, open at the sides to every wind that blows, and every storm of rain it drives along its path.

Passing one of these boats at night, and seeing the great body of fire, exposed as I have just described, that rages and roars beneath the frail pile of painted wood: the machinery not warded off or guarded in any way, but doing its work in the midst of the crowd of idlers and emigrants and children who throng the lower deck: under the management, too, of reckless men whose acquaintance with its mysteries may have been of six months' standing: one feels directly that the wonder is, not that there should be so many fatal accidents, but that any journey should be safely made.

Within, there is one long narrow cabin, the whole length of the boat; from which the staterooms open on both sides. A small portion of it at the stern is partitioned off for the ladies; and the bar is at the opposite extreme. There is a long table down the centre, and at either end a stove. The washing apparatus is forward, on the deck. It is a little better than on board the canal boat, but not much. In all modes of travelling, the American customs, with reference to the means of personal cleanliness and wholesome ablution, are extremely negligent and filthy; and I strongly incline to the belief that a considerable amount of illness is referable to this cause.

We are to be on board the Messenger three days: arriving at Cincinnati (barring accidents) on Monday morning. There are three meals a day. Breakfast at seven, dinner at half-past twelve, supper about six. At each there are a great many small dishes and plates upon the table, with very little in them; so that, although there is every appearance of a mighty "spread," there is seldom really more than a joint: except for those who fancy slices of beet-root, shreds of dried beef, complicated entanglements of yellow pickle, maize, Indian corn, apple sauce, and pumpkin.

Some people fancy all these little dainties together (and sweet preserves besides), by way of relish to their roast pig. They are generally those dyspeptic ladies and gentlemen who eat unheard-of quantities of hot corn bread (almost as good for the digestion as a kneaded pincushion) for breakfast and for supper. Those who do not observe this custom, and who help themselves several times instead, usually suck their knives and forks meditatively until they have decided what to take next; then pull them out of their mouths; put them in the dish; help themselves; and fall to work again. At dinner there is nothing to drink upon the table but great jugs full of cold water. Nobody says anything, at any meal, to anybody. All the passengers are very dismal, and seem to have tremendous secrets weighing on their minds. There is no conversation, no laughter, no cheerfulness, no sociality, except in spitting; and that is done in silent fellowship round the stove, when the meal is over. Every man sits down dull and languid; swallows his fare as if breakfasts, dinners, and suppers were necessities of nature never to be coupled with recreation or enjoyment; and, having bolted his food in a gloomy silence, bolts himself in the same state. But for these animal observances, you might suppose the whole male portion of the company to be the melancholy ghosts of departed book-keepers, who had fallen dead at the desk: such is their weary air of business and calculation. Undertakers on duty would be sprightly beside them; and a collation of funeral baked meats, in comparison with these meals, would be a sparkling festivity.

The people are all alike, too. There is no diversity of character. They travel about on the same errands, say and do the same things in exactly the same manner, and follow in the same dull, cheerless round. All down the long table there is scarcely a man who is in anything different from his neighbor. It is quite a relief to have, sitting opposite, that little girl of fifteen with the loquacious chin: who, to do her justice, acts up to it, and fully identifies Nature's handwriting; for, of all the small chatterboxes that ever invaded the repose of drowsy ladies' cabin, she is the first and foremost. The beautiful girl who sits a little beyond her—farther down the table there—married the young man with the dark whiskers, who sits beyond *her,* only last month. They are going to settle in the very Far West, where he has lived four years, but where she has never been. They were both overturned in a stagecoach the other day (a bad omen anywhere else, where overturns are not so common), and his head, which bears the marks of a recent wound, is bound up still. She was hurt, too, at the same time, and lay insensible for some days; bright as her eyes are now.

Further down still, sits a man who is going some miles beyond their place of destination to "improve" a newly discovered copper mine. He carries the village—that is to be—with him: a few frame cottages, and an apparatus for smelting the copper. He carries its people too. They are partly American and partly Irish, and herd together on the lower deck; where they amused themselves last evening till the night was pretty far advanced, by alternately firing off pistols and singing hymns.

They, and the very few who have been left at table twenty minutes, rise and go away. We do so too; and, passing through our little stateroom, resume our seats in the quiet gallery without.

A fine broad river always, but in some parts much wider than in others: and then there is usually a green island covered with trees, dividing it into two streams. Occasionally we stop for a few minutes, maybe to take in wood, maybe for passengers, at some small town or village (I ought to say city, every place is a city here); but the banks are for the most part deep solitudes, over-

grown with trees, which, hereabouts, are already in leaf
and very green. For miles, and miles, and miles, these
solitudes are unbroken by any sign of human life or trace
of human footstep; nor is anything seen to move about
them but the blue jay, whose color is so bright, and yet
so delicate, that it looks like a flying flower. At lengthened
intervals a log-cabin, with its little space of cleared land
about it, nestles under a rising ground, and sends its
thread of blue smoke curling up into the sky. It stands in
the corner of the poor field of wheat, which is full of
great unsightly stumps, like earthy butchers' blocks. Sometimes the ground is only just now cleared: the felled trees
lying yet upon the soil: and the log-house only this morning begun. As we pass this clearing, the settler leans upon
his axe or hammer, and looks wistfully at the people from
the world. The children creep out of the temporary hut,
which is like a gypsy tent upon the ground, and clap
their hands and shout. The dog only glances round at
us; and then looks up into his master's face again, as if
he were rendered uneasy by any suspension of the common business, and had nothing more to do with pleasures.
And still there is the same eternal foreground. The river
has washed away its banks, and stately trees have fallen
down into the stream. Some have been there so long, that
they are mere dry, grizzly skeletons. Some have just top-
pled over, and, having earth yet about their roots, are
bathing their green heads in the river, and putting forth
new shoots and branches. Some are almost sliding down as
you look at them. And some were drowned so long ago,
that their bleached arms start out from the middle of the
current, and seem to try to grasp the boat, and drag it
under water.

Through such a scene as this the unwieldy machine
takes its hoarse, sullen way: venting, at every revolution
of the paddles, a loud high-pressure blast; enough, one
would think, to waken up the host of Indians who lie
buried in a great mound yonder: so old, that mighty oaks
and other forest trees have struck their roots into its
earth; and so high, that it is a hill even among the hills
that Nature planted round it. The very river, as though
it shared one's feelings of compassion for the extinct
tribes who lived so pleasantly here, in their blessed ignorance of white existence, hundreds of years ago, steals out

of its way to ripple near this mound: and there are few places where the Ohio sparkles more brightly than in the Big Grave Creek.

All this I see as I sit in the little stern-gallery mentioned just now. Evening slowly steals upon the landscape, and changes it before me, when we stop to set some emigrants ashore.

Five men, as many women, and a little girl. All their worldly goods are a bag, a large chest, and an old chair: one old, high-backed, rush-bottomed chair: a solitary settler in itself. They are rowed ashore in the boat, while the vessel stands a little off awaiting its return, the water being shallow. They are landed at the foot of a high bank, on the summit of which are a few log-cabins, attainable only by a long winding path. It is growing dusk: but the sun is very red, and shines in the water, and on some of the tree-tops, like fire.

The men get out of the boat first; help out the women; take out the bag, the chest, the chair; bid the rowers "good-by;" and shove the boat off for them. At the first plash of the oars in the water, the oldest woman of the party sits down in the old chair, close to the water's edge, without speaking a word. None of the others sit down, though the chest is large enough for many seats. They all stand where they landed, as if stricken into stone; and look after the boat. So they remain, quite still and silent: the old woman and her old chair in the centre; the bag and chest upon the shore, without anybody heeding them: all eyes fixed upon the boat. It comes alongside, is made fast, the men jump on board, the engine is put in motion, and we go hoarsely on again. There they stand yet, without the motion of a hand. I can see them, through my glass, when, in the distance and increasing darkness, they are mere specks to the eye: lingering there still: the old woman in the old chair, and all the rest about her: not stirring in the least degree. And thus I slowly lose them.

The night is dark, and we proceed within the shadow of the wooded bank, which makes it darker. After gliding past the sombre maze of boughs for a long time, we come upon an open space where the tall trees are burning. The shape of every branch and twig is expressed in a deep red glow, and as the light wind stirs and ruffles it, they seem to vegetate in fire. It is such a sight as we read of in legends of enchanted forests: saving that it is sad to see these noble works wasting away so awfully, alone; and to think how many years must come and go before the magic that created them will rear their like upon this ground again. But the time will come: and when, in their changed ashes, the growth of centuries unborn has struck its roots, the restless men of distant ages will repair to these again unpeopled solitudes; and their fellows, in cities far away, that slumber now, perhaps, beneath the rolling sea, will read, in language strange to any ears in being now, but very old to them, of primeval forests where the axe was never heard, and where the jungled ground was never trodden by a human foot.

Midnight and sleep blot out these scenes and thoughts: and when the morning shines again, it gilds the house-tops of a lively city, before whose broad paved wharf the boat is moored: with other boats, and flags, and moving wheels, and hum of men around it; as though there were not a solitary or silent rood of ground within the com-pass of a thousand miles.

Cincinnati is a beautiful city; cheerful, thriving, and animated. I have not often seen a place that com-mends itself so favorably and pleasantly to a stranger at the first glance as this does: with its clean houses of red and white, its well-paved roads, and footways of bright tile. Nor does it become less prepossessing on a closer acquaintance. The streets are broad and airy, the shops extremely good, the private residences remarkable for their elegance and neatness. There is something of inven-tion and fancy in the varying styles of these latter erec-tions, which, after the dull company of the steamboat, is perfectly delightful, as conveying an assurance that there are such qualities still in existence. The disposition to orna-ment these pretty villas, and render them attractive, leads to the culture of trees and flowers, and the laying out of well-kept gardens, the sight of which, to those who walk along the streets, is inexpressibly refreshing and agreeable. I was quite charmed with the appearance of the town, and its adjoining suburb of Mount Auburn; from which the city, lying in an amphitheatre of hills, forms a picture of remarkable beauty, and is seen to great advantage.

There happened to be a great Temperance Conven-

tion held here on the day after our arrival; and as the
order of march brought the procession under the windows of the hotel in which we lodged, when they started
in the morning, I had a good opportunity of seeing it. It
comprised several thousand men; the members of various
"Washington Auxiliary Temperance Societies;" and was
marshalled by officers on horseback, who cantered briskly
up and down the line, with scarfs and ribbons of bright
colors fluttering out behind them gayly. There were bands
of music, too, and banners out of number: and it was a
fresh, holiday-looking concourse altogether.

I was particularly pleased to see the Irishmen, who
formed a distinct society among themselves, and mustered
very strong with their green scarfs; carrying their national Harp, and their Portrait of Father Mathew, high
above the people's heads. They looked as jolly and good-
humored as ever; and working (here) the hardest for
their living, and doing any kind of sturdy labor that
came in their way, were the most independent fellows
there, I thought.

The banners were very well painted, and flaunted down
the street famously. There was the smiting of the rock,
and the gushing forth of the waters; and there was a
temperate man with "considerable of a hatchet" (as the
standard-bearer would probably have said), aiming a
deadly blow at a serpent which was apparently about to
spring upon him from the top of a barrel of spirits. But
the chief feature of this part of the show was a huge
allegorical device, borne among the ship carpenters, on
one side whereof the steamboat Alcohol was represented
bursting her boiler and exploding with a great crash,
while upon the other, the good ship Temperance sailed
away with a fair wind, to the heart's content of the captain, crew, and passengers.

After going round the town, the procession repaired to
a certain appointed place, where, as the printed pro-
gramme set forth, it would be received by the children of
the different free schools, "singing Temperance Songs."
I was prevented from getting there in time to hear these
Little Warblers, or to report upon this novel kind of vocal
entertainment: novel, at least, to me: but I found, in a
large open space, each society gathered round its own
banners, and listening in silent attention to its own orator.

The speeches, judging from the little I could hear of them, were certainly adapted to the occasion, as having that degree of relationship to cold water which wet blankets may claim: but the main thing was the conduct and appearance of the audience throughout the day, and that was admirable and full of promise.

Cincinnati is honorably famous for its free schools, of which it has so many that no person's child among its population can, by possibility, want the means of education, which are extended, upon an average, to four thousand pupils annually. I was only present in one of these establishments during the hours of instruction. In the boys' department, which was full of little urchins (varying in their ages, I should say, from six years old to ten or twelve), the master offered to institute an extemporary examination of the pupils in algebra; a proposal which, as I was by no means confident of my ability to detect mistakes in that science, I declined with some alarm. In the girl's school, reading was proposed; and, as I felt tolerably equal to that art, I expressed my willingness to hear a class. Books were distributed accordingly, and some half-dozen girls relieved each other in reading paragraphs from English history. But it seemed to be a dry compilation, infinitely above their powers; and when they had blundered through three or four dreary passages concerning the treaty of Amiens, and other thrilling topics of the same nature (obviously without comprehending ten words), I expressed myself quite satisfied. It is very possible that they only mounted to this exalted stave in the Ladder of Learning for the astonishment of a visitor; and that at other times they keep upon its lower rounds; but I should have been much better pleased and satisfied if I had heard them exercised in simpler lessons which they understood.

As in every other place I visited, the Judges here were gentlemen of high character and attainments. I was in one of the courts for a few minutes, and found it like those to which I have already referred. A nuisance cause was trying; there were not many spectators; and the witnesses, counsel, and jury formed a sort of family circle, sufficiently jocose and snug.

The society with which I mingled was intelligent, courteous, and agreeable. The inhabitants of Cincinnati·are proud of their city, as one of the most interesting in America: and with good reason: for beautiful and thriving as it is now, and containing, as it does, a population of fifty thousand souls, but two and fifty years have passed away since the ground on which it stands (bought at that time for a few dollars) was a wild wood, and its citizens were but a handful of dwellers in scattered log-huts upon the river's shore.

CHAPTER 12

From Cincinnati to Louisville in Another Western Steamboat; and from Louisville to St. Louis in Another. St. Louis.

LEAVING Cincinnati at eleven o'clock in the forenoon, we embarked for Louisville in the Pike steamboat, which, carrying the mails, was a packet of a much better class than that in which we had come from Pittsburg. As this passage does not occupy more than twelve or thirteen hours, we arranged to go ashore that night: not coveting the distinction of sleeping in a stateroom, when it was possible to sleep anywhere else.

There chanced to be on board this boat, in addition to the usual dreary crowd of passengers, one Pitchlynn, a chief of the Choctaw tribe of Indians, who *sent in his card* to me, and with whom I had the pleasure of a long conversation.

He spoke English perfectly well, though he had not begun to learn the language, he told me, until he was a young man grown. He had read many books; and Scott's poetry appeared to have left a strong impression on his mind: especially the opening of The Lady of the Lake, and the great battle scene in Marmion, in which, no doubt from the congeniality of the subjects to his own pursuits and tastes, he had great interest and delight. He appeared to understand correctly all he had read; and whatever fiction had enlisted his sympathy in its belief, had done so keenly and earnestly. I might almost say fiercely. He was dressed in our ordinary every-day costume, which hung about his fine figure loosely, and with indifferent grace.

On my telling him that I regretted not to see him in his
own attire, he threw up his right arm for a moment,
as though he were brandishing some heavy weapon, and
answered, as he let it fall again, that his race was losing
many things besides their dress, and would soon be seen
upon the earth no more: but he wore it at home, he
added proudly.

He told me that he had been away from his home, west
of the Mississippi, seventeen months: and was now returning. He had been chiefly at Washington on some negotiations pending between his Tribe and the Government:
which were not settled yet (he said in a melancholy way),
and he feared never would be: for what could a few poor
Indians do against such well-skilled men of business as the
whites? He had no love for Washington; tired of towns
and cities very soon; and longed for the Forest and the
Prairie.

I asked him what he thought of Congress? He answered,
with a smile, that it wanted dignity in an Indian's eyes.

He would very much like, he said, to see England
before he died; and spoke with much interest about the
great things to be seen there. When I told him of that
chamber in the British Museum wherein are preserved
household memorials of a race that ceased to be, thousands of years ago, he was very attentive, and it was not
hard to see that he had a reference in his mind to the
gradual fading away of his own people.

This led us to speak of Mr. Catlin's gallery, which he
praised highly: observing that his own portrait was
among the collection, and that all the likenesses were "elegant." Mr. Cooper, he said, had painted the Red Man
well; and so would I, he knew, if I would go home with
him and hunt buffaloes, which he was quite anxious I
should do. When I told him that, supposing I went, I
should not be very likely to damage the buffaloes much, he
took it as a great joke and laughed heartily.

He was a remarkably handsome man; some years past
forty, I should judge; with long black hair, an aquiline
nose, broad cheek bones, a sunburnt complexion, and a
very bright, keen, dark, and piercing eye. There were
but twenty thousand of the Choctaws left, he said, and
their number was decreasing every day. A few of his
brother chiefs had been obliged to become civilized, and

to make themselves acquainted with what the whites knew, for it was their only chance of existence. But they were not many; and the rest were as they always had been. He dwelt on this: and said several times that unless they tried to assimilate themselves to their conquerors, they must be swept away before the strides of civilized society.

When we shook hands at parting, I told him he must come to England, as he longed to see the land so much: that I should hope to see him there one day: and that I could promise him he would be well received and kindly treated. He was evidently pleased by this assurance, though he rejoined, with a good-humored smile and an arch shake of his head, that the English used to be very fond of the Red Men when they wanted their help, but had not cared much for them since.

He took his leave; as stately and complete a gentleman of Nature's making as ever I beheld; and moved among the people in the boat, another kind of being. He sent me a lithographed portrait of himself soon afterwards; very like, though scarcely handsome enough; which I have carefully preserved in memory of our brief acquaintance.

There was nothing very interesting in the scenery of this day's journey, which brought us at midnight to Louisville. We slept at the Galt House; a splendid hotel; and were as handsomely lodged as though we had been in Paris, rather than hundreds of miles beyond the Alleghanies.

The city presenting no objects of sufficient interest to detain us on our way, we resolved to proceed next day by another steamboat, the Fulton, and to join it, about noon, at a suburb called Portland, where it would be delayed some time in passing through a canal.

The interval, after breakfast, we devoted to riding through the town, which is regular and cheerful: the streets being laid out at right angles, and planted with young trees. The buildings are smoky and blackened, from the use of bituminous coal, but an Englishman is well used to that appearance, and indisposed to quarrel with it. There did not appear to be much business stirring; and some unfinished buildings and improvements seemed to intimate that the city had been overbuilt in the ardor of "going ahead," and was suffering under the reaction consequent upon such feverish forcing of its powers.

On our way to Portland we passsed a "Magistrate's Office," which amused me, as looking far more like a dame school than any police establishment: for this awful Institution was nothing but a little, lazy, good-for-nothing front parlor, open to the street; wherein two or three figures (I presume the magistrate and his myrmidons) were basking in the sunshine, the very effigies of languor and repose. It was a perfect picture of Justice retired from business for want of customers; her sword and scales sold off; napping comfortably with her legs upon the table.

Here, as elsewhere in these parts, the road was perfectly alive with pigs of all ages; lying about in every direction, fast asleep; or grunting along in quest of hidden dainties. I had always a sneaking kindness for these odd animals, and found a constant source of amusement, when all others failed, in watching their proceedings. As we were riding along this morning, I observed a little incident between two youthful pigs, which was so very human as to be inexpressibly comical and grotesque at the time, though, I dare say, in telling, it is tame enough.

One young gentleman (a very delicate porker with several straws sticking about his nose, betokening recent investigations in a dunghill) was walking deliberately on, profoundly thinking, when suddenly his brother, who was lying in a miry hole unseen by him, rose up immediately before his startled eyes, ghostly with damp mud. Never was pig's whole mass of blood so turned. He started back at least three feet, gazed for a moment, and then shot off as hard as he could go: his excessively little tail vibrating with speed and terror like a distracted pendulum. But, before he had gone very far, he began to reason with himself as to the nature of this frightful appearance; and as he reasoned, he relaxed his speed by gradual degrees; until at last he stopped, and faced about. There was his brother, with the mud upon him glazing in the sun, yet staring out of the very same hole, perfectly amazed at his proceedings! He was no sooner assured of this; and he assured himself so carefully that one may almost say he shaded his eyes with his hand to see the better; than he came back at a round trot, pounced upon him, and summarily took off a piece of his tail; as a caution to him to be careful what he was about for the future, and never to play tricks with his family any more.

We found the steamboat in the canal, waiting for the slow process of getting through the lock, and went on board, where we shortly afterwards had a new kind of visitor in the person of a certain Kentucky Giant whose name is Porter, and who is of the moderate height of seven feet eight inches in his stockings.

There never was a race of people who so completely gave the lie to history as these giants, or whom all the chroniclers have so cruelly libelled. Instead of roaring and ravaging about the world, constantly catering for their cannibal larders, and perpetually going to market in an unlawful manner, they are the meekest people in any man's acquaintance: rather inclining to milk and vegetable diet, and bearing anything for a quiet life. So decidedly are amiability and mildness their characteristics, that I confess I look upon that youth who distinguished himself by the slaughter of these inoffensive persons as a false-hearted brigand, who, pretending to philanthropic motives, was secretly influenced only by the wealth stored up within their castles, and the hope of plunder. And I lean the more to this opinion from finding that even the historian of those exploits, with all his partiality for his hero, is fain to admit that the slaughtered monsters in question were of a very innocent and simple turn; extremely guileless and ready of belief; lending a credulous ear to the most improbable tales; suffering themselves to be easily entrapped into pits; and even (as in the case of the Welsh Giant), with an excess of the hospitable politeness of a landlord, ripping themselves open, rather than hint at the possibility of their guests being versed in the vagabond arts of sleight-of-hand and hocus-pocus.

The Kentucky Giant was but another illustration of the truth of this position. He had a weakness in the region of the knees, and a trustfulness in his long face, which appealed even to five feet nine for encouragement and support. He was only twenty-five years old, he said, and had grown recently, for it had been found necessary to make an addition to the legs of his inexpressibles. At fifteen he was a short boy, and in those days his English father and his Irish mother had rather snubbed him, as being too small of stature to sustain the credit of the family. He added that his health had not been good, though it was better now; but short people are not wanting who whisper that he drinks too hard.

I understand he drives a hackney coach, though how he does it, unless he stands on the foot-board behind, and lies along the roof upon his chest, with his chin in the box, it would be difficult to comprehend. He brought his gun with him, as a curiosity. Christened "The Little Rifle," and displayed outside a shop-window, it would make the fortune of any retail business in Holborn. When he had shown himself and talked a little while, he withdrew with his pocket instrument, and went bobbing down the cabin, among men of six feet high and upwards, like a lighthouse walking among lamp-posts.

Within a few minutes afterwards we were out of the canal, and in the Ohio River again.

The arrangements of the boat were like those of the Messenger, and the passengers were of the same order of people. We fed at the same times, on the same kind of viands, in the same dull manner, and with the same observances. The company appeared to be oppressed by the same tremendous concealments, and had as little capacity of enjoyment or light-heartedness. I never in my life did see such listless, heavy dulness as brooded over these meals: the very recollection of it weighs me down, and makes me, for the moment, wretched. Reading and writing on my knee, in our little cabin, I really dreaded the coming of the hour that summoned us to table; and was as glad to escape from it again as if it had been a penance or a punishment. Healthy cheerfulness and good spirits forming a part of the banquet, I could soak my crusts in the fountain with Le Sage's strolling player, and revel in their glad enjoyment; but sitting down with so many fellow-animals to ward off thirst and hunger as a business; to empty each creature his Yahoo's trough as quickly as he can, and then slink sullenly away; to have these social sacraments stripped of everything but the mere greedy satisfaction of the natural cravings; goes so against the grain with me, that I seriously believe the recollection of these funeral feasts will be a waking nightmare to me all my life.

There was some relief in this boat, too, which there had not been in the other, for the captain (a blunt, good-natured fellow) had his handsome wife with him, who was disposed to be lively and agreeable, as were a few other lady passengers who had their seats about us at the same end of the table. But nothing could have made head against the depressing influence of the general body. There was a magnetism of dulness in them which would have beaten down the most facetious companion that the earth ever knew. A jest would have been a crime, and a smile would have faded into a grinning horror. Such deadly leaden people; such systematic, plodding, weary, insupportable heaviness: such a mass of animated indigestion in respect of all that was genial, jovial, frank, social, or hearty; never, sure, was brought together elsewhere since the world began.

Nor was the scenery, as we approached the junction of the Ohio and Mississippi Rivers, at all inspiriting in its influence. The trees were stunted in their growth; the banks were low and flat; the settlements and log-cabins fewer in number: their inhabitants more wan and wretched than any we had encountered yet. No songs of birds were in the air, no pleasant scents, no moving lights and shadows from swift-passing clouds. Hour after hour, the changeless glare of the hot, unwinking sky shone upon the same monotonous objects. Hour after hour, the river rolled along as wearily and slowly as the time itself.

At length, upon the morning of the third day, we arrived at a spot so much more desolate than any we had yet beheld, that the forlornest places we had passed were, in comparison with it, full of interest. At the junction of the two rivers, on ground so flat and low and marshy, that at certain seasons of the year it is inundated to the housetops, lies a breeding-place of fever, ague, and death; vaunted in England as a mine of Golden Hope, and speculated in, on the faith of monstrous representations, to many people's ruin. A dismal swamp, on which the half-built houses rot away: cleared here and there for the space of a few yards; and teeming, then, with rank, unwholesome vegetation, in whose baleful shade the wretched wanderers who are tempted hither droop, and die, and lay their bones; the hateful Mississippi circling and eddying before it, and turning off upon its southern course, a slimy monster hideous to behold; a hotbed of disease, an ugly sepulchre, a grave uncheered by any gleam of promise: a place without one single quality, in earth or air or water, to commend it: such is this dismal Cairo.

But what words shall describe the Mississippi, great father of rivers, who (praise be to Heaven!) has no young children like him? An enormous ditch, sometimes two or three miles wide, running liquid mud, six miles an hour: its strong and frothy current choked and obstructed everywhere by huge logs and whole forest trees: now twining themselves together in great rafts, from the interstices of which a sedgy, lazy foam works up, to float upon the water's top: now rolling past like monstrous bodies, their tangled roots showing like matted hair; now glancing singly by like giant leeches; and now writhing round and round in the vortex of some small whirlpool like wounded snakes. The banks low, the trees dwarfish, the marshes swarming with frogs, the wretched cabins few and far apart, their inmates hollow-cheeked and pale, the weather very hot, mosquitoes penetrating into every crack and crevice of the boat, mud and slime on everything: nothing pleasant in its aspect, but the harmless lightning which flickers every night upon the dark horizon.

For two days we toiled up this foul stream, striking constantly against the floating timber, or stopping to avoid those more dangerous obstacles, the snags, or sawyers, which are the hidden trunks of trees that have their roots below the tide. When the nights are very dark, the lookout stationed in the head of the boat knows, by the ripple of the water, if any great impediment be near at hand, and rings a bell beside him, which is the signal for the engine to be stopped; but always in the night this bell has work to do, and, after every ring, there comes a blow which renders it no easy matter to remain in bed.

The decline of day here was very gorgeous; tingeing the firmament deeply with red and gold, up to the very keystone of the arch above us. As the sun went down behind the bank, the slightest blades of grass upon it seemed to become as distinctly visible as the arteries in the skeleton of a leaf, and when, as it slowly sank, the red and golden bars upon the water grew dimmer, and dimmer yet, as if they were sinking too; and all the glowing colors of departing day paled, inch by inch, before the sombre night; the scene became a thousand times more lonesome and more dreary than before, and all its influences darkened with the sky.

We drank the muddy water of this river while we were upon it. It is considered wholesome by the natives, and is something more opaque than gruel. I have seen water like it at the Filter shops, but nowhere else.

On the fourth night after leaving Louisville we reached St. Louis, and here I witnessed the conclusion of an incident, trifling enough in itself, but very pleasant to see, which had interested me during the whole journey.

There was a little woman on board, with a little baby; and both little woman and little child were cheerful, good-looking, bright-eyed, and fair to see. The little woman had been passing a long time with her sick mother in New York, and had left her home in St. Louis in that condition in which ladies who truly love their lords desire to be. The baby was born in her mother's house; and she had not seen her husband (to whom she was now returning) for twelve months: having left him a month or two after their marriage.

Well, to be sure there never was a little woman so full of hope, and tenderness, and love, and anxiety as this little woman was: and all day long she wondered whether "He" would be at the wharf; and whether "He" had got her letter; and whether, if she sent the baby ashore by somebody else, "He" would know it, meeting it in the street: which, seeing that he had never set eyes upon it in his life, was not very likely in the abstract, but was probable enough to the young mother. She was such an artless little creature; and was in such a sunny, beaming, hopeful state; and let out all this matter, clinging close about her heart, so freely; that all the other lady passengers entered into the spirit of it as much as she; and the captain (who heard all about it from his wife) was wondrous sly, I promise you: inquiring, every time we met at table, as in forgetfulness, whether she expected anybody to meet her at St. Louis, and whether she would want to go ashore the night we reached it (but he supposed she wouldn't), and cutting many other dry jokes of that nature. There was one little, weazen, dried-apple-faced old woman, who took occasion to doubt the constancy of husbands in such circumstances of bereavement; and there was another lady (with a lapdog) old enough to moralize on the lightness of human affections, and yet not so old that she could help nursing the baby now and then, or laughing with the rest when the little woman called it by its father's name, and asked it all manner of fantastic questions concerning him in the joy of her heart.

It was something of a blow to the little woman, that when we were within twenty miles of our destination, it became clearly necessary to put this baby to bed. But she got over it with the same good-humor; tied a handkerchief round her head; and came out into the little gallery with the rest. Then, such an oracle as she became in reference to the localities! and such facetiousness as was displayed by the married ladies! and such sympathy as was shown by the single ones! and such peals of laughter as the little woman herself (who would just as soon have cried) greeted every jest with!

At last there were the lights of St. Louis, and here was the wharf, and those were the steps: and the little woman, covering her face with her hands, and laughing (or seeming to laugh) more than ever, ran into her own cabin, and shut herself up. I have no doubt that, in the charming inconsistency of such excitement, she stopped her ears, lest she should hear "Him" asking for her: but I did not see her do it.

Then a great crowd of people rushed on board, though the boat was not yet made fast, but was wandering about, among the other boats, to find a landing-place; and everybody looked for the husband: and nobody saw him: when, in the midst of us all—Heaven knows how she ever got there—there was the little woman clinging with both arms tight round the neck of a fine, good-looking, sturdy young fellow! and, in a moment afterwards, there she was again, actually clapping her little hands for joy, as she dragged him through the small door of her small cabin, to look at the baby as he lay asleep!

We went to a large hotel, called the Planter's House: built like an English hospital, with long passages and bare walls, and skylights above the room-doors for the free circulation of air. There were a great many boarders in it; and as many lights sparkled and glistened from the windows down into the street below, when we drove up, as if it had been illuminated on some occasion of rejoicing. It is an excellent house, and the proprietors have most bountiful notions of providing the creature comforts. Dining alone with my wife in our own room one day, I counted fourteen dishes on the table at once.

In the old French portion of the town the thoroughfares are narrow and crooked, and some of the houses
are very quaint and picturesque: being built of wood,
with tumble-down galleries before the windows, approach-
able by stairs, or rather ladders, from the street. There
are queer little barbers' shops, and drinking-houses too,
in this quarter; and abundance of crazy old tenements
with blinking casements, such as may be seen in Flanders.
Some of these ancient habitations, with high garret gable
windows perking into the roofs, have a kind of French
shrug about them; and, being lop-sided with age, appear
to hold their heads askew besides, as if they were gri-
macing in astonishment at the American Improvements.

It is hardly necessary to say that these consist of wharfs
and warehouses, and new buildings in all directions; and
of a great many vast plans which are still "progressing."
Already, however, some very good houses, broad streets,
and marble-fronted shops have gone so far ahead as to be
in a state of completion; and the town bids fair, in a few
years, to improve considerably: though it is not likely
ever to vie, in point of elegance or beauty, with Cincinnati.

The Roman Catholic religion, introduced here by the
early French settlers, prevails extensively. Among the
public institutions are a Jesuit College; a convent for "the
Ladies of the Sacred Heart;" and a large chapel attached
to the college, which was in course of erection at the time
of my visit, and was intended to be consecrated on the
second of December in the next year. The architect of
this building is one of the reverend fathers of the school,
and the works proceed under his sole direction. The
organ will be sent from Belgium.

In addition to these establishments, there is a Roman
Catholic cathedral, dedicated to St. Francis Xavier; and
a hospital, founded by the munificence of a deceased
resident, who was a member of that church. It also sends
missionaries from hence among the Indian tribes.

The Unitarian church is represented, in this remote
place, as in most other parts of America, by a gentleman
of great worth and excellence. The poor have good reason
to remember and bless it; for it befriends them, and aids
the cause of rational education, without any sectarian or
selfish views. It is liberal in all its actions; of kind construction; and of wide benevolence.

There are three free schools already erected and in

full operation in this city. A fourth is building, and will soon be opened.

No man ever admits the unhealthiness of the place he dwells in (unless he is going away from it), and I shall therefore, I have no doubt, be at issue with the inhabitants of St. Louis in questioning the perfect salubrity of its climate, and in hinting that I think it must rather dispose to fever in the summer and autumnal seasons. Just adding, that it is very hot, lies among great rivers, and has vast tracts of undrained swampy land around it, I leave the reader to form his own opinion.

As I had a great desire to see a Prairie before turning back from the furthest point of my wanderings; and as some gentlemen of the town had, in their hospitable consideration, an equal desire to gratify me; a day was fixed, before my departure, for an expedition to the Looking-Glass Prairie, which is within thirty miles of the town. Deeming it possible that my readers may not object to know what kind of thing such a gypsy party may be at that distance from home, and among what sort of objects it moves, I will describe the jaunt in another chapter.

CHAPTER 13

A Jaunt to the Looking-Glass Prairie and Back.

I MAY premise that the word Prairie is variously pronounced *paraaer, parearer,* and *paroarer.* The latter mode of pronunciation is, perhaps, the most in favor.

We were fourteen in all, and all young men: indeed, it is a singular though very natural feature in the society of these distant settlements, that it is mainly composed of adventurous persons in the prime of life, and has very few gray heads among it. There were no ladies: the trip being a fatiguing one: and we were to start at five o'clock in the morning punctually.

I was called at four, that I might be certain of keeping nobody waiting; and having got some bread and milk for breakfast, threw up the window and looked down into the street, expecting to see the whole party busily astir, and great preparations going on below. But, as everything was very quiet, and the street presented that hopeless aspect with which five o'clock in the morning is familiar elsewhere, I deemed it as well to go to bed again, and went accordingly.

I woke again at seven o'clock, and by that time the party had assembled, and were gathered round, one light carriage, with a very stout axle-tree; one something on wheels like an amateur carrier's cart; one double phaeton of great antiquity and unearthly construction; one gig with a great hole in its back, and a broken head; and one rider on horseback, who was to go on before. I got into the first coach with three companions; the rest bestowed themselves in the other vehicles; two large baskets were made fast to the lightest; two large stone jars in wicker cases, technically known as demijohns, were consigned to the "least rowdy" of the party for safe keeping; and the procession moved off to the ferry-boat, in which it was to cross the river bodily, men, horses, carriages, and all, as the manner in these parts is.

We got over the river in due course, and mustered again before a little wooden box on wheels, hove down all aslant in a morass, with "MERCHANT TAILOR" painted in very large letters over the door. Having settled the order of proceeding and the road to be taken, we started off once more, and began to make our way through an ill-favored Black Hollow, called, less expressively, the American Bottom.

The previous day had been—not to say hot, for the term is weak and lukewarm in its power of conveying an idea of the temperature. The town had been on fire; in a blaze. But at night it had come on to rain in torrents, and all night long it had rained without cessation. We had a pair of very strong horses, but travelled at the rate of little more than a couple of miles an hour, through one unbroken slough of black mud and water. It had no variety but in depth. Now it was only half over the wheels, now it hid the axle-tree, and now the coach sank down in it almost to the windows. The air resounded in all directions with the loud chirping of the frogs, who, with the pigs (a coarse, ugly breed, as unwholesome-looking as though they were the spontaneous growth of the country), had the whole scene to themselves. Here and there we passed a log-hut; but the wretched cabins were wide apart and thinly scattered, for though the soil is very rich in this place, few people can exist in such a deadly atmosphere. On either side of the track, if it deserve the name, was the thick "bush;" and everywhere was stagnant, slimy, rotten, filthy water.

As it is the custom in these parts to give a horse a gallon or so of cold water whenever he is in a foam with heat, we halted for that purpose at a log inn in the wood, far removed from any other residence. It consisted of one room, bare-roofed and bare-walled of course, with a loft above. The ministering priest was a swarthy young savage in a shirt of cotton print like bed-furniture, and a pair of ragged trousers. There were a couple of young boys, too, nearly naked, lying idly by the well; and they, and he, and *the* traveller at the inn, turned out to look at us.

The traveller was an old man, with a gray, grisly beard two inches long, a shaggy moustache of the same hue, and enormous eyebrows; which almost obscured his lazy, semi-drunken glance, as he stood regarding us with folded arms: poising himself alternately upon his toes and heels. On being addressed by one of the party, he drew nearer, and said, rubbing his chin (which scraped under his horny hand like fresh gravel beneath a nailed shoe), that he was from Delaware, and had lately bought a farm "down there," pointing into one of the marshes where the stunted trees were thickest. He was "going," he added, to St. Louis, to fetch his family, whom he had left behind; but he seemed in no great hurry to bring on these incumbrances, for when we moved away, he loitered back into the cabin, and was plainly bent on stopping there so long as his money lasted. He was a great politician, of course, and explained his opinions at some length to one of our company; but I only remember that he concluded with two sentiments, one of which was, Somebody forever; and the other, Blast everybody else! which is by no means a bad abstract of the general creed in these matters.

When the horses were swollen out to about twice their natural dimensions (there seems to be an idea here that this kind of inflation improves their going), we went forward again, through mud and mire, and damp, and festering heat, and brake and bush, attended always by the music of the frogs and pigs, until nearly noon, when we halted at a place called Belleville.

Belleville was a small collection of wooden houses, huddled together in the very heart of the bush and swamp. Many of them had singularly bright doors of red and yellow; for the place had been lately visited by a travelling painter, "who got along," as I was told, "by eating his way." The Criminal Court was sitting, and was at that moment trying some criminals for horse-stealing: with whom it would most likely go hard: for live-stock of all kinds, being necessarily very much exposed in the woods, is held by the community in rather higher value than human life; and, for this reason, juries generally make a point of finding all men indicted for cattle-stealing, guilty, whether or no.

The horses belonging to the bar, the judge, and wit-

nesses, were tied to temporary racks set up roughly
in the road; by which is to be understood a forest path,
nearly knee deep in mud and slime.

There was an hotel in this place, which, like all hotels
in America, had its large dining-room for the public
table. It was an odd, shambling, low-roofed outhouse, half
cow-shed and half kitchen, with a coarse brown canvas
table-cloth, and tin sconces stuck against the walls, to hold
candles at supper-time. The horseman had gone forward
to have coffee and some eatables prepared, and they were
by this time nearly ready. He had ordered "wheat bread
and chicken fixings," in preference to "corn bread and
common doings." The latter kind of refection includes only
pork and bacon. The former comprehends broiled ham,
sausages, veal cutlets, steaks, and such other viands of that
nature as may be supposed, by a tolerably wide poetical
construction, to "fix" a chicken comfortably in the di-
gestive organs of any lady or gentleman.

On one of the door-posts at this inn was a tin plate,
whereon was inscribed, in characters of gold, "Doctor
Crocus;" and on a sheet of paper, pasted up by the side
of this plate, was a written announcement that Doctor
Crocus would that evening deliver a lecture on Phrenology for the benefit of the Belleville public; at a charge for
admission of so much a head.

Straying upstairs during the preparation of the chicken
fixings, I happened to pass the Doctor's chamber; and as
the door stood wide open, and the room was empty, I
made bold to peep in.

It was a bare, unfurnished, comfortless room, with an
unframed portrait hanging up at the head of the bed; a
likeness, I take it, of the Doctor, for the forehead was
fully displayed, and great stress was laid by the artist upon
its phrenological developments. The bed itself was covered
with an old patchwork counterpane. The room was destitute of carpet or of curtain. There was a damp fire-place
without any stove, full of wood ashes; a chair, and a very
small table; and on the last-named piece of furniture was
displayed, in grand array, the Doctor's library, consist-
ing of some half-dozen greasy old books.

Now, it certainly looked about the last apartment on
the whole earth out of which any man would be likely to
get anything to do him good. But the door, as I have said,

stood coaxingly open, and plainly said, in conjunction with the chair, the portrait, the table, and the books, "Walk in, gentlemen, walk in! Don't be ill, gentlemen, when you may be well in no time. Doctor Crocus is here, gentlemen, the celebrated Doctor Crocus! Doctor Crocus has come all this way to cure you, gentlemen. If you haven't heard of Doctor Crocus, it's your fault, gentlemen, who live a little way out of the world here: not Doctor Crocus's. Walk in, gentlemen, walk in!"

In the passage below, when I went downstairs again, was Doctor Crocus himself. A crowd had flocked in from the Court House, and a voice from among them called out to the landlord, "Colonel! introduce Doctor Crocus."

"Mr. Dickens," says the colonel, "Doctor Crocus."

Upon which Doctor Crocus, who is a tall, fine-looking Scotchman, but rather fierce and warlike in appearance for a professor of the peaceful art of healing, bursts out of the concourse with his right arm extended, and his chest thrown out as far as it will possibly come, and says,—

"Your countryman, sir!"

Whereupon Doctor Crocus and I shake hands; and Doctor Crocus looks as if I didn't by any means realize his expectations, which in a linen blouse, and a great straw hat with a green ribbon, and no gloves, and my face and nose profusely ornamented with the stings of mosquitoes and the bites of bugs, it is very likely I did not.

"Long in these parts, sir?" says I.

"Three or four months, sir," says the Doctor.

"Do you think of soon returning to the old country, sir?" says I.

Doctor Crocus makes no verbal answer, but gives me an imploring look, which says so plainly, "Will you ask me that again a little louder, if you please?" that I repeat the question.

"Think of soon returning to the old country, sir?" repeats the Doctor.

"To the old country, sir," I rejoin.

Doctor Crocus looks round upon the crowd to observe the effect he produces, rubs his hands, and says, in a very loud voice,—

"Not yet awhile, sir, not yet. You won't catch me at that just yet, sir. I am a little too fond of freedom for *that,* sir. Ha, ha! It's not so easy for a man to tear himself from a free country such as this is, sir. Ha, ha! No, no! Ha, ha! None of that till one's obliged to do it, sir. No, no!"

As Doctor Crocus says these latter words, he shakes his head knowingly, and laughs again. Many of the bystanders shake their heads in concert with the Doctor, and laugh too, and look at each other as much as to say, "A pretty bright and first-rate sort of chap is Crocus!" and, unless I am very much mistaken, a good many people went to the lecture that night who never thought about phrenology, or about Doctor Crocus either, in all their lives before.

From Belleville we went on, through the same desolate kind of waste, and constantly attended, without the interval of a moment, by the same music; until, at three o'clock in the afternoon, we halted once more at a village called Lebanon to inflate the horses again, and give them some corn besides: of which they stood much in need. Pending this ceremony, I walked into the village, where I met a full-sized dwelling-house coming downhill at a round trot, drawn by a score or more of oxen.

The public-house was so very clean and good a one, that the managers of the jaunt resolved to return to it, and put up there for the night, if possible. This course decided on, and the horses being well refreshed, we again pushed forward, and came upon the Prairie at sunset.

It would be difficult to say why, or how—though it was possibly from having heard and read so much about it—but the effect on me was disappointment. Looking towards the setting sun, there lay, stretched out before my view, a vast expanse of level ground; unbroken, save by one thin line of trees, which scarcely amounted to a scratch upon the great blank; until it met the glowing sky, wherein it seemed to dip: mingling with its rich colors, and mellowing in its distant blue. There it lay, a tranquil sea or lake without water, if such a simile be admissible, with the day going down upon it: a few birds wheeling here and there: and solitude and silence reigning paramount around. But the grass was not yet high; there were bare black patches on the ground; and the few wild flowers that the eye could see were poor and scanty. Great as the picture was, its very flatness and extent, which left nothing to the imagination, tamed it down and cramped its interest. I felt little of that sense of freedom and exhilaration which a Scottish heath inspires, or even our English downs awaken. It was lonely and wild, but oppressive in its barren monotony. I felt that, in traversing the Prairies, I could never abandon myself to the scene, forgetful of all else; as I should do instinctively, were the heather underneath my feet, or an iron-bound coast beyond; but should often glance towards the distant and frequently receding line of the horizon, and wish it gained and passed. It is not a scene to be forgotten, but it is scarcely one, I think (at all events, as I saw it), to remember with much pleasure, or to covet the looking on again in after life.

We encamped near a solitary log-house, for the sake of its water, and dined upon the plain. The baskets contained roast fowls, buffalo's tongue (an exquisite dainty, by the way), ham, bread, cheese, and butter, biscuits, champagne, sherry; lemon and sugar for punch; and abundance of rough ice. The meal was delicious, and the entertainers were the soul of kindness and good-humor. I have often recalled that cheerful party to my pleasant recollection since, and shall not easily forget, in junketings nearer home with friends of older date, my boon companions on the Prairie.

Returning to Lebanon that night, we lay at the little inn at which we had halted in the afternoon. In point of cleanliness and comfort it would have suffered by no comparison with any village alehouse of a homely kind in England.

Rising at five o'clock next morning, I took a walk about the village: none of the houses were strolling about today, but it was early for them yet, perhaps: and then amused myself by lounging in a kind of farmyard behind the tavern, of which the leading features were, a strange jumble of rough sheds for stables; a rude colonnade, built as a cool place of summer resort; a deep well; a great earthen mound for keeping vegetables in, in winter-time; and a pigeon-house, whose little apertures looked, as they do in all pigeon-houses, very much too small for the admission of the plump and swelling-breasted birds who were strutting about it, though they tried to get in never so hard. That interest exhausted, I took a survey of the inn's two parlors, which were decorated with col-

ored prints of Washington and President Madison, and of
a white-faced young lady (much speckled by the flies),
who held up her gold neck-chain for the admiration of
the spectator, and informed all admiring comers that she
was "Just Seventeen:" although I should have thought her
older. In the best room were two oil portraits of the kit-
cat size, representing the landlord and his infant son;
both looking as bold as lions, and staring out of the canvas with an intensity that would have been cheap at any
price. They were painted, I think, by the artist who had
touched up the Belleville doors with red and gold; for I
seemed to recognize his style immediately.

After breakfast we started to return by a different way
from that which we had taken yesterday, and coming up
at ten o'clock with an encampment of German emigrants
carrying their goods in carts, who had made a rousing
fire which they were just quitting, stopped there to refresh. And very pleasant the fire was; for, hot though it
had been yesterday, it was quite cold to-day, and the
wind blew keenly. Looming in the distance, as we rode
along, was another of the ancient Indian burial-places,
called the Monks' Mound; in memory of a body of fanat-
ics of the order of La Trappe, who founded a desolate
convent there many years ago, when there were no settlers within a thousand miles, and were all swept off by
the pernicious climate: in which lamentable fatality few rational people will suppose, perhaps, that society experienced any very severe deprivation.

The track of to-day had the same features as the track
of yesterday. There was the swamp, the bush, the perpetual chorus of frogs, the rank unseemly growth, the unwholesome steaming earth. Here and there, and frequently too, we encountered a solitary broken-down
wagon, full of some new settler's goods. It was a pitiful
sight to see one of these vehicles deep in the mire; the
axle-tree broken; the wheel lying idly by its side; the man
gone miles away, to look for assistance; the woman seated
among their wandering household goods, with a baby at
her breast, a picture of forlorn, dejected patience; the
team of oxen crouching down mournfully in the mud, and
breathing forth such clouds of vapor from their mouths
and nostrils, that all the damp mist and fog around seemed
to have come direct from them.

In due time we mustered once again before the merchant tailor's, and, having done so, crossed over to the city in the ferry-boat: passing, on the way, a spot called Bloody Island, the duelling-ground of St. Louis, and so designated in honor of the last fatal combat fought there, which was with pistols, breast to breast. Both combatants fell dead upon the ground; and possibly some rational people may think of them, as of the gloomy madmen on the Monks' Mound, that they were no great loss to the community.

CHAPTER 14

*Return to Cincinnati. A Stage-Coach Ride
from that City to Columbus, and thence
to Sandusky. So, by Lake Erie, to the
Falls of Niagara.*

As I had a desire to travel through the interior of the
State of Ohio, and to "strike the lakes," as the phrase is,
at a small town called Sandusky, to which that route would
conduct us on our way to Niagara, we had to return
from St. Louis by the way we had come, and to retrace
our former track as far as Cincinnati.

The day on which we were to take leave of St. Louis
being very fine; and the steamboat, which was to have
started I don't know how early in the morning, postpon-
ing, for the third or fourth time, her departure until
the afternoon; we rode forward to an old French village
on the river, called properly Carondelet, and nicknamed
Vide Poche, and arranged that the packet should call
for us there.

The place consisted of a few poor cottages and two or
three public-houses; the state of whose larders certainly
seemed to justify the second designation of the village, for
there was nothing to eat in any of them. At length, however, by going back some half a mile or so, we found a
solitary house where ham and coffee were procurable;
and there we tarried to await the advent of the boat,
which would come in sight from the green before the
door, a long way off.

It was a neat, unpretending village tavern, and we took

212

our repast in a quaint little room with a bed in it, decorated with some old oil-paintings, which in their time had probably done duty in a Catholic chapel or monastery. The fare was very good, and served with great cleanliness. The house was kept by a characteristic old couple, with whom we had a long talk, and who were perhaps a very good sample of that kind of people in the West.

The landlord was a dry, tough, hard-faced old fellow (not so very old either, for he was but just turned sixty, I should think), who had been out with the militia in the last war with England, and had seen all kinds of service—except a battle; and he had been very near seeing that, he added: very near. He had all his life been restless and locomotive, with an irresistible desire for change; and was still the son of his old self: for, if he had nothing to keep him at home, he said (slightly jerking his hat and his thumb towards the window of the room in which the old lady sat, as we stood talking in front of the house), he would clean up his musket, and be off to Texas to-morrow morning. He was one of the very many descendants of Cain proper to this continent, who seem destined from their birth to serve as pioneers in the great human army: who gladly go on from year to year extending its outposts, and leaving home after home behind them; and die at last, utterly regardless of their graves being left thousands of miles behind, by the wandering generation who succeed.

His wife was a domesticated, kind-hearted old soul, who had come with him "from the queen city of the world," which, it seemed, was Philadelphia; but had no love for this Western country, and, indeed, had little reason to bear it any; having seen her children, one by one, die here of fever, in the full prime and beauty of their youth. Her heart was sore, she said, to think of them; and to talk on this theme, even to strangers, in that blighted place, so far from her old home, eased it somewhat, and became a melancholy pleasure.

The boat appearing towards evening, we bade adieu to the poor old lady and her vagrant spouse, and, making for the nearest landing-place, were soon on board the Messenger again, in our old cabin, and steaming down the Mississippi.

If the coming up this river, slowly making head against the stream, be an irksome journey, the shooting down it with the turbid current is almost worse; for then the boat, proceeding at the rate of twelve or fifteen miles an hour, has to force its passage through a labyrinth of floating logs, which, in the dark, it is often impossible to see beforehand or avoid. All that night the bell was never silent for five minutes at a time; and after every ring the vessel reeled again, sometimes beneath a single blow, sometimes beneath a dozen dealt in quick succession, the lightest of which seemed more than enough to beat in her frail keel, as though it had been pie-crust. Looking down upon the filthy river after dark, it seemed to be alive with monsters, as these black masses rolled upon the surface, or came starting up again, head first, when the boat, in ploughing her way among a shoal of such obstructions, drove a few among them, for the moment, under water. Sometimes the engine stopped during a long interval, and then before her and behind, and gathering close about her on all sides, were so many of these ill-favored obstacles that she was fairly hemmed in; the centre of a floating island; and was constrained to pause until they parted somewhere, as dark clouds will do before the wind, and opened by degrees a channel out.

In good time next morning, however, we came again in sight of the detestable morass called Cairo: and, stopping there to take in wood, lay alongside a barge, whose starting timbers scarcely held together. It was moored to the bank, and on its side was painted "Coffee House;" that being, I suppose, the floating paradise to which the people fly for shelter when they lose their houses for a month or two beneath the hideous waters of the Mississippi. But, looking southward from this point, we had the satisfaction of seeing that intolerable river dragging its slimy length and ugly freight abruptly off towards New Orleans; and, passing a yellow line which stretched across the current, were again upon the clear Ohio, never, I trust, to see the Mississippi more, saving in troubled dreams and nightmares. Leaving it for the company of its sparkling neighbor was like the transition from pain to ease, or the awakening from a horrible vision to cheerful realities.

We arrived at Louisville on the fourth night, and gladly availed ourselves of its excellent hotel. Next day we went on in the Ben Franklin, a beautiful mail steamboat, and reached Cincinnati shortly after midnight. Being by this time nearly tired of sleeping upon shelves, we had remained awake to go ashore straightway; and, groping a passage across the dark decks of other boats, and among labyrinths of engine machinery and leaking casks of molasses, we reached the streets, knocked up the porter at the hotel where we had stayed before, and were, to our great joy, safely housed soon afterwards.

We rested but one day at Cincinnati, and then resumed our journey to Sandusky. As it comprised two varieties of stage-coach travelling, which, with those I have already glanced at, comprehend the main characteristics of this mode of transit in America, I will take the reader as our fellow-passenger, and pledge myself to perform the distance with all possible despatch.

Our place of destination, in the first instance, is Columbus. It is distant about a hundred and twenty miles from Cincinnati, but there is a macadamized road (rare blessing!) the whole way, and the rate of travelling upon it is six miles an hour.

We start at eight o'clock in the morning, in a great mail-coach, whose huge cheeks are so very ruddy and plethoric that it appears to be troubled with a tendency of blood to the head. Dropsical it certainly is, for it will hold a dozen passengers inside. But, wonderful to add, it is very clean and bright, being nearly new; and rattles through the streets of Cincinnati gayly.

Our way lies through a beautiful country, richly cultivated, and luxuriant in its promise of an abundant harvest. Sometimes we pass a field where the strong bristling stalks of Indian corn look like a crop of walking-sticks, and sometimes an enclosure where the green wheat is springing up among a labyrinth of stumps; the primitive worm-fence is universal, and an ugly thing it is; but the farms are neatly kept, and, save for these differences, one might be travelling just now in Kent.

We often stop to water at a roadside inn, which is always dull and silent. The coachman dismounts and fills his bucket, and holds it to the horses' heads. There is scarcely ever any one to help him; there are seldom any loungers standing round; and never any stable company with jokes to crack. Sometimes, when we have changed our team, there is a difficulty in starting again, arising out of the prevalent mode of breaking a young horse: which is to catch him, harness him against his will, and put him in a stage-coach without further notice: but we get on somehow or other, after a great many kicks and a violent struggle; and jog on as before again.

Occasionally, when we stop to change, some two or three half-drunken loafers will come loitering out with their hands in their pockets, or will be seen kicking their heels in rocking-chairs, or lounging on the window-sill, or sitting on a rail within the colonnade: they have not often anything to say, though, either to us or to each other, but sit there idly staring at the coach and horses. The landlord of the inn is usually among them, and seems, of all the party, to be the least connected with the business of the house. Indeed, he is, with reference to the tavern, what the driver is in relation to the coach and passengers: whatever happens in his sphere of action, he is quite indifferent, and perfectly easy in his mind.

The frequent change of coachmen works no change or variety in the coachman's character. He is always dirty, sullen, and taciturn. If he be capable of smartness of any kind, moral or physical, he has a faculty of concealing it which is truly marvellous. He never speaks to you as you sit beside him on the box, and if you speak to him, he answers (if at all) in monosyllables. He points out nothing on the road, and seldom looks at anything: being, to all appearance, thoroughly weary of it, and of existence generally. As to doing the honors of his coach, his business, as I have said, is with the horses. The coach follows because it is attached to them and goes on wheels: not because you are in it. Sometimes, towards the end of a long stage, he suddenly breaks out into a discordant fragment of an election song, but his face never sings along with him: it is only his voice, and not often that.

He always chews and always spits, and never encumbers himself with a pocket-handkerchief. The consequences to the box passenger, especially when the wind blows towards him, are not agreeable.

Whenever the coach stops, and you can hear the voices of the inside passengers; or whenever any bystander addresses them, or any one among them; or they address each other; you will hear one phrase repeated over and over and over again to the most extraordinary extent. It is an ordinary and unpromising phrase enough, being neither more nor less than "Yes, sir;" but it is adapted to every variety of circumstance, and fills up every pause in the conversation. Thus:

The time is one o'clock at noon. The scene, a place where we are to stay to dine on this journey. The coach drives up to the door of an inn. The day is warm, and there are several idlers lingering about the tavern, and waiting for the public dinner. Among them is a stout gentleman in a brown hat, swinging himself to and fro in a rocking-chair on the pavement.

As the coach stops, a gentleman in a straw hat looks out of the window.

STRAW HAT (to the stout gentleman in the rocking-chair). I reckon that's Judge Jefferson, ain't it?

BROWN HAT (still swinging; speaking very slowly; and without any emotion whatever). Yes, sir.

STRAW HAT. Warm weather, Judge.

BROWN HAT. Yes, sir.

STRAW HAT. There was a snap of cold last week.

BROWN HAT. Yes, sir.

STRAW HAT. Yes, sir.

A pause, they look at each other very seriously.

STRAW HAT. I calculate you'll have got through that case of the corporation, Judge, by this time, now?

BROWN HAT. Yes, sir.

STRAW HAT. How did the verdict go, sir?

BROWN HAT. For the defendant, sir.

STRAW HAT (interrogatively). Yes, sir?

BROWN HAT (affirmatively). Yes, sir.

BOTH (musingly, as each gazes down the street). Yes, sir.

Another pause. They look at each other again, still more seriously than before.

BROWN HAT. This coach is rather behind its time to-day, I guess.

STRAW HAT (doubtingly). Yes, sir.

BROWN HAT (looking at his watch). Yes, sir; nigh upon two hours.

STRAW HAT (raising his eyebrows in very great surprise). Yes, sir!

BROWN HAT (decisively, as he puts up his watch). Yes, sir.

ALL THE OTHER INSIDE PASSENGERS (among themselves). Yes, sir.

COACHMAN (in a very surly tone). No, it ain't.

STRAW HAT (to the coachman). Well, I don't know, sir. We were a pretty tall time coming that last fifteen mile. That's a fact.

The coachman making no reply, and plainly declining to enter into any controversy on a subject so far removed from his sympathies and feelings, another passenger says, "Yes, sir;" and the gentleman in the straw hat, in acknowledgment of his courtesy, says, "Yes, sir," to him in return. The straw hat then inquires of the brown hat whether that coach in which he (the straw hat) then sits is not a new one? To which the brown hat again makes answer, "Yes, sir."

STRAW HAT. I thought so. Pretty loud smell of varnish, sir?

BROWN HAT. Yes, sir.

ALL THE OTHER INSIDE PASSENGERS. Yes, sir.

BROWN HAT (to the company in general). Yes, sir.

The conversational powers of the company having been by this time pretty heavily taxed, the straw hat opens the door and gets out; and all the rest alight also. We dine soon afterwards with the boarders in the house, and have nothing to drink but tea and coffee. As they are both very bad, and the water is worse, I ask for brandy; but it is a Temperance Hotel, and spirits are not to be had for love or money. This preposterous forcing of unpleasant drinks down the reluctant throats of travellers is not at all uncommon in America, but I never discovered that the scruples of such wincing landlords induced them to preserve any unusually nice balance between the quality of their fare and their scale of charges: on the contrary, I rather suspected them of diminishing the one and exalting the other, by way of recompense for the loss of their profit on the sale of spirituous liquors. After all, perhaps, the plainest course for persons of such tender consciences would be, a total abstinence from tavern-keeping.

Dinner over, we get into another vehicle which is ready at the door (for the coach has been changed in the in-

AS THE COACH STOPS, A GENTLEMAN IN A STRAW HAT LOOKS OUT OF THE WINDOW.

terval), and resume our journey; which continues through the same kind of country until evening, when we come to the town where we are to stop for tea and supper; and having delivered the mail-bags at the Post Office, ride through the usual wide street, lined with the usual stores and houses (the drapers always having hung up at their door, by way of sign, a piece of bright red cloth), to the hotel where this meal is prepared. There being many boarders here, we sit down a large party, and a very melancholy one as usual. But there is a buxom hostess at the head of the table, and opposite, a simple Welsh school-master with his wife and child; who came here, on a speculation of greater promise than performance, to teach the classics: and they are sufficient subjects of interest until the meal is over, and another coach is ready. In it we go on once more, lighted by a bright moon, until midnight; when we stop to change the coach again, and remain for half an hour or so in a miserable room, with a blurred lithograph of Washington over the smoky fireplace, and a mighty jug of cold water on the table: to which refreshment the moody passengers do so apply themselves that they would seem to be, one and all, keen patients of Doctor Sangrado. Among them is a very little boy, who chews tobacco like a very big one; and a droning gentleman who talks arithmetically and statistically on all subjects, from poetry downwards; and who always speaks in the same key, with exactly the same emphasis, and with very grave deliberation. He came outside just now, and told me how that the uncle of a certain young lady who had been spirited away and married by a certain captain lived in these parts; and how this uncle was so valiant and ferocious that he shouldn't wonder if he were to follow the said captain to England, "and shoot him down in the street, wherever he found him;" in the feasibility of which strong measure I, being for the moment rather prone to contradiction, from feeling half asleep and very tired, declined to acquiesce: assuring him that if the uncle did resort to it, or gratified any other little whim of the like nature, he would find himself one morning prematurely throttled at the Old Bailey; and that he would do well to make his will before he went, as he would certainly want it before he had been in Britain very long.

On we go all night, and by and by the day begins to

break, and presently the first cheerful rays of the warm sun come slanting on us brightly. It sheds its light upon a miserable waste of sodden grass, and dull trees, and squalid huts, whose aspect is forlorn and grievous in the last degree. A very desert in the wood, whose growth of green is dank and noxious like that upon the top of standing water: where poisonous fungus grows in the rare footprint on the oozy ground, and sprouts like witches' coral from the crevices in the cabin wall and floor; it is a hideous thing to lie upon the very threshold of a city. But it was purchased years ago, and as the owner cannot be discovered, the State has been unable to reclaim it. So there it remains, in the midst of cultivation and improvement, like ground accursed, and made obscene and rank by some great crime.

We reached Columbus shortly before seven o'clock, and stayed there, to refresh, that day and night: having excellent apartments in a very large unfinished hotel called the Neill House, which were richly fitted with the polished wood of the black walnut, and opened on a handsome portico and stone veranda, like rooms in some Italian mansion. The town is clean and pretty, and of course is "going to be" much larger. It is the seat of the State legislature of Ohio, and lays claim, in consequence, to some consideration and importance.

There being no stage-coach next day upon the road we wished to take, I hired "an extra," at a reasonable charge, to carry us to Tiffin; a small town from whence there is a railroad to Sandusky. This extra was an ordinary four-horse stage-coach, such as I have described, changing horses and drivers, as the stage-coach would, but was exclusively our own for the journey. To insure our having horses at the proper stations, and being incommoded by no strangers, the proprietors sent an agent on the box, who was to accompany us the whole way through; and thus attended, and bearing with us, besides, a hamper full of savory cold meats, and fruit, and wine; we started off again, in high spirits, at half-past six o'clock next morning, very much delighted to be by ourselves, and disposed to enjoy even the roughest journey.

It was well for us that we were in this humor, for the road we went over that day was certainly enough to have shaken tempers that were not resolutely at Set Fair down

to some inches below Stormy. At one time we were all
flung together in a heap at the bottom of the coach, and
at another we were crushing our heads against the roof.
Now one side was down deep in the mire, and we were
holding on to the other. Now the coach was lying on the
tails of the two wheelers; and now it was rearing up in
the air, in a frantic state, with all four horses standing
on the top of an insurmountable eminence, looking coolly
back at it, as though they would say, "Unharness us. It
can't be done." The drivers on these roads, who certainly
get over the road in a manner which is quite miraculous,
so twist and turn the team about in forcing a passage,
corkscrew fashion, through the bogs and swamps, that it
was quite a common circumstance, on looking out of the
window, to see the coachman, with the ends of a pair of
reins in his hands, apparently driving nothing, or playing
at horses, and the leaders staring at one unexpectedly
from the back of the coach, as if they had some idea of
getting up behind. A great portion of the way was over
what is called a corduroy road, which is made by throwing trunks of trees into a marsh, and leaving them to
settle there. The very slightest of the jolts with which the
ponderous carriage fell from log to log was enough, it
seemed, to have dislocated all the bones in the human
body. It would be impossible to experience a similar set
of sensations in any other circumstances, unless, perhaps,
in attempting to go up to the top of St. Paul's in an omni-
bus. Never, never once, that day, was the coach in any
position, attitude, or kind of motion to which we are accustomed in coaches. Never did it make the smallest approach to one's experience of the proceedings of any sort
of vehicle that goes on wheels.

Still, it was a fine day, and the temperature was delicious, and though we had left Summer behind us in the
west, and were fast leaving Spring, we were moving towards Niagara and home. We alighted in a pleasant wood
towards the middle of the day, dined on a fallen tree,
and leaving our best fragments with a cottager, and our
worst with the pigs (who swarm in this part of the country like grains of sand on the seashore, to the great comfort of our commissariat in Canada), we went forward
again gayly.

As night came on, the track grew narrower and narrower, until at last it so lost itself among the trees, that

the driver seemed to find his way by instinct. We had the comfort of knowing, at least, that there was no danger of his falling asleep, for every now and then a wheel would strike against an unseen stump with such a jerk, that he was fain to hold on pretty tight and pretty quick, to keep himself upon the box. Nor was there any reason to dread the least danger from furious driving, inasmuch as over that broken ground the horses had enough to do to walk; as to shying, there was no room for that; and a herd of wild elephants could not have run away in such a wood with such a coach at their heels. So we stumbled along, quite satisfied.

These stumps of trees are a curious feature in American travelling. The varying illusions they present to the unaccustomed eye, as it grows dark, are quite astonishing in their number and reality. Now there is a Grecian urn in the centre of a lonely field; now there is a woman weeping at a tomb; now a very commonplace old gentleman in a white waistcoat, with a thumb thrust into each armhole of his coat; now a student poring on a book; now a crouching Negro; now a horse, a dog, a cannon, an armed man; a hunchback throwing off his cloak and stepping forth into the light. They were often as entertaining to me as so many glasses in a magic lantern, and never took their shapes at my bidding, but seemed to force themselves upon me, whether I would or no; and, strange to say, I sometimes recognized in them counterparts of figures once familiar to me in pictures attached to childish books, forgotten long ago.

It soon became too dark, however, even for this amusement, and the trees were so close together that their dry branches rattled against the coach on either side, and obliged us all to keep our heads within. It lightened, too, for three whole hours; each flash being very bright, and blue, and long; and as the vivid streaks came darting in among the crowded branches, and the thunder rolled gloomily above the tree-tops, one could scarcely help thinking that there were better neighborhoods at such a time than thick woods afforded.

At length, between ten and eleven o'clock at night, a few feeble lights appeared in the distance, and Upper Sandusky, an Indian village, where we were to stay till morning, lay before us.

They were gone to bed at the log-inn, which was the

only house of entertainment in the place, but soon answered to our knocking, and got some tea for us in a sort of kitchen or common room, tapestried with old newspapers, pasted against the wall. The bedchamber to which my wife and I were shown was a large, low, ghostly room; with a quantity of withered branches on the hearth, and two doors without any fastening, opposite to each other, both opening on the black night and wild country, and so contrived that one of them always blew the other open: a novelty in domestic architecture which I do not remember to have seen before, and which I was somewhat disconcerted to have forced on my attention after getting into bed, as I had a considerable sum in gold, for our travelling expenses, in my dressing-case. Some of the luggage, however, piled against the panels, soon settled this difficulty, and my sleep would not have been very much affected that night, I believe, though it had failed to do so.

My Boston friend climbed up to bed somewhere in the roof, where another guest was already snoring hugely. But, being bitten beyond his power of endurance, he turned out again, and fled for shelter to the coach, which was airing itself in front of the house. This was not a very politic step as it turned out, for the pigs scenting him, and looking upon the coach as a kind of pie with some manner of meat inside, grunted round it so hideously, that he was afraid to come out again, and lay there shivering till morning. Nor was it possible to warm him when he did come out, by means of a glass of brandy; for in Indian villages, the legislature, with a very good and wise intention, forbids the sale of spirits by tavern-keepers. The precaution, however, is quite inefficacious, for the Indians never fail to procure liquor of a worse kind, at a dearer price, from travelling peddlers.

It is a settlement of the Wyandot Indians who inhabit this place. Among the company at breakfast was a mild old gentleman, who had been for many years employed by the United States Government in conducting negotiations with the Indians, and who had just concluded a treaty with these people by which they bound themselves, in consideration of a certain annual sum, to remove next year to some land provided for them west of the Mississippi, and a little way beyond St. Louis. He gave me a moving account of their strong attachment to the familiar scenes of their infancy, and in particular to the burial-places of their kindred; and of their great reluctance to leave them. He had witnessed many such removals, and always with pain, though he knew that they departed for their own good. The question whether this tribe should go or stay had been discussed among them a day or two before, in a hut erected for the purpose, the logs of which still lay upon the ground before the inn. When the speaking was done, the ayes and noes were ranged on opposite sides, and every male adult voted in his turn. The moment the result was known, the minority (a large one) cheerfully yielded to the rest, and withdrew all kind of opposition.

We met some of these poor Indians afterwards, riding on shaggy ponies. They were so like the meaner sort of gypsies, that if I could have seen any of them in England, I should have concluded, as a matter of course, that they belonged to that wandering and restless people.

Leaving this town directly after breakfast, we pushed forward again, over a rather worse road than yesterday, if possible, and arrived about noon at Tiffin, where we parted with the extra. At two o'clock we took the railroad; the travelling on which was very slow, its construction being indifferent, and the ground wet and marshy; and arrived at Sandusky in time to dine that evening. We put up at a comfortable little hotel on the brink of Lake Erie, lay there that night, and had no choice but to wait there next day, until a steamboat bound for Buffalo appeared. The town, which was sluggish and uninteresting enough, was something like the back of an English watering-place out of the season.

Our host, who was very attentive and anxious to make us comfortable, was a handsome middle-aged man, who had come to this town from New England, in which part of the country he was "raised." When I say that he constantly walked in and out of the room with his hat on; and stopped to converse in the same free-and-easy state; and lay down on our sofa, and pulled his newspaper out of his pocket, and read it at his ease; I merely mention these traits as characteristic of the country: not at all as being matter of complaint, or as having been disagreeable to me. I should undoubtedly be offended by such proceedings at home, because there they are not the

custom, and where they are not, they would be imper-
tinences; but, in America, the only desire of a good-
natured fellow of this kind is to treat his guests hospitably
and well; and I had no more right, and I can truly say no
more disposition, to measure his conduct by our English
rule and standard, than I had to quarrel with him for
not being of the exact stature which would qualify him for
admission into the Queen's Grenadier Guards. As little
inclination had I to find fault with a funny old lady
who was an upper domestic in this establishment, and who,
when she came to wait upon us at any meal, sat herself
down comfortably in the most convenient chair, and, producing a large pin to pick her teeth with, remained
performing that ceremony, and steadfastly regarding us
meanwhile with much gravity and composure (now and
then pressing us to eat a little more), until it was time to
clear away. It was enough for us that whatever we wished
done was done with great civility and readiness, and a
desire to oblige, not only here, but everywhere else; and
that all our wants were, in general, zealously anticipated.

We were taking an early dinner at this house, on the
day after our arrival, which was Sunday, when a steamboat came in sight, and presently touched at the wharf.
As she proved to be on her way to Buffalo, we hurried on
board with all speed, and soon left Sandusky far behind
us.

She was a large vessel of five hundred tons, and handsomely fitted up, though with high-pressure engines;
which always conveyed that kind of feeling to me which
I should be likely to experience, I think, if I had lodgings
on the first floor of a powder-mill. She was laden with
flour, some casks of which commodity were stored upon
the deck. The captain coming up to have a little conversation, and to introduce a friend, seated himself astride of
one of these barrels, like a Bacchus of private life; and
pulling a great clasp-knife out of his pocket, began to
"whittle" it as he talked, by paring thin slices off the edges.
And he whittled with such industry and hearty good-will,
that but for his being called very soon, it must have
disappeared bodily, and left nothing in its place but grist
and shavings.

After calling at one or two flat places, with low dams
stretching out into the lake, whereon were stumpy light-

houses, like windmills without sails, the whole looking
like a Dutch vignette, we came at midnight to Cleveland,
where we lay all night, and until nine o'clock next morning.

I entertained quite a curiosity in reference to this
place, from having seen at Sandusky a specimen of its
literature in the shape of a newspaper, which was very
strong indeed upon the subject of Lord Ashburton's recent arrival at Washington, to adjust the points in dispute
between the United States Government and Great Britain:
informing its readers that as America had "whipped"
England in her infancy, and whipped her again in her
youth, so it was clearly necessary that she must whip
her once again in her maturity: and pledging its credit
to all True Americans, that if Mr. Webster did his duty
in the approaching negotiations, and sent the English
Lord home again in double-quick time, they should, within
two years, sing "Yankee Doodle in Hyde Park, and Hail
Columbia in the scarlet courts of Westminster!" I found
it a pretty town, and had the satisfaction of beholding the
outside of the office of the journal from which I have just
quoted. I did not enjoy the delight of seeing the wit who
indited the paragraphs in question, but I have no doubt he
is a prodigious man in his way, and held in high repute
by a select circle.

There was a gentleman on board, to whom, as I un-
intentionally learned through the thin partition which
divided our stateroom from the cabin in which he and
his wife conversed together, I was unwittingly the occasion
of very great uneasiness. I don't know why or wherefore,
but I appeared to run in his mind perpetually, and to
dissatisfy him very much. First of all I heard him say:
and the most ludicrous part of the business was, that he
said it in my very ear, and could not have communicated
more directly with me, if he had leaned upon my shoulder,
and whispered me: "Boz is on board still, my dear."
After a considerable pause he added, complainingly, "Boz
keeps himself very close:" which was true enough, for I
was not very well, and was lying down, with a book. I
thought he had done with me after this, but I was deceived; for a long interval having elapsed, during which
I imagine him to have been turning restlessly from side to
side, and trying to go to sleep, he broke out again with,

"I suppose *that* Boz will be writing a book by and by, and putting all our names in it!" at which imaginary consequence of being on board a boat with Boz, he groaned, and became silent.

We called at the town of Erie at eight o'clock that night, and lay there an hour. Between five and six next morning we arrived at Buffalo, where we breakfasted; and, being too near the Great Falls to wait patiently anywhere else, we set off by the train, the same morning at nine o'clock, to Niagara.

It was a miserable day; chilly and raw; a damp mist falling; and the trees in that northern region quite bare and wintry. Whenever the train halted, I listened for the roar; and was constantly straining my eyes in the direction where I knew the Falls must be, from seeing the river rolling on towards them; every moment expecting to behold the spray. Within a few minutes of our stopping, not before, I saw two great white clouds rising up slowly and majestically from the depths of the earth. That was all. At length we alighted: and then, for the first time, I heard the mighty rush of water, and felt the ground tremble underneath my feet.

The bank is very steep, and was slippery with rain and half-melted ice. I hardly know how I got down, but I was soon at the bottom, and climbing, with two English officers who were crossing and had joined me, over some broken rocks, deafened by the noise, half blinded by the spray, and wet to the skin. We were at the foot of the American Fall. I could see an immense torrent of water tearing headlong down from some great height, but had no idea of shape, or situation, or anything but vague immensity.

When we were seated in the little ferry-boat, and were crossing the swollen river immediately before both cataracts, I began to feel what it was: but I was in a manner stunned, and unable to comprehend the vastness of the scene. It was not until I came on Table Rock, and looked— Great Heaven, on what a fall of bright green water!— that it came upon me in its full might and majesty.

Then, when I felt how near to my Creator I was standing, the first effect, and the enduring one—instant and lasting—of the tremendous spectacle, was Peace. Peace of Mind, tranquillity, calm recollections of the

Dead, great thoughts of Eternal Rest and Happiness: nothing of gloom or terror. Niagara was at once stamped upon my heart, an Image of Beauty; to remain there, changeless and indelible, until its pulses cease to beat, forever.

Oh, how the strife and trouble of daily life receded from my view, and lessened in the distance, during the ten memorable days we passed on that Enchanted Ground! What voices spoke from out the thundering water; what faces, faded from the earth, looked out upon me from its gleaming depths; what Heavenly promise glistened in those angels' tears, the drops of many hues, that showered around, and twined themselves about the gorgeous arches which the changing rainbows made!

I never stirred in all that time from the Canadian side, whither I had gone at first. I never crossed the river again; for I knew there were people on the other shore, and in such a place it is natural to shun strange company. To wander to and fro all day, and see the cataracts from all points of view; to stand upon the edge of the Great Horseshoe Fall, marking the hurried water gathering strength as it approached the verge, yet seeming, too, to pause before it shot into the gulf below; to gaze from the river's level up at the torrent as it came streaming down; to climb the neighboring heights and watch it through the trees, and see the wreathing water in the rapids hurrying on to take its fearful plunge; to linger in the shadow of the solemn rocks three miles below; watching the river as, stirred by no visible cause, it heaved and eddied and awoke the echoes, being troubled yet, far down beneath the surface, by its giant leap; to have Niagara before me, lighted by the sun and by the moon, red in the day's decline, and gray as evening slowly fell upon it; to look upon it every day, and wake up in the night and hear its ceaseless voice: this was enough.

I think in every quiet season now, still do those waters roll and leap, and roar and tumble, all day long; still are the rainbows spanning them, a hundred feet below. Still, when the sun is on them, do they shine and glow like molten gold. Still, when the day is gloomy, do they fall like snow, or seem to crumble away like the front of a great chalk cliff, or roll down the rock like dense white smoke. But always does the mighty stream appear to die as it comes down, and always from its unfathomable grave arises that tremendous ghost of spray and mist, which is never laid: which has haunted this place with the same dread solemnity since Darkness brooded on the deep, and that first flood before the Deluge—Light—came rushing on Creation at the word of God.

CHAPTER 15

In Canada: Toronto; Kingston; Montreal; Quebec; St. John's. In the United States again: Lebanon; the Shaker Village; West Point.

I wish to abstain from instituting any comparison, or drawing any parallel whatever, between the social features of the United States and those of the British possessions in Canada. For this reason, I shall confine myself to a very brief account of our journeyings in the latter territory.

But, before I leave Niagara, I must advert to one disgusting circumstance, which can hardly have escaped the observation of any decent traveller who has visited the Falls.

On Table Rock there is a cottage belonging to a Guide, where little relics of the place are sold, and where visitors register their names in a book kept for the purpose. On the wall of the room in which a great many of these volumes are preserved, the following request is posted: "Visitors will please not copy nor extract the remarks and poetical effusions from the registers and albums kept here."

But for this intimation, I should have let them lie upon the tables on which they were strewn with careful negligence, like books in a drawing-room: being quite satisfied with the stupendous silliness of certain stanzas with an anticlimax at the end of each, which were framed and hung up on the wall. Curious, however, after reading this announcement, to see what kind of morsels were so carefully preserved, I turned a few leaves, and found them scrawled all over with the vilest and the filthiest ribaldry that ever human hogs delighted in.

It is humiliating enough to know that there are among men brutes so obscene and worthless, that they can delight in laying their miserable profanations upon the very steps of Nature's greatest altar. But that these should be hoarded up for the delight of their fellow-swine, and kept in a public place where any eyes may see them, is a disgrace to the English language in which they are written (though I hope few of these entries have been made by Englishmen), and a reproach to the English side, on which they are preserved.

The quarters of our soldiers at Niagara are finely and airily situated. Some of them are large detached houses on the plain above the Falls, which were originally designed for hotels; and in the evening-time, when the women and children were leaning over the balconies watching the men as they played at ball and other games upon the grass before the door, they often presented a little picture of cheerfulness and animation which made it quite a pleasure to pass that way.

At any garrisoned point where the line of demarcation between one country and another is so very narrow as at Niagara, desertion from the ranks can scarcely fail to be of frequent occurrence: and it may be reasonably supposed that when the soldiers entertain the wildest and maddest hopes of the fortune and independence that await them on the other side, the impulse to play traitor, which such a place suggests to dishonest minds, is not weakened. But it very rarely happens that the men who do desert are happy or contented afterwards; and many instances have been known in which they have confessed their grievous disappointment, and their earnest desire to return to their old service, if they could but be assured of pardon, or of lenient treatment. Many of their comrades, notwithstanding, do the like from time to time; and instances of loss of life in the effort to cross the river with this object are far from being uncommon. Several men were drowned in the attempt to swim across, not long ago; and one, who had the madness to trust himself upon a table as a raft, was swept down to the whirlpool, where his mangled body eddied round and round some days.

I am inclined to think that the noise of the Falls is very much exaggerated; and this will appear the more probable when the depth of the great basin in which the water is received is taken into account. At no time during our stay there was the wind at all high or boisterous, but we never heard them three miles off, even at the very quiet time of sunset, though we often tried.

Queenston, at which place the steamboats start for Toronto (or I should rather say at which place they call, for their wharf is at Lewiston, on the opposite shore), is situated in a delicious valley, through which the Niagara River, in color a very deep green, pursues its course. It is approached by a road that takes its winding way among the heights by which the town is sheltered; and, seen from this point, is extremely beautiful and picturesque. On the most conspicuous of these heights stood a monument erected by the Provincial Legislature in memory of General Brock, who was slain in a battle with the American Forces, after having won the victory. Some vagabond, supposed to be a fellow of the name of Lett, who is now, or who lately was, in prison as a felon, blew up this monument two years ago, and it is now a melancholy ruin, with a long fragment of iron railing hanging dejectedly from its top, and waving to and fro like a wild ivy branch or broken vine stem. It is of much higher importance than it may seem, that this statue should be repaired at the public cost, as it ought to have been long ago. Firstly, because it is beneath the dignity of England to allow a memorial raised in honor of one of her defenders to remain in this condition, on the very spot where he died. Secondly, because the sight of it in its present state, and the recollection of the unpunished outrage which brought it to this pass, is not very likely to soothe down border feelings among English subjects here, or compose their border quarrels and dislikes.

I was standing on the wharf at this place, watching the passengers embarking in a steamboat which preceded that whose coming we awaited, and participating in the anxiety with which a sergeant's wife was collecting her few goods together—keeping one distracted eye hard upon the porters, who were hurrying them on board, and the other on a hoopless washing tub for which, as being the most utterly worthless of all her movables, she seemed to entertain particular affection—when three or four soldiers with a recruit came up, and went on board.

The recruit was a likely young fellow enough, strongly built and well made, but by no means sober: indeed, he had all the air of a man who had been more or less drunk for some days. He carried a small bundle over his shoulder, slung at the end of a walking-stick, and had a short pipe in his mouth. He was as dusty and dirty as recruits usually are, and his shoes betokened that he had travelled on foot some distance, but he was in a very jocose state, and shook hands with this soldier, and clapped that one on the back, and talked and laughed continually, like a roaring idle dog as he was.

The soldiers rather laughed at this blade than with him: seeming to say, as they stood straightening their canes in their hands, and looking coolly at him over their glazed stocks, "Go on, my boy, while you may! you'll know better by and by:" when suddenly the novice, who had been backing towards the gangway in his noisy merriment, fell overboard before their eyes, and splashed heavily down into the river between the vessel and the dock.

I never saw such a good thing as the change that came over these soldiers in an instant. Almost before the man was down, their professional manner, their stiffness and constraint, were gone, and they were filled with the most violent energy. In less time than is required to tell it, they had him out again, feet first, with the tails of his coat flapping over his eyes, everything about him hanging the wrong way, and the water streaming off at every thread in his threadbare dress. But the moment they set him upright, and found that he was none the worse, they were soldiers again, looking over their glazed stocks more composedly than ever.

The half-sobered recruit glanced round for a moment, as if his first impulse were to express some gratitude for his preservation, but seeing them with this air of total unconcern, and having his wet pipe presented to him with an oath by the soldier who had been by far the most anxious of the party, he stuck it in his mouth, thrust his hands into his moist pockets, and, without even shaking the water off his clothes, walked on board whistling; not to say as if nothing had happened, but as if he had meant to do it, and it had been a perfect success.

Our steamboat came up directly this had left the wharf,

AND HAVING HIS WET PIPE PRESENTED TO HIM.

and soon bore us to the mouth of the Niagara: where the stars and stripes of America flutter on one side, and the Union Jack of England on the other: and so narrow is the space between them that the sentinels in either fort can often hear the watchword of the other country given. Thence we emerged on Lake Ontario, an inland sea; and by half-past six o'clock were at Toronto.

The country round this town, being very flat, is bare of scenic interest; but the town itself is full of life and motion, bustle, business, and improvement. The streets are well paved, and lighted with gas; the houses are large and good; the shops excellent. Many of them have a display of goods in their windows, such as may be seen in thriving county towns in England; and there are some which would do no discredit to the metropolis itself. There is a good stone prison here; and there are, besides, a handsome church, a Courthouse, public offices, many commodious private residences, and a Government Observatory for noting and recording the magnetic variations. In the College of Upper Canada, which is one of the public establishments of the city, a sound education in every department of polite learning can be had at a very moderate expense: the annual charge for the instruction of each pupil not exceeding nine pounds sterling. It has pretty good endowments in the way of land, and is a valuable and useful institution.

The first stone of a new college had been laid but a few days before by the Governor General. It will be a handsome, spacious edifice, approached by a long avenue, which is already planted and made available as a public walk. The town is well adapted for wholesome exercise at all seasons, for the footways in the thoroughfares which lie beyond the principal streets are planked like floors, and kept in very good and clean repair.

It is a matter of deep regret that political differences should have run high in this place, and led to most discreditable and disgraceful results. It is not long since guns were discharged from a window in this town at the successful candidates in an election, and the coachman of one of them was actually shot in the body, though not dangerously wounded. But one man was killed on the same occasion; and from the very window whence he received his death, the very flag which shielded his murderer (not

only in the commission of his crime, but from its consequences) was displayed again on the occasion of the public
ceremony performed by the Governor General to which
I have just adverted. Of all the colors in the rainbow,
there is but one which could be so employed: I need not
say that flag was orange.

The time of leaving Toronto for Kingston is noon. By
eight o'clock next morning the traveller is at the end of
his journey, which is performed by steamboat upon Lake
Ontario, calling at Port Hope and Coburg, the latter a
cheerful, thriving little town. Vast quantities of flour form
the chief item in the freight of these vessels. We had no
fewer than one thousand and eighty barrels on board between Coburg and Kingston.

The latter place, which is now the seat of government
in Canada, is a very poor town, rendered still poorer in
the appearance of its market-place by the ravages of a
recent fire. Indeed, it may be said of Kingston, that one
half of it appears to be burnt down, and the other half not
to be built up. The Government House is neither elegant
nor commodious, yet it is almost the only house of any
importance in the neighborhood.

There is an admirable jail here, well and wisely governed, and excellently regulated in every respect. The
men were employed as shoemakers, ropemakers, black-
smiths, tailors, carpenters, and stone-cutters; and in building a new prison, which was pretty far advanced towards completion. The female prisoners were occupied
in needlework. Among them was a beautiful girl of twenty,
who had been there nearly three years. She acted as
bearer of secret despatches for the self-styled Patriots
on Navy Island during the Canadian Insurrection: sometimes dressing as a girl, and carrying them in her stays;
sometimes attiring herself as a boy, and secreting them
in the lining of her hat. In the latter character she
always rode as a boy would, which was nothing to her, for
she could govern any horse that any man could ride, and
could drive four-in-hand with the best whip in those parts.
Setting forth on one of her patriotic missions, she
appropriated to herself the first horse she could lay her
hands on; and this offence had brought her where I saw
her. She had quite a lovely face, though, as the reader may
suppose from this sketch of her history, there was a

lurking devil in her bright eye, which looked out pretty sharply from between her prison bars.

There is a bomb-proof fort here of great strength, which occupies a bold position, and is capable, doubtless, of doing good service; though the town is much too close upon the frontier to be long held, I should imagine, for its present purpose in troubled times. There is also a small navy-yard, where a couple of Government steamboats were building, and getting on vigorously.

We left Kingston for Montreal on the tenth of May, at half-past nine in the morning, and proceeded in a steamboat down the St. Lawrence River. The beauty of this noble stream at almost any point, but especially in the commencement of this journey, when it winds its way among the Thousand Islands, can hardly be imagined. The number and constant successions of these islands, all green and richly wooded; their fluctuating sizes, some so large that for half an hour together one among them will appear as the opposite bank of the river, and some so small that they are mere dimples on its broad bosom; their infinite variety of shapes; and the numberless combinations of beautiful forms which the trees growing on them present; all form a picture fraught with uncommon interest and pleasure.

In the afternoon we shot down some rapids where the river boiled and bubbled strangely, and where the force and headlong violence of the current were tremendous. At seven o'clock we reached Dickenson's Landing, whence travellers proceed for two or three hours by stage-coach: the navigation of the river being rendered so dangerous and difficult in the interval, by rapids, that steamboats do not make the passage. The number and length of those *portages,* over which the roads are bad, and the travelling slow, render the way between the towns of Montreal and Kingston somewhat tedious.

Our course lay over a wide, unenclosed tract of country at a little distance from the river-side, whence the bright warning lights on the dangerous parts of the St. Lawrence shone vividly. The night was dark and raw, and the way dreary enough. It was nearly ten o'clock when we reached the wharf where the next steamboat lay; and went on board, and to bed.

She lay there all night, and started as soon as it was

day. The morning was ushered in by a violent thunder-storm, and was very wet, but gradually improved and brightened up. Going on deck after breakfast, I was amazed to see floating down with the stream a most gigantic raft, with some thirty or forty wooden houses upon it, and at least as many flag masts, so that it looked like a nautical street. I saw many of these rafts afterwards, but never one so large. All the timber, or "lumber," as it is called in America, which is brought down the St. Lawrence, is floated down in this manner. When the raft reaches its place of destination, it is broken up; the materials are sold; and the boatmen return for more.

At eight we landed again, and travelled by a stage-coach for four hours through a pleasant and well-cultivated country, perfectly French in every respect: in the appearance of the cottages; the air, language, and dress of the peasantry, the signboards on the shops and taverns; and the Virgin's shrines and crosses by the way-side. Nearly every common laborer and boy, though he had no shoes to his feet, wore round his waist a sash of some bright color: generally red: and the women, who were working in the fields and gardens, and doing all kinds of husbandry, wore, one and all, great flat straw hats with most capacious brims. There were Catholic Priests and Sisters of Charity in the village streets; and images of the Saviour at the corners of crossroads, and in other public places.

At noon we went on board another steamboat, and reached the village of Lachine, nine miles from Montreal, by three o'clock. There we left the river, and went on by land.

Montreal is pleasantly situated on the margin of the St. Lawrence, and is backed by some bold heights, about which there are charming rides and drives. The streets are generally narrow and irregular, as in most French towns of any age; but, in the more modern parts of the city, they are wide and airy. They display a great variety of very good shops; and both in the town and suburbs there are many excellent private dwellings. The granite quays are remarkable for their beauty, solidity, and extent.

There is a very large Catholic cathedral here, recently erected; with two tall spires, of which one is yet unfin-

ished. In the open space in front of this edifice stands a
solitary, grim-looking, square brick tower, which has a
quaint and remarkable appearance, and which the wise-
acres of the place have consequently determined to pull
down immediately. The Government House is very superior to that at Kingston, and the town is full of life and
bustle. In one of the suburbs is a plank road—not foot-
path—five or six miles long, and a famous road it is too.
All the rides in the vicinity were made doubly interesting
by the bursting out of spring, which is here so rapid,
that it is but a day's leap from barren winter to the
blooming youth of summer.

The steamboats to Quebec perform the journey in
the night; that is to say, they leave Montreal at six in the
evening, and arrive in Quebec at six next morning. We
made this excursion during our stay in Montreal (which
exceeded a fortnight), and were charmed by its interest
and beauty.

The impression made upon the visitor by this Gibraltar
of America: its giddy heights; its citadel suspended, as it
were, in the air; its picturesque steep streets and frowning
gateways; and the splendid views which burst upon the
eye at every turn: is at once unique and lasting.

It is a place not to be forgotten, or mixed up in the
mind with other places, or altered for a moment in the
crowd of scenes a traveller can recall. Apart from the realities of this most picturesque city, there are associations
clustering about it which would make a desert rich
in interest. The dangerous precipice along whose rocky
front Wolfe and his brave companions climbed to glory;
the Plains of Abraham, where he received his mortal
wound; the fortress so chivalrously defended by Mont-
calm; and his soldier's grave, dug for him, while yet alive,
by the bursting of a shell; are not the least among them,
or among the gallant incidents of history. That is a noble
Monument, too, and worthy of two great nations, which
perpetuates the memory of both brave generals, and on
which their names are jointly written.

The city is rich in public institutions and in Catholic
churches and charities, but it is mainly in the prospect
from the site of the Old Government House, and from
the Citadel, that its surpassing beauty lies. The exquisite
expanse of country, rich in field and forest, mountain

height and water, which lies stretched out before the view, with miles of Canadian villages, glancing in long white streaks, like veins along the landscape; the motley crowd of gables, roofs, and chimney-tops in the old hilly town immediately at hand; the beautiful St. Lawrence sparkling and flashing in the sunlight; and the tiny ships below the rock from which you gaze, whose distant rigging looks like spiders' webs against the light, while casks and barrels on their decks dwindle into toys, and busy mariners become so many puppets: all this, framed by a sunken window in the fortress, and looked at from the shadowed room within, forms one of the brightest and most enchanting pictures that the eye can rest upon.

In the spring of the year, vast numbers of emigrants, who have newly arrived from England or from Ireland, pass between Quebec and Montreal, on their way to the backwoods and new settlements of Canada. If it be an entertaining lounge (as I very often found it) to take a morning stroll upon the quay at Montreal, and see them grouped in hundreds on the public wharves about their chests and boxes, it is matter of deep interest to be their fellow-passenger on one of these steamboats, and, mingling with the concourse, see and hear them unobserved.

The vessel in which we returned from Quebec to Montreal was crowded with them, and at night they spread their beds between decks (those who had beds, at least), and slept so close and thick about our cabin door, that the passage to and fro was quite blocked up. They were nearly all English; from Gloucestershire the greater part; and had had a long winter passage out; but it was wonderful to see how clean the children had been kept, and how untiring in their love and self-denial all the poor parents were.

Cant as we may, and as we shall to the end of all things, it is very much harder for the poor to be virtuous than it is for the rich; and the good that is in them shines the brighter for it. In many a noble mansion lives a man, the best of husbands and of fathers, whose private worth in both capacities is justly lauded to the skies. But bring him here, upon this crowded deck. Strip from his fair young wife her silken dress and jewels, unbind her braided hair, stamp early wrinkles on her brow, pinch her pale cheek with care and much privation, array her faded form in coarsely patched attire, let there be nothing but his love to set her forth or deck her out, and you shall put it to the proof indeed. So change his station in the world, that he shall see in those young things who climb about his knee: not records of his wealth and name: but little wrestlers with him for his daily bread; so many poachers on his scanty meal; so many units to divide his every sum of comfort, and farther to reduce its small amount. In lieu of the endearments of childhood in its sweetest aspect, heap upon him all its pains and wants, its sicknesses and ills, its fretfulness, caprice, and querulous endurance: let its prattle be, not of engaging infant fancies, but of cold, and thirst, and hunger: and if his fatherly affection outlive all this, and he be patient, watchful, tender; careful of his children's lives, and mindful always of their joys and sorrows; then send him back to Parliament, and Pulpit, and to Quarter Sessions, and when he hears fine talk of the depravity of those who live from hand to mouth, and labor hard to do it, let him speak up, as one who knows, and tell those holders forth that they, by parallel with such a class, should be High Angels in their daily lives, and lay but humble siege to Heaven at last.

Which of us shall say what he would be, if such realities, with small relief or change all through his days, were his? Looking round upon these people; far from home, houseless, indigent, wandering, weary with travel and hard living: and seeing how patiently they nursed and tended their young children; how they consulted ever their wants first, then half supplied their own; what gentle ministers of hope and faith the women were; how the men profited by their example; and how very, very seldom even a moment's petulance or harsh complaint broke out among them: I felt a stronger love and honor of my kind come glowing on my heart, and wished to God there had been many Atheists in the better part of human nature there, to read this simple lesson in the book of Life.

We left Montreal for New York again on the thirtieth of May; crossing to La Prairie, on the opposite shore of the St. Lawrence, in a steamboat; we then took the railroad to St. John's, which is on the brink of Lake Champlain. Our last greeting in Canada was from the English officers in the pleasant barracks at that place (a class of gentlemen who had made every hour of our visit memorable by their hospitality and friendship) ; and, with "Rule Britannia" sounding in our ears, we soon left it far behind.

But Canada has held, and always will retain, a foremost place in my remembrance. Few Englishmen are prepared to find it what it is. Advancing quietly; old differences settling down, and being fast forgotten; public feeling and private enterprise alike in a sound and wholesome state; nothing of flush or fever in its system, but health and vigor throbbing in its steady pulse: it is full of hope and promise. To me—who had been accustomed to think of it as something left behind in the strides of advancing society, as something neglected and forgotten, slumbering and wasting in its sleep—the demand for labor and the rates of wages; the busy quays of Montreal; the vessels taking in their cargoes, and discharging them; the amount of shipping in the different ports; the commerce, roads, and public ,works, all made *to last;* the respectability and character of the public journals; and the amount of rational comfort and happiness which honest industry may earn: were very great surprises. The steamboats on the lakes, in their conveniences, cleanliness, and safety; in the gentlemanly character and bearing of their captains; and in the politeness and perfect comfort of their social regulations; are unsurpassed even by the famous Scotch vessels, deservedly so much esteemed at home. The inns are usually bad; because the custom of boarding at hotels is not so general here as in the States, and the British officers, who form a large portion of the society of every town, live chiefly at the regimental messes: but, in every other respect, the traveller in Canada will find as good provision for his comfort as in any place I know.

There is one American boat—the vessel which carried us on Lake Champlain, from St. John's to Whitehall— which I praise very highly, but no more than it deserves, when I say that it is superior even to that in which we went from Queenston to Toronto, or to that in which we travelled from the latter place to Kingston, or, I have no doubt I may add, to any other in the world. This steamboat, which is called the Burlington, is a perfectly exquisite achievement of neatness, elegance, and order. The decks are drawing-rooms; the cabins are boudoirs, choicely fur-

nished and adorned with prints, pictures, and musical instruments; every nook and corner in the vessel is a perfect
curiosity of graceful comfort and beautiful contrivance.
Captain Sherman, her commander, to whose ingenuity
and excellent taste these results are solely attributable,
has bravely and worthily distinguished himself on more
than one trying occasion: not least among them in having
the moral courage to carry British troops, at a time
(during the Canadian rebellion) when no other conveyance was open to them. He and his vessel are held in
universal respect, both by his own countrymen and ours;
and no man ever enjoyed the popular esteem, who, in his
sphere of action, won and wore it better than this
gentleman.

By means of this floating palace we were soon in the
United States again, and called that evening at Burlington; a pretty town, where we lay an hour or so. We
reached Whitehall, where we were to disembark, at six
next morning; and might have done so earlier, but that
these steamboats lie by for some hours in the night, in
consequence of the lake becoming very narrow at that
part of the journey, and difficult of navigation in the dark.
Its width is so contracted at one point, indeed, that they
are obliged to warp round by means of a rope.

After breakfasting at Whitehall, we took the stage-coach
for Albany: a large and busy town, where we arrived
between five and six o'clock that afternoon; after a very
hot day's journey, for we were now in the height of summer again. At seven we started for New York on board a
great North River steamboat, which was so crowded with
passengers that the upper deck was like the box lobby of
a theatre between the pieces, and the lower one like Tot-
tenham Court Road on a Saturday night. But we slept
soundly, notwithstanding, and soon after five o'clock next
morning reached New York.

Tarrying here only that day and night to recruit after
our late fatigues, we started off once more upon our last
journey in America. We had yet five days to spare before
embarking for England, and I had a great desire to see
"the Shaker Village," which is peopled by a religious sect
from whom it takes its name.

To this end, we went up the North River again as far
as the town of Hudson, and there hired an extra to carry
us to Lebanon, thirty miles distant: and of course another

and a different Lebanon from that village where I slept on the night of the Prairie trip.

The country through which the road meandered was rich and beautiful; the weather very fine; and for many miles the Kaatskill Mountains, where Rip Van Winkle and the ghastly Dutchmen played at ninepins one memorable gusty afternoon, towered in the blue distance like stately clouds. At one point, as we ascended a steep hill, athwart whose base a railroad, yet constructing, took its course, we came upon an Irish colony. With means at hand of building decent cabins, it was wonderful to see how clumsy, rough, and wretched its hovels were. The best were poor protection from the weather; the worst let in the wind and rain through wide breaches in the roofs of sodden grass, and in the walls of mud; some had neither door nor window; some had nearly fallen down, and were imperfectly propped up by stakes and poles; all were ruinous and filthy. Hideously ugly old women and very buxom young ones, pigs, dogs, men, children, babies, pots, kettles, dunghills, vile refuse, rank straw, and standing water all wallowing together in an inseparable heap, composed the furniture of every dark and dirty hut.

Between nine and ten o'clock at night we arrived at Lebanon; which is renowned for its warm baths, and for a great hotel, well adapted, I have no doubt, to the gregarious taste of those seekers after health or pleasure who repair here, but inexpressibly comfortless to me. We were shown into an immense apartment, lighted by two dim candles, called the drawing-room: from which there was a descent, by a flight of steps, to another vast desert called the dining-room: our bedchambers were among certain long rows of little whitewashed cells, which opened from either side of a dreary passage; and were so like rooms in a prison that I half expected to be locked up when I went to bed, and listened involuntarily for the turning of the key on the outside. There need be baths somewhere in the neighborhood, for the other washing arrangements were on as limited a scale as I ever saw, even in America: indeed, these bedrooms were so very bare of even such common luxuries as chairs, that I should say they were not provided with enough of anything, but that I bethink myself of our having been most bountifully bitten all night.

The house is very pleasantly situated, however, and we

had a good breakfast. That done, we went to visit our place of destination, which was some two miles off, and the way to which was soon indicated by a finger-post, whereon was painted, "To the Shaker Village."

As we rode along, we passed a party of Shakers, who were at work upon the road; who wore the broadest of all broad-brimmed hats; and were in all visible respects such very wooden men, that I felt about as much sympathy for them, and as much interest in them, as if they had been so many figure-heads of ships. Presently we came to the beginning of the village, and, alighting at the door of a house where the Shaker manufactures are sold, and which is the headquarters of the elders, requested permission to see the Shaker worship.

Pending the conveyance of this request to some person in authority, we walked into a grim room, where several grim hats were hanging on grim pegs, and the time was grimly told by a grim clock, which uttered every tick with a kind of struggle, as if it broke the grim silence reluctantly, and under protest. Ranged against the wall were six or eight stiff, high-backed chairs, and they partook so strongly of the general grimness, that one would much rather have sat on the floor than incurred the smallest obligation to any of them.

Presently, there stalked into this apartment a grim old Shaker, with eyes as hard, and dull, and cold as the great round metal buttons on his coat and waist-coat; a sort of calm goblin. Being informed of our desire, he produced a newspaper wherein the body of elders, whereof he was a member, had advertised, but a few days before, that in consequence of certain unseemly interruptions which their worship had received from strangers, their chapel was closed to the public for the space of one year.

As nothing was to be urged in opposition to this reasonable arrangement, we requested leave to make some trifling purchases of Shaker goods; which was grimly conceded. We accordingly repaired to a store in the same house, and on the opposite side of the passage, where the stock was presided over by something alive in a russet case, which the elder said was a woman; and which I suppose *was* a woman, though I should not have suspected it.

On the opposite side of the road was their place of worship: a cool, clean edifice of wood, with large windows and green blinds: like a spacious summer-house. As there was no getting into this place, and nothing was to be done but walk up and down, and look at it and the other buildings in the village (which were chiefly of wood, painted a dark red like English barns, and composed of many stories like English factories), I have nothing to communicate to the reader beyond the scanty results I gleaned the while our purchases were making.

These people are called Shakers from their peculiar form of adoration, which consists of a dance, performed by the men and women of all ages, who arrange themselves for that purpose in opposite parties: the men first divesting themselves of their hats and coats, which they gravely hang against the wall before they begin; and tying a ribbon round their shirt-sleeves, as though they were going to be bled. They accompany themselves with a droning, humming noise, and dance until they are quite exhausted, alternately advancing and retiring in a preposterous sort of trot. The effect is said to be unspeakably absurd: and if I may judge from a print of this ceremony which I have in my possession; and which, I am informed by those who have visited the chapel, is perfectly accurate; it must be infinitely grotesque.

They are governed by a woman, and her rule is understood to be absolute, though she has the assistance of a council of elders. She lives, it is said, in strict seclusion, in certain rooms above the chapel, and is never shown to profane eyes. If she at all resemble the lady who presided over the store, it is a great charity to keep her as close as possible, and I cannot too strongly express my perfect concurrence in this benevolent proceeding.

All the possessions and revenues of the settlement are thrown into a common stock, which is managed by the elders. As they have made converts among people who were well to do in the world, and are frugal and thrifty, it is understood that this fund prospers: the more especially as they have made large purchases of land. Nor is this at Lebanon the only Shaker settlement: there are, I think, at least three others.

They are good farmers, and all their produce is eagerly purchased and highly esteemed. "Shaker seeds," "Shaker herbs," and "Shaker distilled waters" are commonly announced for sale in the shops of towns and cities. They are good breeders of cattle, and are kind and merciful to the brute creation. Consequently, Shaker beasts seldom fail to find a ready market.

They eat and drink together, after the Spartan model, at a great public table. There is no union of the sexes; and every Shaker, male and female, is devoted to a life of celibacy. Rumor has been busy upon this theme, but here again I must refer to the lady of the store, and say, that if many of the sister Shakers resemble her, I treat all such slander as bearing on its face the strongest marks of wild improbability. But that they take as proselytes persons so young that they cannot know their own minds, and cannot possess much strength of resolution in this or any other respect, I can assert from my own observation of the extreme juvenility of certain youthful Shakers whom I saw at work among the party on the road.

They are said to be good drivers of bargains, but to be honest and just in their transactions, and even in horse-dealing to resist those thievish tendencies which would seem, for some undiscovered reason, to be almost inseparable from that branch of traffic. In all matters they hold their own course quietly, live in their gloomy, silent commonwealth, and show little desire to interfere with other people.

This is well enough, but nevertheless I cannot, I confess, incline towards the Shakers; view them with much favor, or extend towards them any very lenient construction. I so abhor, and from my soul detest, that bad spirit, no matter by what class or sect it may be entertained, which would strip life of its healthful graces, rob youth of its innocent pleasures, pluck from maturity and age their pleasant ornaments, and make existence but a narrow path towards the grave: that odious spirit which, if it could have had full scope and sway upon the earth, must have blasted and made barren the imaginations of the greatest men, and left them, in their power of raising up enduring images before their fellow-creatures yet unborn, no better than the beasts: that, in these very broad-brimmed hats and very sombre coats—in stiff-necked, solemn-visaged piety, in short, no matter what its garb, whether it have cropped hair as in a Shaker village, or long nails as in a Hindu temple—I recognize the worst among the enemies of Heaven and Earth, who turn the water at the marriage feasts of this poor world, not into wine, but gall. And if there must be people vowed to crush the harmless fancies and the love of innocent delights and gayeties, which are a part of human nature: as much a part of it as any other love or hope that is our common portion: let them, for me, stand openly revealed among the ribald and licentious; the very idiots know that *they* are not on the Immortal road, and will despise them, and avoid them readily.

Leaving the Shaker village with a hearty dislike of the old Shakers, and a hearty pity for the young ones: tempered by the strong probability of their running away as they grow older and wiser, which they not uncommonly do: we returned to Lebanon, and so to Hudson, by the way we had come upon the previous day. There we took steamboat down the North River towards New York, but stopped, some four hours' journey short of it, at West Point, where we remained that night, and all next day, and next night too.

In this beautiful place: the fairest among the fair and lovely Highlands of the North River: shut in by deep green heights and ruined forts, and looking down upon the distant town of Newburgh, along a glittering path of sunlit water, with here and there a skiff, whose white sail often bends on some new tack as sudden flaws of wind come down upon her from the gullies in the hills: hemmed in, besides, all round, with memories of Washington and events of the revolutionary war: is the Military School of America.

It could not stand on more appropriate ground, and any ground more beautiful can hardly be. The course of education is severe, but well devised and manly. Through June, July, and August, the young men encamp upon the spacious plain whereon the college stands; and all the year their military exercises are performed there daily. The term of study at this institution, which the State requires from all cadets, is four years; but, whether it be from the rigid nature of the discipline, or the national impatience of restraint, or both causes combined, not more than half the number who begin their studies here ever remain to finish them.

The number of cadets being about equal to that of the members of Congress, one is sent here from every Congressional district: its members influencing the selection. Commissions in the service are distributed on the same principle. The dwellings of the various Professors are beautifully situated; and there is a most excellent hotel for strangers, though it has the two drawbacks of being a total-abstinence house (wines and spirits being forbidden to the students), and of serving the public meals at rather uncomfortable hours; to wit, breakfast at seven, dinner at one, and supper at sunset.

The beauty and freshness of this calm retreat, in the very dawn and greenness of summer—it was then the beginning of June—were exquisite indeed. Leaving it upon the sixth, and returning to New York, to embark for England on the succeeding day, I was glad to think that among the last memorable beauties which had glided past us, and softened in the bright perspective, were those whose pictures, traced by no common hand, are fresh in most men's minds; not easily to grow old, or fade beneath the dust of Time: the Kaatskill Mountains, Sleepy Hollow, and the Tappaan Zee.

CHAPTER 16

The Passage Home.

I NEVER had so much interest before, and very likely I shall never have so much interest again, in the state of the wind as on the long-looked-for morning of Tuesday, the Seventh of June. Some nautical authority had told me, a day or two previous, "Anything with west in it will do;" so when I darted out of bed at daylight, and, throwing up the window, was saluted by a lively breeze from the northwest, which had sprung up in the night, it came upon me so freshly, rustling with so many happy associations, that I conceived upon the spot a special regard for all airs blowing from that quarter of the compass, which I shall cherish, I dare say, until my own wind has breathed its last frail puff, and withdrawn itself forever from the mortal calendar.

The pilot had not been slow to take advantage of this favorable weather, and the ship, which yesterday had been in such a crowded dock that she might have retired from trade for good and all, for any chance she seemed to have of going to sea, was now full sixteen miles away. A gallant sight she was, when we, fast gaining on her in a steamboat, saw her in the distance riding at anchor; her tall masts pointing up in graceful lines against the sky, and every rope and spar expressed in delicate and thread-like outline: gallant, too, when, we being all aboard, the anchor came up to the sturdy chorus, "Cheerily, men, oh, cheerily!" and she followed proudly in the towing steamboat's wake: but bravest and most gallant of all when the tow-rope being cast adrift, the canvas fluttered from her masts, and, spreading her white wings, she soared away upon her free and solitary course.

In the after-cabin we were only fifteen passengers in all, and the greater part were from Canada, where some of us had known each other. The night was rough and squally, so were the next two days, but they flew by quickly, and we were soon as cheerful and as snug a party, with an honest, manly-hearted captain at our head, as ever came to the resolution of being mutually agreeable, on land or water.

We breakfasted at eight, lunched at twelve, dined at three, and took our tea at half-past seven. We had abundance of amusements, and dinner was not the least among them: firstly, for its own sake; secondly, because of its extraordinary length: its duration, inclusive of all the long pauses between the courses, being seldom less than two hours and a half; which was a subject of never-failing entertainment. By way of beguiling the tediousness of these banquets, a select association was formed at the lower end of the table, below the mast, to whose distinguished president modesty forbids me to make any further allusion, which, being a very hilarious and jovial institution, was (prejudice apart) in high favor with the rest of the community, and particularly with a black steward, who lived for three weeks in a broad grin at the marvellous humor of these incorporated worthies.

Then we had chess for those who played it, whist, cribbage, books, backgammon, and shovelboard. In all weathers, fair or foul, calm or windy, we were every one on deck, walking up and down in pairs, lying in the boats, leaning over the side, or chatting in a lazy group together. We had no lack of music, for one played the accordion, another the violin, and another (who usually began at six o'clock A.M.) the key-bugle: the combined effect of which instruments, when they all played different tunes, in different parts of the ship, at the same time, and within hearing of each other, as they sometimes did (everybody being intensely satisfied with his own performance), was sublimely hideous.

When all these means of entertainment failed, a sail would heave in sight; looming, perhaps, the very spirit of a ship, in the misty distance, or passing us so close that through our glasses we could see the people on her decks, and easily make out her name, and whither she was bound. For hours together we could watch the dolphins and porpoises as they rolled and leaped and dived around the vessel; or those small creatures ever on the wing, the Mother Carey's chickens, which had borne us company from New York Bay, and for a whole fortnight fluttered about the vessel's stern. For some days we had a dead calm, or very light winds, during which the crew amused themselves with fishing, and hooked an unlucky dolphin, who expired, in all his rainbow colors, on the deck: an event of such importance in our barren calendar, that afterwards we dated from the dolphin, and made the day on which he died an era.

Besides all this, when we were five or six days out, there began to be much talk of icebergs, of which wandering islands an unusual number had been seen by the vessels that had come into New York a day or two before we left that port, and of whose dangerous neighborhood we were warned by the sudden coldness of the weather, and the sinking of the mercury in the barometer. While these tokens lasted, a double lookout was kept, and many dismal tales were whispered, after dark, of ships that had struck upon the ice and gone down in the night; but the wind obliging us to hold a southward course, we saw none of them, and the weather soon grew bright and warm again.

The observation every day at noon, and the subsequent working of the vessel's course, was, as may be supposed, a feature in our lives of paramount importance; nor were there wanting (as there never are) sagacious doubters of the captain's calculations, who, so soon as his back was turned, would, in the absence of compasses, measure the chart with bits of string, and ends of pocket-handkerchiefs, and points of snuffers, and clearly prove him to be wrong by an odd thousand miles or so. It was very edifying to see these unbelievers shake their heads and frown, and hear them hold forth strongly upon navigation: not that they knew anything about it, but that they always mistrusted the captain in calm weather, or when the wind was adverse. Indeed, the mercury itself is not so variable as this class of passengers, whom you will see, when the ship is going nobly through the water, quite pale with admiration, swearing that the captain beats all captains ever known, and even hinting at subscriptions for a piece of plate; and who, next morning, when the breeze has lulled, and all the sails hang useless in the idle air, shake their despondent heads again, and say, with screwed-up lips, they hope that the captain is a sailor—but they shrewdly doubt him.

It even became an occupation in the calm to wonder when the wind *would* spring up in the favorable quarter, where, it was clearly shown by all the rules and precedents, it ought to have sprung up long ago. The first mate, who whistled for it zealously, was much respected for his perseverance, and was regarded, even by the unbelievers, as a first-rate sailor. Many gloomy looks would be cast upward through the cabin skylights at the flapping sails while dinner was in progress; and some, growing bold in ruefulness, predicted that we should land about the middle of July. There are always on board ship a Sanguine One and a Despondent One. The latter character carried it hollow at this period of the voyage, and triumphed over the Sanguine One at every meal, by inquiring where he supposed the Great Western (which left New York a week after us) was *now:* and where he supposed the Cunard steam-packet was *now:* and what he thought of sailing vessels as compared with steamships *now:* and so beset his life with pestilent attacks of that kind, that he, too, was obliged to affect despondency for very peace and quietude.

These were additions to the list of entertaining incidents, but there was still another source of interest. We carried in the steerage nearly a hundred passengers: a little world of poverty: and, as we came to know individuals among them by sight, from looking down upon the deck where they took the air in the daytime, and cooked their food, and very often ate it too, we became curious to know their histories, and with what expectations they had gone out to America, and on what errands they were going home, and what their circumstances were. The information we got on these heads from the carpenter, who had charge of these people, was often of the strangest kind. Some of them had been in America but three days, some but three months, and some had gone out in the last voyage of that very ship in which they were now returning home. Others had sold their clothes to raise the passage-money, and had hardly rags to cover them; others

had no food, and lived upon the charity of the rest: and
one man, it was discovered nearly at the end of the
voyage, not before—for he kept his secret close, and did
not court compassion—had had no sustenance whatever
but the bones and scraps of fat he took from the plates
used in the after-cabin dinner, when they were put out to
be washed.

The whole system of shipping and conveying these unfortunate persons is one that stands in need of thorough
revision. If any class deserve to be protected and assisted
by the Government, it is that class who are banished from
their native land in search of the bare means of subsist-
ence. All that could be done for these poor people by the
great compassion and humanity of the captain and officers
was done, but they require much more. The law is bound,
at least upon the English side, to see that too many of
them are not put on board one ship: and that their accommodations are decent: not demoralizing and profligate. It is bound, too, in common humanity, to declare
that no man shall be taken on board without his stock of
provisions being previously inspected by some proper officer, and pronounced moderately sufficient for his support upon the voyage. It is bound to provide, or to
require that there be provided, a medical attendant;
whereas in these ships there are none, though sickness
of adults, and deaths of children, on the passage are matters of the very commonest occurrence. Above all, it is
the duty of any Government, be it monarchy or republic,
to interpose and put an end to that system by which a firm
of traders in emigrants purchase of the owners the whole
'tween-decks of a ship, and send on board as many
wretched people as they can lay hold of, on any terms they
can get, without the smallest reference to the conveniences
of the steerage, the number of berths, the slightest
separation of the sexes, or anything but their own immediate profit. Nor is even this the worst of the vicious
system: for, certain crimping agents of these houses, who
have a percentage on all the passengers they inveigle, are
constantly travelling about those districts where poverty
and discontent are rife, and tempting the credulous into
more misery, by holding out monstrous inducements to
emigration which can never be realized.

The history of every family we had on board was pretty

much the same. After hoarding up, and borrowing, and begging, and selling everything to pay the passage, they had gone out to New York, expecting to find its streets paved with gold; and had found them paved with very hard and very real stones. Enterprise was dull; laborers were not wanted; jobs of work were to be got, but the payment was not. They were coming back, even poorer than they went. One of them was carrying an open letter from a young English artisan, who had been in New York a fortnight, to a friend near Manchester, whom he strongly urged to follow him. One of the officers brought it to me as a curiosity. "This is the country, Jem," said the writer. "I like America. There is no despotism here; that's the great thing. Employment of all sorts is going a-begging, and wages are capital. You have only to choose a trade, Jem, and be it. I haven't made choice of one yet, but I shall soon. *At present, I haven't quite made up my mind whether to be a carpenter or a tailor.*"

There was yet another kind of passenger, and but one more, who, in the calm and the light winds, was a constant theme of conversation and observation among us. This was an English sailor, a smart, thorough-built, English man-of-war's man from his hat to his shoes, who was serving in the American navy, and, having got leave of absence, was on his way home to see his friends. When he presented himself to take and pay for his passage, it had been suggested to him that, being an able seaman, he might as well work it and save the money, but this piece of advice he very indignantly rejected: saying, "He'd be damned but for once he'd go aboard ship as a gentleman." Accordingly, they took his money, but he no sooner came aboard than he stowed his kit in the forecastle, arranged to mess with the crew, and, the very first time the hands were turned up, went aloft like a cat, before anybody. And all through the passage there he was, first at the braces, outermost on the yards, perpetually lending a hand everywhere, but always with a sober dignity in his manner, and a sober grin on his face, which plainly said, "I do it as a gentleman. For my own pleasure, mind you!"

At length and at last, the promised wind came up in right good earnest, and away we went before it, with every stitch of canvas set, slashing through the water nobly. There was a grandeur in the motion of the splendid ship, as, overshadowed by her mass of sails, she rode at a furious pace upon the waves, which filled one with an indescribable sense of pride and exultation. As she plunged into a foaming valley, how I loved to see the green waves, bordered deep with white, come rushing on astern, to buoy her upward at their pleasure, and curl about her as she stooped again, but always own her for their haughty mistress still! On, on we flew, with changing lights upon the water, being now in the blessed region of fleecy skies; a bright sun lighting us by day, and a bright moon by night; the vane pointing directly homeward, alike the truthful index to the favoring wind and to our cheerful hearts; until at sunrise, one fair Monday morning—the twenty-seventh of June, I shall not easily forget the day—there lay before us old Cape Clear, God bless it, showing, in the mist of early morning, like a cloud: the brightest and most welcome cloud, to us, that ever hid the face of Heaven's fallen sister—Home.

Dim speck as it was in the wide prospect, it made the sunrise a more cheerful sight, and gave to it that sort of human interest which it seems to want at sea. There, as elsewhere, the return of day is inseparable from some sense of renewed hope and gladness; but the light shining on the dreary waste of water, and showing it in all its vast extent of loneliness, presents a solemn spectacle, which even night, veiling it in darkness and uncertainty, does not surpass. The rising of the moon is more in keeping with the solitary ocean; and has an air of melancholy grandeur, which, in its soft and gentle influence, seems to comfort while it saddens. I recollect, when I was a very young child, having a fancy that the reflection of the moon in water was a path to heaven, trodden by the spirits of good people on their way to God; and this old feeling often came over me again, when I watched it on a tranquil night at sea.

The wind was very light on this same Monday morning, but it was still in the right quarter, and so, by slow degrees, we left Cape Clear behind, and sailed along within sight of the coast of Ireland. And how merry we all were, and how loyal to the George Washington, and how full of mutual congratulations, and how venturesome in predicting the exact hour at which we should arrive at Liverpool, may be easily imagined and readily under-

stood. Also, how heartily we drank the captain's health
that day at dinner; and how restless we became about
packing up; and how two or three of the most sanguine
spirits rejected the idea of going to bed at all that
night as something it was not worth while to do, so
near the shore, but went nevertheless, and slept soundly;
and how to be so near our journey's end was like a
pleasant dream, from which one feared to wake.

The friendly breeze freshened again next day, and on
we went once more before it gallantly; descrying now
and then an English ship going homeward under short-
ened sail, while we, with every inch of canvas crowded on,
dashed gayly past, and left her far behind. Towards evening the weather turned hazy, with a drizzling rain; and
soon became so thick, that we sailed, as it were, in a cloud.
Still we swept onward like a phantom ship, and many an
eager eye glanced up to where the Lookout on the mast
kept watch for Holyhead.

At length his long-expected cry was heard, and at the
same moment there shone out from the haze and mist
ahead a gleaming light, which presently was gone, and
soon returned, and soon was gone again. Whenever it
came back, the eyes of all on board brightened and
sparkled like itself: and there we all stood, watching this
revolving light upon the rock at Holyhead, and praising
it for its brightness and its friendly warning, and lauding
it, in short, above all other signal lights that ever were
displayed, until it once more glimmered faintly in the
distance, far behind us.

Then, it was time to fire a gun for a pilot; and, almost
before its smoke had cleared away, a little boat with a
light at her masthead came bearing down upon us, through
the darkness, swiftly. And presently, our sails being backed,
she ran alongside; and the hoarse pilot, wrapped and
muffled in pea-coats and shawls to the very bridge of his
weather-ploughed-up nose, stood bodily among us on the
deck. And I think, if that pilot had wanted to borrow fifty
pounds for an indefinite period on no security, we should
have engaged to lend it to him, among us, before his boat
had dropped astern, or, (which is the same thing) before every scrap of news in the paper he brought with
him had become the common property of all on board.

We turned in pretty late that night, and turned out

pretty early next morning. By six o'clock we clustered on the deck, prepared to go ashore; and looked upon the spires and roofs, and smoke, of Liverpool. By eight we all sat down in one of its hotels, to eat and drink together for the last time. And by nine we had shaken hands all round, and broken up our social company forever.

The country, by the railroad, seemed, as we rattled through it, like a luxuriant garden. The beauty of the fields (so small they looked!), the hedgerows, and the trees; the pretty cottages, the beds of flowers, the old churchyards, the antique houses, and every well-known object; the exquisite delights of that one journey crowding, in the short compass of a summer's day, the joy of many years, and winding up with Home, and all that makes it dear; no tongue can tell, or pen of mine describe.

CHAPTER 17

Slavery.

THE upholders of slavery in America—of the atrocities of which system I shall not write one word for which I have not ample proof and warrant—may be divided into three great classes.

The first are those more moderate and rational owners of human cattle who have come into the possession of them as , so many coins in their trading capital, but who admit the frightful nature of the Institution in the abstract, and perceive the dangers to society with which it is fraught: dangers which, however distant they may be, or howsoever tardy in their coming on, are as certain to fall upon its guilty head as is the Day of Judgment.

The second consists of all those owners, breeders, users, buyers, and sellers of slaves, who will, until the bloody chapter has a bloody end, own, breed, use, buy, and sell them at all hazards; who doggedly deny the horrors of the system, in the teeth of such a mass of evidence as never was brought to bear on any other subject, and to which the experience of every day contributes its immense amount; who would, at this or any other moment, gladly involve America in a war, civil or foreign, provided that it had for its sole end and object the assertion of their right to perpetuate slavery, and to whip and work and torture slaves, unquestioned by any human authority, and unassailed by any human power; who, when they speak of Freedom, mean the Freedom to oppress their kind, and to be savage, merciless, and cruel; and of whom every man on his own ground, in Republican America, is a more exacting, and a sterner, and a less responsible despot than the Caliph Haroun Alraschid in his angry robe of scarlet.

The third, and not the least numerous or influential, is composed of all that delicate gentility which cannot bear a superior, and cannot brook an equal; of that class whose Republicanism means, "I will not tolerate a man above me: and, of those below, none must approach too near;" whose pride, in a land where voluntary servitude is shunned as a disgrace, must be ministered to by slaves; and whose inalienable rights can only have their growth in Negro wrongs.

It has been sometimes urged that, in the unavailing efforts which have been made to advance the cause of Human Freedom in the republic of America (strange cause for history to treat of!), sufficient regard has not been had to the existence of the first class of persons; and it has been contended that they are hardly used, in being confounded with the second. This is, no doubt, the case; noble instances of pecuniary and personal sacrifice have already had their growth among them; and it is much to be regretted that the gulf between them and the advocates of emancipation should have been widened and deepened by any means: the rather as there are, beyond dispute, among these slave-owners, many kind masters who are tender in the exercise of their unnatural power. Still it is to be feared that this injustice is inseparable from the state of things with which humanity and truth are called upon to deal. Slavery is not a whit the more endurable because some hearts are to be found which can partially resist its hardening influences; nor can the indignant tide of honest wrath stand still, because in its onward course it overwhelms a few who are comparatively innocent among a host of guilty.

The ground most commonly taken by these better men among the advocates of slavery is this: "It is a bad system; and for myself I would willingly get rid of it, if I could; most willingly. But it is not so bad as you in England take it to be. You are deceived by the representations of the emancipationists. The greater part of my slaves are much attached to me. You will say that I do not allow them to be severely treated; but I will put it to you whether you believe that it can be a general practice to treat them inhumanly, when it would impair their value, and would be obviously against the interests of their masters."

Is it the interest of any man to steal, to game, to waste

his health and mental faculties by drunkenness, to lie, forswear himself, indulge hatred, seek desperate revenge, or do murder? No. All these are roads to ruin. And why, then, do men tread them? Because such inclinations are among the vicious qualities of mankind. Blot out, ye friends of slavery, from the catalogue of human passions, brutal lust, cruelty, and the abuse of irresponsible power (of all earthly temptations the most difficult to be resisted), and when ye have done so, and not before, we will inquire whether it be the interest of a master to lash and maim the slaves, over whose lives and limbs he has an absolute control!

But again: this class, together with that last one I have named, the miserable aristocracy spawned of a false republic, lift up their voices and exclaim, "Public opinion is all-sufficient to prevent such cruelty as you denounce." Public opinion! Why, public opinion in the slave States *is* slavery, is it not? Public opinion in the slave States has delivered the slaves over to the gentle mercies of their masters. Public opinion has made the laws, and denied the slaves legislative protection. Public opinion has knotted the lash, heated the branding-iron, loaded the rifle, and shielded the murderer. Public opinion threatens the abolitionist with death, if he venture to the South; and drags him with a rope about his middle, in broad unblushing noon, through the first city in the East. Public opinion has, within a few years, burned a slave alive at a slow fire in the city of St. Louis; and public opinion has to this day maintained upon the bench that estimable Judge who charged the Jury, impanelled there to try his murderers, that their most horrid deed was an act of public opinion, and, being so, must not be punished by the laws the public sentiment had made. Public opinion hailed this doctrine with a howl of wild applause, and set the prisoners free, to walk the city, men of mark, and influence, and station, as they had been before.

Public opinion! what class of men have an immense preponderance over the rest of the community in their power of representing public opinion in the legislature? The slave-owners. They send from their twelve States one hundred members, while the fourteen free States, with a free population nearly double, return but a hundred and forty-two. Before whom do the presidential candidates bow down the most humbly, on whom do they fawn the most fondly, and for whose tastes do they cater the most assiduously in their servile protestations? The slave-owners always.

Public opinion! hear the public opinion of the free South as expressed by its own members in the House of Representatives at Washington. "I have a great respect for the chair," quoth North Carolina, "I have a great respect for the chair as an officer of the House, and a great respect for him personally; nothing but that respect prevents me from rushing to the table, and tearing that petition which has just been presented for the abolition of slavery in the District of Columbia to pieces."—"I warn the abolitionists," says South Carolina, "ignorant, infuriated barbarians as they are, that if chance shall throw any of them into our hands, he may expect a felon's death."—"Let an abolitionist come within the borders of South Carolina," cries a third; mild Carolina's colleague; "and if we can catch him, we will try him, and, notwithstanding the interference of all the governments on earth, including the Federal Government, we will HANG him."

Public opinion has made this law.—It has declared that in Washington, in that city which takes its name from the father of American liberty, any justice of the peace may bind with fetters any Negro passing down the street, and thrust him into jail: no offence on the black man's part is necessary. The justice says, "I choose to think this man a runaway:" and locks him up. Public opinion empowers the man of law, when this is done, to advertise the Negro in the newspapers, warning his owner to come and claim him, or he will be sold to pay the jail fees. But supposing he is a free black, and has no owner, it may naturally be presumed that he is set at liberty. No: HE IS SOLD TO RECOMPENSE HIS JAILER. This has been done again, and again, and again. He has no means of proving his freedom; has no adviser, messenger, or assistance of any sort or kind; no investigation into his case is made, or inquiry instituted. He, a free man, who may have served for years, and bought his liberty, is thrown into jail on no process, for no crime, and on no pretence of crime: and is sold to pay the jail fees. This seems incredible, even of America, but it is the law.

Public opinion is deferred to in such cases as the following; which is headed in the newspapers—

"Interesting Law-case.

"An interesting case is now on trial in the Supreme Court, arising out of the following facts. A gentleman residing in Maryland had allowed an aged pair of his slaves substantial though not legal freedom for several years. While thus living, a daughter was born to them, who grew up in the same liberty, until she married a free negro, and went with him to reside in Pennsylvania. They had several children, and lived unmolested until the original owner died, when his heir attempted to regain them; but the magistrate before whom they were brought decided that he had no jurisdiction in the case. *The owner seized the woman and her children in the night, and carried them to Maryland.*"

"Cash for negroes," "cash for negroes," "cash for negroes," is the heading of advertisements in great capitals down the long columns of the crowded journals. Woodcuts of a runaway Negro with manacled hands, crouching beneath a bluff pursuer in top-boots, who, having caught him, grasps him by the throat, agreeably diversify the pleasant text. The leading article protests against "that abominable and hellish doctrine of abolition, which is repugnant alike to every law of God and nature." The delicate mamma, who smiles her acquiescence in this sprightly writing as she reads the paper in her cool piazza, quiets her youngest child who clings about her skirts by promising the boy "a whip to beat the little niggers with."—But the Negroes, little and big, are protected by public opinion.

Let us try this public opinion by another test, which is important in three points of view: first, as showing how desperately timid of the public opinion slave-owners are in their delicate descriptions of fugitive slaves in widely circulated newspapers; secondly, as showing how perfectly contented the slaves are, and how very seldom they run away; thirdly, as exhibiting their entire freedom from scar, or blemish, or any mark of cruel infliction, as their pictures are drawn, not by lying abolitionists, but by their own truthful masters.

The following are a few specimens of the advertisements in the public papers. It is only four years since the oldest among them appeared; and others of the same nature continue to be published every day in shoals.

"Ran away, Negress Caroline. Had on a collar with one prong turned down."

"Ran away, a black woman, Betsy. Had an iron bar on her right leg."

"Ran away, the negro Manuel. Much marked with irons."

"Ran away, the negress Fanny. Had on an iron band about her neck."

"Ran away, a negro boy about twelve years old. Had round his neck a chain dog-collar with 'De Lampert' engraved on it."

"Ran away, the negro Hown. Has a ring of iron on his left foot. Also, Grise, *his wife,* having a ring and chain on the left leg."

"Ran away, a negro boy named James. Said boy was ironed when he left me."

"Committed to jail, a man who calls his name John. He has a clog of iron on his right foot which will weigh four or five pounds."

"Detained at the police jail, the negro wench Myra. Has several marks of LASHING, and has irons on her feet."

"Ran away, a negro woman and two children. A few days before she went off, I burnt her with a hot iron, on the left side of her face. I tried to make the letter M."

"Ran away, a negro man named Henry; his left eye out, some scars from a dirk on and under his left arm, and much scarred with the whip."

"One hundred dollars reward, for a negro fellow, Pompey, 40 years old. He is branded on the left jaw."

"Committed to jail, a negro man. Has no toes on the left foot."

"Ran away, a negro woman named Rachel. Has lost all her toes except the large one."

"Ran away, Sam. He was shot a short time since through the hand, and has several shots in his left arm and side."

"Ran away, my negro man Dennis. Said negro has been shot in the left arm between the shoulder and elbow, which has paralyzed the left hand."

"Ran away, my negro man named Simon. He has been shot badly, in his back and right arm."

"Ran away, a negro named Arthur. Has a considerable scar across his breast and each arm, made by a knife; loves to talk much of the goodness of God."

"Twenty-five dollars reward for my man Isaac. He has

a scar on his forehead, caused by a blow; and one on his back, made by a shot from a pistol."

"Ran away, a negro girl called Mary. Has a small scar over her eye, a good many teeth missing, the letter A is branded on her cheek and forehead."

"Ran away, negro Ben. Has a scar on his right hand; his thumb and forefinger being injured by being shot last fall. A part of the bone came out. He has also one or two large scars on his back and hips."

"Detained at the jail, a mulatto, named Tom. Has a scar on the right cheek, and appears to have been burned with powder on the face."

"Ran away, a negro man named Ned. Three of his fingers are drawn into the palm of his hand by a cut. Has a scar on the back of his neck, nearly half round, done by a knife."

"Was committed to jail, a negro man. Says his name is Josiah. His back very much scarred by the whip: and branded on the thigh and hips in three or four places, thus (J M). The rim of his right ear has been bit or cut off."

"Fifty dollars reward, for my fellow Edward. He has a scar on the corner of his mouth, two cuts on and under his arm, and the letter E on his arm."

"Ran away, negro boy Ellie. Has a scar on one of his arms from the bite of a dog."

"Ran away, from the plantation of James Surgette, the following negroes: Randal, has one ear cropped; Bob, has lost one eye; Kentucky Tom, has one jaw broken."

"Ran away, Anthony. One of his ears cut off, and his left hand cut with an axe."

"Fifty dollars reward for the negro Jim Blake. Has a piece cut out of each ear, and the middle finger of the left hand cut off to the second joint."

"Ran away, a negro woman named Maria. Has a scar on one side of her cheek, by a cut. Some scars on her back."

"Ran away, the Mulatto wench Mary. Has a cut on the left arm, a scar on the left shoulder, and two upper teeth missing."

I should say, perhaps, in explanation of this latter piece of description, that, among the other blessings which public opinion secures to the Negroes, is the common practice of violently punching out their teeth. To make them wear iron collars by day and night, and to worry them with dogs, are practices almost too ordinary to deserve mention.

"Ran away, my man Fountain. Has holes in his ears, a scar on the right side of his forehead, has been shot in the hind parts of his legs, and is marked on the back with the whip."

"Two hundred and fifty dollars reward for my negro man Jim. He is much marked with shot in his right thigh. The shot entered on the outside, half-way between the hip and knee joints."

"Brought to jail, John. Left ear cropt."

"Taken up, a negro man. Is very much scarred about the face and body, and has the left ear bit off."

"Ran away, a black girl named Mary. Has a scar on her cheek, and the end of one of her toes cut off."

"Ran away, my mulatto woman, Judy. She has had her right arm broke."

"Ran away, my negro man, Levi. His left hand has been burnt, and I think the end of his forefinger is off."

"Ran away, a negro man NAMED WASHINGTON. Has lost a part of his middle finger, and the end of his little finger."

"Twenty-five dollars reward for my man John. The tip of his nose is bit off."

"Twenty-five dollars reward for the negro slave Sally. Walks *as though* crippled in the back."

"Ran away, Joe Dennis. Has a small notch in one of his ears."

"Ran away, negro boy, Jack. Has a small crop out of his left ear."

"Ran away, a negro man, named Ivory. Has a small piece cut out of the top of each ear."

While upon the subject of ears, I may observe that a distinguished abolitionist in New York once received a Negro's ear, which had been cut off close to the head, in a general post letter. It was forwarded by the free and independent gentleman who had caused it to be amputated, with a polite request that he would place the specimen in his "collection."

I could enlarge this catalogue with broken arms, and broken legs, and gashed flesh, and missing teeth, and lacerated backs, and bites of dogs, and brands of red-hot irons innumerable: but, as my readers will be sufficiently sickened and repelled already, I will turn to another branch of the subject.

These advertisements, of which a similar collection might be made for every year, and month, and week, and day; and which are coolly read in families as things of course, and as a part of the current news and small talk; will serve to show how very much the slaves profit by public opinion, and how tender it is in their behalf. But it may be worth while to inquire how the slave-owners, and the class of society to which great numbers of them belong, defer to public opinion in their conduct, not to their slaves, but to each other; how they are accustomed to restrain their passions; what their bearing is among themselves; whether they are fierce or gentle, whether their social customs be brutal, sanguinary, and violent, or bear the impress of civilization and refinement.

That we may have no partial evidence from abolitionists in this inquiry either, I will once more turn to their own newspapers, and I will confine myself, this time, to a selection from paragraphs which appeared from day to day during my visit to America, and which refer to occurrences happening while I was there. The italics in these extracts, as in the foregoing, are my own.

These cases did not ALL occur, it will be seen, in territory actually belonging to legalized Slave States, though most, and those the very worst among them, did, as their counterparts constantly do; but the position of the scenes of action in reference to places immediately at hand, where slavery is the law; and the strong resemblance between that class of outrages and the rest; lead to the just presumption that the character of the parties concerned was formed in slave districts, and brutalized by slave customs.

"Horrible Tragedy.

"By a slip from *The Southport Telegraph,* Wisconsin, we learn that the Hon. Charles C. P. Arndt, Member of the Council for Brown county, was shot dead *on the floor of the Council chamber,* by James R. Vinyard, Member from Grant county. *The affair* grew out of a nomination for Sheriff of Grant county. Mr. E. S. Baker was nominated and supported by Mr. Arndt. This nomination was opposed by Vinyard, who wanted the appointment to vest in his own brother. In the course of debate, the deceased made some statements which Vinyard pronounced false, and made use of violent and insulting language, dealing largely in personalities, to which Mr. A. made no reply. After the adjournment, Mr. A. stepped up to Vinyard, and requested him to retract, which he refused to do, repeating the offensive words. Mr. Arndt then made a blow at Vinyard, who drew back a pace, drew a pistol, and shot him dead.

"The issue appears to have been provoked on the part of Vinyard, who was determined at all hazards to defeat the appointment of Baker, and who, himself defeated, turned his ire and revenge upon the unfortunate Arndt."

"The Wisconsin Tragedy.

"Public indignation runs high in the territory of Wisconsin, in relation to the murder of C. C. P. Arndt, in the Legislative Hall of the Territory. Meetings have been held in different counties of Wisconsin, denouncing *the practice of secretly bearing arms in the Legislative chambers of the country.* We have seen the account of the expulsion of James R. Vinyard, the perpetrator of the bloody deed, and are amazed to hear, that, after this expulsion by those who saw Vinyard kill Mr. Arndt in the presence of his aged father, who was on a visit to see his son, little dreaming that he was to witness his murder, *Judge Dunn has discharged Vinyard on bail.* The Miners' Free Press speaks *in terms of merited rebuke* at the outrage upon the feelings of the people of Wisconsin. Vinyard was within arm's length of Mr. Arndt, when he took such deadly aim at him, that he never spoke. Vinyard might at pleasure, being so near, have only wounded him, but he chose to kill him."

"Murder.

"By a letter in a St. Louis paper of the 14th, we notice a terrible outrage at Burlington, Iowa. A Mr. Bridgman having had a difficulty with a citizen of the place, Mr.

Ross; a brother-in-law of the latter provided himself with one of Colt's revolving pistols, met Mr. B. in the street, *and discharged the contents of five of the barrels at him: each shot taking effect.* Mr. B., though horribly wounded, and dying, returned the fire, and killed Ross on the spot."

"Terrible death of Robert Potter.

"From the 'Caddo Gazette,' of the 12th inst., we learn the frightful death of Colonel Robert Potter. . . . He was beset in his house by an enemy, named Rose. He sprang from his couch, seized his gun, and, in his night clothes, rushed from the house. For about two hundred yards his speed seemed to defy his pursuers; but, getting entangled in a thicket, he was captured. Rose told him *that he intended to act a generous part,* and give him a chance for his life. He then told Potter that he might run, and he should not be interrupted till he reached a certain distance. Potter started at the word of command, and before a gun was fired he had reached the lake. His first impulse was to jump into the water and dive for it, which he did. Rose was close behind him, and formed his men on the bank ready to shoot him as he rose. In a few seconds he came up to breathe; and scarce had his head reached the surface of the water when it was completely riddled with the shot of their guns, and he sank, to rise no more!"

"Murder in Arkansas.

"We understand *that a severe rencontre came off* a few days since in the Seneca Nation, between Mr. Loose, the sub-agent of the mixed band of the Senecas, Quapaw, and Shawnees, and Mr. James Gillespie, of the mercantile firm of Thomas G. Allison and Co., of Maysville, Benton County, Ark., in which the latter was slain with a bowie-knife. Some difficulty had for some time existed between the parties. It is said that Major Gillespie brought on the attack with a cane. A severe conflict ensued, during which two pistols were fired by Gillespie and one by Loose. Loose then stabbed Gillespie with one of those never-failing weapons, a bowie-knife. The death of Major G. is much regretted, as he was a liberal-minded and energetic man.

Since the above was in type, we have learned that Major Allison has stated to some of our citizens in town that Mr. Loose gave the first blow. We forbear to give any particulars, as *the matter will be the subject of judicial investigation.*"

"Foul Deed.

"The steamer Thames, just from Missouri river, brought us a handbill, offering a reward of 500 · dollars, for the person who assassinated Lilburn W. Baggs, late Governor of this State, at Independence, on the night of the 6th inst. Governor Baggs, it is stated in a written memorandum, was not dead, but mortally wounded.

"Since the above was written, we received a note from the clerk of the Thames, giving the following particulars. Gov. Baggs was shot by some villain on Friday, 6th inst., in the evening, while sitting in a room in his own house in Independence. His son, a boy, hearing a report, ran into the room, and found the Governor sitting in his chair, with his jaw fallen down, and his head leaning back: on discovering the injury done to his father, he gave the alarm. Foot tracks were found in the garden below the window, and a pistol picked up supposed to have been overloaded, and thrown from the hand of the scoundrel who fired it. Three buck shots of a heavy load took effect; one going through his mouth, one into the brain, and another probably in or near the brain; all going into the back part of the neck and head. The Governor was still alive on the morning of the 7th; but no hopes for his recovery by his friends, and but slight hopes from his physicians.

"A man was suspected, and the Sheriff most probably has possession of him by this time.

"The pistol was one of a pair stolen some days previous from a baker in Independence, and the legal authorities have the description of the other."

"Rencontre.

"An unfortunate *affair* took place on Friday evening in Chartres Street, in which one of our most respectable citizens received a dangerous wound, from a poignard, in the abdomen. From the Bee (New Orleans) of yesterday, we learn the following particulars. It appears that an article was published in the French side of the paper on Monday last, containing some strictures on the Artillery Battalion for firing their guns on Sunday morning, in answer to those from the Ontario and Woodbury, and thereby much alarm was caused to the families of those persons who were out all night preserving the peace of the city. Major C. Gally, Commander of the battalion, resenting this, called at the office and demanded the author's name; that of Mr. P. Arpin was given to him, who was absent at the time. Some angry words then passed with one of the proprietors, and a challenge followed; the friends of both parties tried to arrange the affair, but failed to do so. On Friday evening, about seven o'clock, Major Gally met Mr. P. Arpin in Chartres Street, and accosted him. 'Are you Mr. Arpin?'

" 'Yes, sir.'

" 'Then I have to tell you that you are a ——' (applying an appropriate epithet).

" 'I shall remind you of your. words, sir.'

" 'But I have said I would break my cane on your shoulders.'

" 'I know it, but I have not yet received the blow.'

"At these words, Major Gally, having a cane in his hands, struck Mr. Arpin across the face, and the latter drew a poignard from his pocket and stabbed Major Gally in the abdomen.

"Fears are entertained that the wound will be mortal. *We understand that Mr. Arpin has given security for his appearance at the Criminal Court to answer the charge.*"

"Affray in Mississippi.

"On the 27th ult., in an affray near Carthage, Leake county, Mississippi, between James Cottingham and John Wilburn, the latter was shot by the former, and so horribly wounded, that there was no hope of his recovery. On the 2d instant, there was an affray at Carthage between A. C. Sharkey and George Goff, in which the latter was shot, and thought mortally wounded. Sharkey delivered himself up to the authorities, *but changed his mind and escaped!*"

"Personal Encounter.

"An encounter took place in Sparta, a few days since, between the barkeeper of an hotel, and a man named Bury. It appears that Bury had become somewhat noisy, *and that the barkeeper, determined to preserve order, had threatened to shoot Bury,* whereupon Bury drew a pistol and shot the barkeeper down. He was not dead at the last accounts, but slight hopes were entertained of his recovery."

"Duel.

"The clerk of the steamboat *Tribune* informs us that another duel was fought on Tuesday last, by Mr. Robbins, a bank officer in Vicksburg, and Mr. Fall, the editor of the Vicksburg Sentinel. According to the arrangement, the parties had six pistols each, which, after the word 'Fire!' *they were to discharge as fast as they pleased.* Fall fired two pistols without effect. Mr. Robbins's first shot took effect in Fall's thigh, who fell, and was unable to continue the combat."

"Affray in Clarke County.

"An *unfortunate affray* occurred in Clarke county (Mo.) near Waterloo, on Tuesday the 19th ult., which originated in settling the partnership concerns of Messrs. M'Kane and M'Allister, who had been engaged in the business of distilling, and resulted in the death of the latter, who was shot down by Mr. M'Kane, because of his attempting to take possession of seven barrels of whiskey, the property of M'Kane, which had been knocked off to M'Allister at a sheriff's sale at one dollar per barrel. M'Kane immediately fled, *and at the latest dates had not been taken.*

"*This unfortunate affray* caused considerable excitement in the neighborhood, as both the parties were men with large families depending upon them and stood well in the community."

I will quote but one more paragraph, which, by reason of its monstrous absurdity, may be a relief to these atrocious deeds.

"Affair of Honor.

"We have just heard the particulars of a meeting which took place on Six Mile Island, on Tuesday, between two young bloods of our city: Samuel Thurston, *aged fifteen,* and William Hine, *aged thirteen years.* They were attended by young gentlemen of the same age. The weapons used on the occasion were a couple of Dickson's best rifles; the distance, thirty yards. They took one fire, without any damage being sustained by either party, except the ball of Thurston's gun passing through the crown of Hine's hat. *Through the intercession of the Board of Honor,* the challenge was withdrawn, and the difference amicably adjusted."

If the reader will picture to himself the kind of Board of Honor which amicably adjusted the difference between these two little boys, who in any other part of the world would have been amicably adjusted on two porters' backs, and soundly flogged with birchen rods, he will be possessed, no doubt, with as strong a sense of its ludicrous character as that which sets me laughing whenever its image rises up before me.

Now, I appeal to every human mind imbued with the commonest of common sense, and the commonest of common humanity; to all dispassionate, reasoning creatures, of any shade of opinion: and ask, with these revolting evidences of the state of society which exists in and about the slave districts of America before them, can they have a doubt of the real condition of the slave, or can they for a moment make a compromise between the institution or any of its flagrant fearful features, and their own just consciences? Will they say of any tale of cruelty and horror, however aggravated in degree, that it is improbable, when they can turn to the public prints, and, running, read such signs as these, laid before them by the men who rule the slaves: in their own acts, and under their own hands?

Do we not know that the worst deformity and ugliness of slavery are at once the cause and the effect of the reckless license taken by these freeborn outlaws? Do we not know that the man who has been born and bred among its wrongs; who has seen in his childhood husbands obliged, at the word of command, to flog their wives; women, indecently compelled to hold up their own garments that men might lay the heavier stripes upon their legs, driven and harried by brutal overseers in their time of travail, and becoming mothers on the field of toil, under the very lash itself; who has read in youth, and seen his virgin sisters read, descriptions of runaway men and women, and their disfigured persons, which could not be published elsewhere of so much stock upon a farm, or at a show of beasts:—do we not know that that man, whenever his wrath is kindled up, will be a brutal savage? Do we not know that as he is a coward in his domestic life, stalking among his shrinking men and women slaves armed with his heavy whip, so he will be a coward out of doors, and, carrying cowards' weapons hidden in his breast, will shoot men down and stab them when he quarrels? And if our reason did not teach us this and much beyond; if we were such idiots as to close our eyes to that fine mode of training which rears up such men; should we not know that they who among their equals stab and pistol in the legislative halls, and in the counting-house, and on the market-place, and in all the elsewhere peaceful pursuits of life, must be to their dependants, even though they were free servants, so many merciless and unrelenting tyrants?

What! shall we declaim against the ignorant peasantry of Ireland, and mince the matter when these American taskmasters are in question? Shall we cry shame on the brutality of those who hamstring cattle: and spare the lights of Freedom upon earth who notch the ears of men and women, cut pleasant posies in the shrinking flesh, learn to write with pens of red-hot iron on the human face, rack their poetic fancies for liveries of mutilation which their slaves shall wear for life and carry to the grave, break living limbs as did the soldiery who mocked and slew the Saviour of the world, and set defenceless creatures up for targets? Shall we whimper over legends of the tortures practised on each other by the Pagan Indians, and smile upon the cruelties of Christian men? Shall we, so long as these things last, exult above the scattered remnants of that stately race, and triumph in the white enjoyment of their broad possessions? Rather, for me, restore the forest and the Indian village; in lieu of stars and stripes, let some poor feather flutter in the breeze; replace the streets and squares by wigwams; and though the death-song of a hundred haughty warriors fill the air, it will be music to the shriek of one unhappy slave.

On one theme, which is commonly before our eyes, and in respect of which our national character is changing fast, let the plain Truth be spoken, and let us not, like dastards, beat about the bush by hinting at the Spaniard and the fierce Italian. When knives are drawn by Englishmen in conflict, let it be said and known: "We owe this change to Republican Slavery. These are the weapons of Freedom. With sharp points and edges such as these, Liberty in America hews and hacks her slaves; or, failing that pursuit, her sons devote them to a better use, and turn them on each other."

CHAPTER 18

Concluding Remarks.

THERE are many passages in this book where I have been
at some pains to resist the temptation of troubling my
readers with my own deductions and conclusions: preferring that they should judge for themselves, from such
premises as I have laid before them. My only object in
the outset was, to carry them with me faithfully wheresoever I went: and that task I have discharged.

But I may be pardoned if, on such a theme as the general character of the American people, and the general
character of their social system, as presented to a stranger's eyes, I desire to express my own opinions in a few
words, before I bring these volumes to a close.

They are, by nature, frank, brave, cordial, hospitable,
and affectionate. Cultivation and refinement seem but to
enhance their warmth of heart and ardent enthusiasm;
and it is the possession of these latter qualities in a most
remarkable degree which renders an educated American
one of the most endearing and most generous of
friends. I never was so won upon as by this class; never
yielded up my full confidence and esteem so readily and
pleasurably as to them; never can make again, in half a
year, so many friends for whom I seem to entertain
the regard of half a life.

These qualities are natural, I implicitly believe, to the
whole people. That they are, however, sadly sapped and
blighted in their growth among the mass; and that there
are influences at work which endanger them still more, and

give but little present promise of their healthy restoration, is a truth that ought to be told.

It is an essential part of every national character to pique itself mightily upon its faults, and to deduce tokens of its virtue or its wisdom from their very exaggeration. One great blemish in the popular mind of America, and the prolific parent of an innumerable brood of evils, is Universal Distrust. Yet the American citizen plumes himself upon this spirit, even when he is sufficiently dispassionate to perceive the ruin it works; and will often adduce it, in spite of his own reason, as an instance of the great sagacity and acuteness of the people, and their superior shrewdness and independence.

"You carry," says the stranger, "this jealousy and distrust into every transaction of public life. By repelling worthy men from your legislative assemblies, it has bred up a class of candidates for the suffrage, who, in their every act, disgrace your Institutions and your people's choice. It has rendered you so fickle, and so given to change, that your inconstancy has passed into a proverb; for you no sooner set up an idol firmly than you are sure to pull it down and dash it into fragments: and this because, directly you reward a benefactor, or a public servant, you distrust him, merely because he *is* rewarded; and immediately apply yourselves to find out, either that you have been too bountiful in your acknowledgments, or he remiss in his deserts. Any man who attains a high place among you, from the President downwards, may date his downfall from that moment; for any printed lie that any notorious villain pens, although it militate directly against the character and conduct of a life, appeals at once to your distrust, and is believed. You will strain at a gnat in the way of trustfulness and confidence, however fairly won and well deserved; but you will swallow a whole caravan of camels, if they be laden with unworthy doubts and mean suspicions. Is this well, think you, or likely to elevate the character of the governors or the governed among you?"

The answer is invariably the same: "There's freedom of opinion here, you know. Every man thinks for himself, and we are not to be easily over-reached. That's how our people come to be suspicious."

Another prominent feature is the love of "smart" dealing: which gilds over many a swindle and gross breach of trust; many a defalcation, public and private; and enables many a knave to hold his head up with the best, who well deserves a halter: though it has not been without its retributive operation, for this smartness has done more in a few years to impair the public credit, and to cripple the public resources, than dull honesty, however rash, could have effected in a century. The merits of a broken speculation, or a bankruptcy, or of a successful scoundrel, are not gauged by its or his observance of the golden rule, "Do as you would be done by," but are considered with reference to their smartness. I recollect, on both occasions of our passing that ill-fated Cairo on the Mississippi, remarking on the bad effects such gross deceits must have, when they exploded, in generating a want of confidence abroad, and discouraging foreign investment: but I was given to understand that this was a very smart scheme, by which a deal of money had been made: and that its smartest feature was, that they forgot these things abroad in a very short time, and speculated again as freely as ever. The following dialogue I have held a hundred times: "Is it not a very disgraceful circumstance that such a man as So-and-so should be acquiring a large property by the most infamous and odious means, and, notwithstanding all the crimes of which he has been guilty, should be tolerated and abetted by your citizens? He is a public nuisance, is he not?"—"Yes, sir."—"A convicted liar?"—"Yes, sir."—"He has been kicked, and cuffed, and caned?"—"Yes, sir."—"And he is utterly dishonorable, debased, and profligate?"—"Yes, sir."—"In the name of wonder, then, what is his merit?"—"Well, sir, he is a smart man."

In like manner, all kinds of deficient and impolitic usages are referred to the national love of trade; though, oddly enough, it would be a weighty charge against a foreigner that he regarded the Americans as a trading people. The love of trade is assigned as a reason for that comfortless custom, so very prevalent in country towns, of married persons living in hotels, having no fireside of their own, and seldom meeting, from early morning until late at night, but at the hasty public meals. The love of trade is a reason why the literature of America is to remain forever unprotected: "For we are a trading people, and don't care for poetry:" though we *do,* by the way, profess to be very proud of our poets: while healthful amusements, cheerful means of recreation, and wholesome fancies must fade before the stern utilitarian joys of trade.

These three characteristics are strongly presented at every turn, full in the stranger's view. But, the foul growth of America has a more tangled root than this; and it strikes its fibres deep in its licentious Press.

Schools may be erected, East, West, North, and South; pupils be taught, and masters reared, by scores upon scores of thousands; colleges may thrive, churches may be crammed, temperance may be diffused, and advancing knowledge in all other forms walk through the land with giant strides: but while the newspaper press of America is in, or near, its present abject state, high moral improvement in that country is hopeless. Year by year, it must and will go back; year by year, the tone of public feeling must sink lower down; year by year, the Congress and the Senate must become of less account before all decent men; and year by year, the memory of the Great Fathers of the Revolution must be outraged more and more, in the bad life of their degenerate child.

Among the herd of journals which are published in the States, there are some, the reader scarcely need be told, of character and credit. From personal intercourse with accomplished gentlemen connected with publications of this class, I have derived both pleasure and profit. But the name of these is Few, and of the others Legion; and the influence of the good is powerless to counteract the mortal poison of the bad.

Among the gentry of America; among the well-informed and moderate; in the learned professions; at the bar and on the bench: there is, as there can be, but one opinion, in reference to the vicious character of these infamous journals. It is sometimes contended—I will not say strangely, for it is natural to seek excuses for such a disgrace—that their influence is not so great as a visitor would suppose. I must be pardoned for saying that there is no warrant for this plea, and that every fact and circumstance tends directly to the opposite conclusion.

When any man, of any grade of desert in intellect or character, can climb to any public distinction, no matter what, in America, without first grovelling down upon the earth, and bending the knee before this monster of depravity; when any private excellence is safe from its attacks; when any social confidence is left unbroken by it, or any tie of social decency and honor is held in the least regard; when any man in that Free Country has freedom of opinion, and presumes to think for himself, and speak for himself, without humble reference to a censorship which, for its rampant ignorance and base dishonesty, he utterly loathes and despises in his heart; when those who most acutely feel its infamy, and the reproach it casts upon the nation, and who most denounce it to each other, dare to set their heels upon, and crush it openly, in the sight of all men: then I will believe that its influence is lessening, and men are returning to their manly senses. But while that Press has its evil eye in every house, and its black hand in every appointment in the state, from a president to a postman; while, with ribald slander for its only stock in trade, it is the standard literature of an enormous class, who must find their reading in a newspaper, or they will not read at all; so long must its odium be upon the country's head, and so long must the evil it works be plainly visible in the Republic.

To those who are accustomed to the leading English journals, or to the respectable journals of the Continent of Europe; to those who are accustomed to anything else in print and paper; it would be impossible, without an amount of extract for which I have neither space nor inclination, to convey an adequate idea of this frightful engine in America. But, if any man desire confirmation of my statement on this head, let him repair to any place in this city of London, where scattered numbers of these publications are to be found; and there let him form his own opinion.[1]

[1] NOTE TO THE ORIGINAL EDITION.—Or let him refer to an able and perfectly truthful article in *The Foreign Quarterly Review*, published in the present month of October; to which my attention has been attracted, since these sheets have been passing through the press. He will find some specimens there, by no means remarkable to any man who has been in America, but sufficiently striking to one who has not.

It would be well, there can be no doubt, for the American people as a whole, if they loved the Real less, and the Ideal somewhat more. It would be well, if there were greater encouragement to lightness of heart and gayety, and a wider cultivation of what is beautiful, without being eminently and directly useful. But here I think the general remonstrance, "We are a new country," which is so often advanced as an excuse for defects which are quite unjustifiable, as being of right only the slow growth of an old one, may be very reasonably urged: and I yet hope to hear of there being some other national amusement in the United States, besides newspaper politics.

They certainly are not a humorous people, and their temperament always impressed me as being of a dull and gloomy character. In shrewdness of remark, and a certain cast-iron quaintness, the Yankees, or people of New England, unquestionably take the lead; as they do in most other evidences of intelligence. But in travelling about, out of the large cities—as I have remarked in former parts of these volumes—I was quite oppressed by the prevailing seriousness and melancholy air of business: which was so general and unvarying, that, at every new town I came to, I seemed to meet the very same people whom I had left behind me at the last. Such defects as are perceptible in the national manners seem, to me, to be referable, in a great degree, to this cause: which has generated a dull, sullen persistence in coarse usages, and rejected the graces of life as undeserving of attention. There is no doubt that Washington, who was always most scrupulous and exact on points of ceremony, perceived the tendency towards this mistake, even in his time, and did his utmost to correct it.

I cannot hold, with other writers on these subjects, that the prevalence of various forms of Dissent in America is in any way attributable to the non-existence there of an Established Church: indeed, I think the temper of the people, if it admitted of such an Institution being founded amongst them, would lead them to desert it, as a matter of course, merely because it *was* established. But, supposing it to exist, I doubt its probable efficacy in summoning the wandering sheep to one great fold, simply because of the immense amount of Dissent which prevails at home; and because I do not find in America any one form of religion with which we in Europe, or even in England, are unacquainted. Dissenters resort thither in great numbers, as other people do, simply because it is a land of resort; and great settlements of them are founded, because ground can be purchased, and towns and villages reared, where there were none of the human creation before. But even the Shakers emigrated from England; our country is not unknown to Mr. Joseph Smith, the apostle of Mormonism, or to his benighted disciples; I have beheld religious scenes myself, in some of our populous towns, which can hardly be surpassed by an American camp-meeting; and I am not aware that any instance of superstitious imposture on the one hand, and superstitious credulity on the other, has had its origin in the United States, which we cannot more than parallel by the precedents of Mrs. Southcote, Mary Tofts the rabbit-breeder, or even Mr. Thom of Canterbury: which latter case arose some time after the dark ages had passed away.

The Republican Institutions of America undoubtedly lead the people to assert their self-respect and their equality; but a traveller is bound to bear those Institutions in his mind, and not hastily to resent the near approach of a class of strangers who, at home, would keep aloof. This characteristic, when it was tinctured with no foolish pride, and stopped short of no honest service, never offended me; and I very seldom, if ever, experienced its rude or unbecoming display. Once or twice it was comically developed, as in the following case; but this was an amusing incident, and not the rule, or near it.

I wanted a pair of boots at a certain town, for I had none to travel in, but those with the memorable cork soles, which were much too hot for the fiery decks of a steamboat. I therefore sent a message to an artist in boots, importing, with my compliments, that I should be happy to see him, if he would do me the polite favor to call. He very kindly returned for answer, that he would "look round" at six o'clock that evening.

I was lying on the sofa, with a book and a wine-glass, at about that time, when the door opened, and a gentleman in a stiff cravat, within a year or two on either side of thirty, entered, in his hat and gloves; walked up to the looking-glass; arranged his hair; took off his gloves; slowly produced a measure from the uttermost depths of his coat-pocket; and requested me, in a languid tone, to "unfix" my straps. I complied, but looked with some curiosity at his hat, which was still upon his head. It might have been that, or it might have been the heat—but he took it off. Then, he sat himself down on a chair opposite to me; rested an arm on each knee; and, leaning forward very much, took from the ground, by a great effort, the specimen of metropolitan workmanship which I had just pulled off: whistling pleasantly as he did so. He turned it over and over; surveyed it with a contempt no language can express; and inquired if I wished him to fix me a boot like *that?* I courteously replied that, provided the boots were large enough, I would leave the rest to him; that, if convenient and practicable, I should not object to their bearing some resemblance to the model then before him; but that I would be entirely guided by, and would beg to leave the whole subject to, his judgment and discretion. "You ain't partickler about this scoop in the heel I suppose, then?" says he. "We don't foller that here." I repeated my last observation. He looked at himself in the glass again; went closer to it to dash a grain or two of dust out of the corner of his eye; and settled his cravat. All this time my leg and foot were in the air. "Nearly ready, sir?" I inquired. "Well, pretty nigh," he said; "keep steady." I kept as steady as I could, both in foot and face; and having by this time got the dust out, and found his pencil-case, he measured me, and made the necessary notes. When he had finished, he fell into his old attitude, and, taking up the boot again, mused for some time. "And this," he said at last, "is an English boot, is it? This is a London boot, eh?" "That, sir," I replied, "is a London boot." He mused over it again, after the manner of Hamlet with Yorick's skull; nodded his head, as who should say, "I pity the Institutions that led to the production of this boot;" rose; put up his pencil, notes, and paper—glancing at himself in the glass all the time— put on his hat; drew on his gloves very slowly; and finally walked out. When he had been gone about a minute, the door re-opened, and his hat and his head re-appeared. He looked round the room, and at the boot again, which was still lying on the floor; appeared thoughtful for a minute, and then said, "Well, good arternoon." "Good afternoon, sir," said I: and that was the end of the interview.

There is but one other head on which I wish to offer a remark; and that has reference to the public health. In so vast a country, where there are thousands of millions of acres of land yet unsettled and uncleared, and on every rood of which vegetable decomposition is annually taking place; where there are so many great rivers, and such opposite varieties of climate; there cannot fail to be a great amount of sickness at certain seasons. But I may venture to say, after conversing with many members of the medical profession in America, that I am not singular in the opinion that much of the disease which does prevail might be avoided, if a few common precautions were observed. Greater means of personal cleanliness are indispensable to this end; the custom of hastily swallowing large quantities of animal food three times a day, and rushing back to sedentary pursuits after each meal, must be changed; the gentler sex must go more wisely clad, and take more healthful exercise; and in the latter clause the males must be included also. Above all, in public institutions, and throughout the whole of every town and city, the system of ventilation, and drainage, and removal of impurities requires to be thoroughly revised. There is no local Legislature in America which may not study Mr. Chadwick's excellent Report upon the Sanitary Condition of our Laboring Classes with immense advantage.

I have now arrived at the close of this book. I have little reason to believe, from certain warnings I have had since I returned to England, that it will be tenderly or favorably received by the American people; and, as I have written the Truth in relation to the mass of those who form their judgments and express their opinions, it will be seen that I have no desire to court, by any adventitious means, the popular applause.

It is enough for me to know that what I have set down in these pages cannot cost me a single friend on the other side of the Atlantic, who is, in anything, deserving of the name. For the rest, I put my trust, implicitly, in the spirit in which they have been conceived and penned; and I can bide my time.

I have made no reference to my reception, nor have I suffered it to influence me in what I have written; for, in either case, I should have offered but a sorry acknowledgment, compared with what I bear within my breast, towards those partial readers of my former books across the Water, who met me with an open hand, and not with one that closed upon an iron muzzle.

POSTSCRIPT

AT a Public Dinner given to me on Saturday, the 18th of April, 1868, in the City of New York, by two hundred representatives of the Press of the United States of America, I made the following observations among others:

"So much of my voice has lately been heard in the land, that I might have been contented with troubling you no further from my present standing-point, were it not a duty with which I henceforth charge myself, not only here, but on every suitable occasion, whatsoever and wheresoever, to express my high and grateful sense of my second reception in America, and to bear my honest testimony to the national generosity and magnanimity. Also, to declare how astounded I have been by the amazing changes I have seen around me on every side,—changes moral, changes physical, changes in the amount of land subdued and peopled, changes in the rise of vast new cities, changes in the growth of older cities almost out of recognition, changes in the graces and amenities of life, changes in the Press, without whose advancement no advancement can take place anywhere. Nor am I, believe me, so arrogant as to suppose that in five and twenty years there have been no changes in me, and that I had nothing to learn and no extreme impressions to correct when I was here first. And this brings me to a point on which I have, ever since I landed in the United States last November, observed a strict silence, though sometimes tempted to break it, but in reference to which I will, with your good leave, take you into my confidence now. Even the Press, being human, may be sometimes mistaken or misinformed, and I rather think that I have in one or two rare instances observed its information to be not strictly accurate with reference to myself. Indeed, I have, now and again, been more surprised by printed news that I have read of myself, than by any printed news that I have ever read in my present state of existence. Thus, the vigor and perseverance with which I have for some months past been collecting materials for, and hammering away at, a new book on America has much astonished me; seeing that all that time my declaration has been perfectly well known to my publishers on both sides of the Atlantic, that no consideration on earth would induce me to write one. But what I have intended, what I have resolved upon (and this is the confidence I seek to place in you) is, on my return to England, in my own person, in my own Journal, to bear, for the behoof of my countrymen, such testimony to the gigantic changes in this country as I have hinted at to-night. Also, to record that wherever I have been, in the smallest places equally with the largest, I have been received with unsurpassable politeness, delicacy, sweet temper, hospitality, consideration, and with unsurpassable respect for the privacy daily enforced upon me by the nature of my avocation here, and the state of my health. This testimony, so long as I live, and so long as my descendants have any legal right in my books, I shall cause to be republished, as an appendix to every copy of those two books of mine in which I have referred to America. And this I will do and cause to be done, not in mere love and thankfulness, but because I regard it as an act of plain justice and honor."

I said these words with the greatest earnestness that I could lay upon them, and I repeat them in print here with equal earnestness. So long as this book shall last, I hope that they will form a part of it, and will be fairly read as inseparable from my experiences and impressions of America.

CHARLES DICKENS.

May, 1868.